"Part deux of Mastropolo's tour de force of ghost signs in New York City provides not only a visual glimpse of the city's vintage signage but also a veritable walk back in time when industrial activity made the city buzz. These are the remnants of the factories that served a growing city, the restaurants that fed its workers, the department stores that fascinated, and more. Mastropolo is that true expert that turns a fleeting observation into a lifelong exploration."

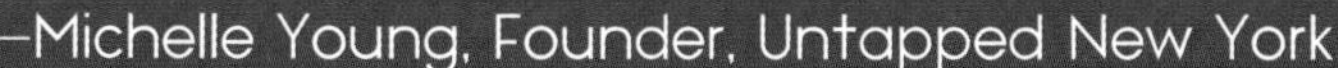

—Michelle Young, Founder, Untapped New York

"Mastropolo's latest installment chronicling the ghost signs of Manhattan highlights some truly fading legends. From my personal favorites in Union Square to a collage of hidden gems in the Fashion District, this book offers great coverage across all the smaller neighborhoods formed within Uptown's localized past, hidden within plain sight."

—Craig Winslow, Artist & Founder, Light Capsules

GHOST SIGNS 2

CLUES TO UPTOWN NEW YORK'S PAST

FRANK MASTROPOLO

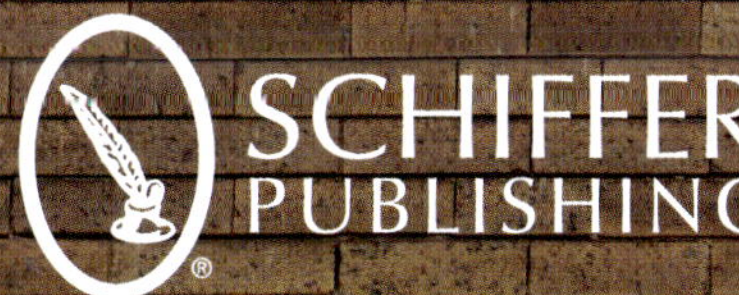

4880 Lower Valley Road • Atglen, PA 19310

Other Schiffer Books by Frank Mastropolo
Ghost Signs: Clues to Downtown New York's Past, ISBN 978-0-7643-5831-9

Other Schiffer Books on Related Subjects
Ghosts of New York City, Therese Lanigan-Schmidt, ISBN 978-0-7643-1714-9

Abandoned NYC, Will Ellis, ISBN 978-0-7643-4761-0

Swing Street: The Rise and Fall of New York's 52nd Street Jazz Scene: An Illustrated Tribute, 1930-1950, Leo T. Sullivan, ISBN 978-0-7643-5973-6

Library of Congress Control Number: 2019936105

Designed by Jack Chappell
Cover design by Jack Chappell
Image postproduction by Pete Mastropolo
All text and color photography by the author © Frank Mastropolo

Type set in High Life/Noir/Avenir

ISBN: 978-0-7643-6362-7
Printed in Serbia

Schiffer Publishing, Ltd.
4880 Lower Valley Road
Atglen, PA 19310
Phone: (610) 593-1777; Fax: (610) 593-2002
Email: Info@schifferbooks.com
Web: www.redfeathermbs.com

Study the past, if you would divine the future.

—Confucius

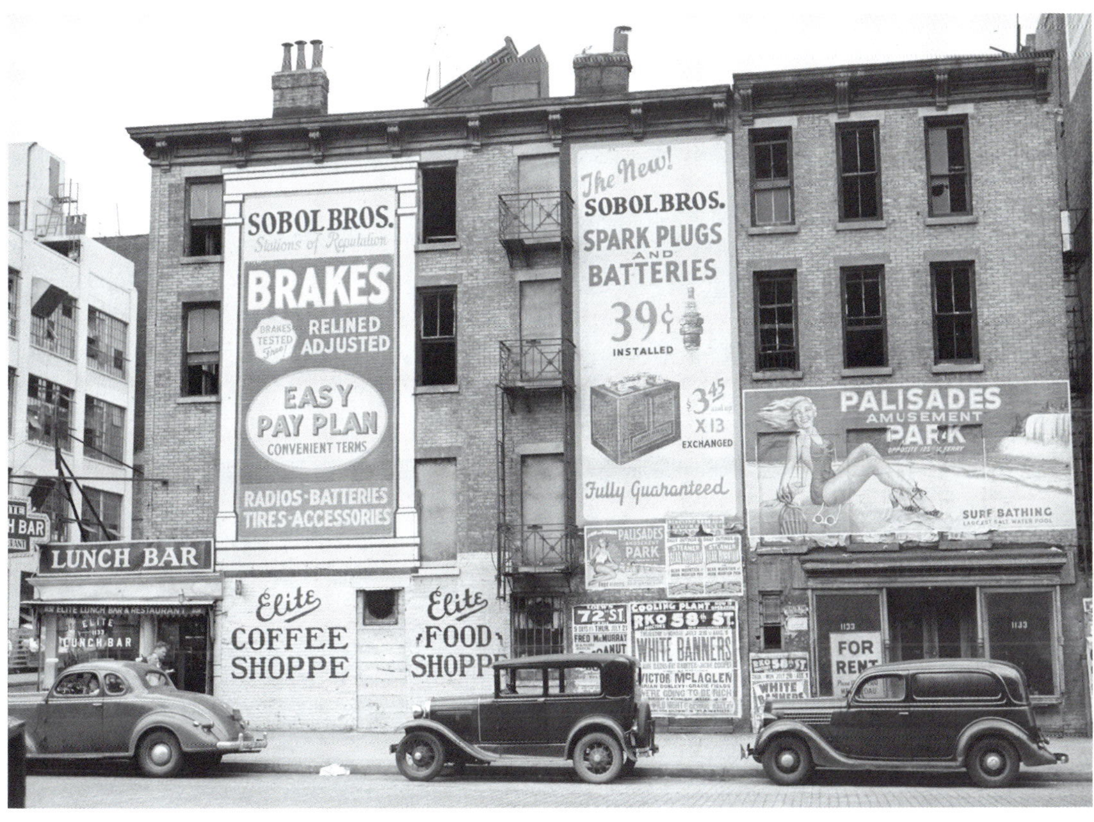

1133 First Avenue, 1938. *Courtesy of the Farm Security Administration, Office of War Information Photograph Collection, Library of Congress*

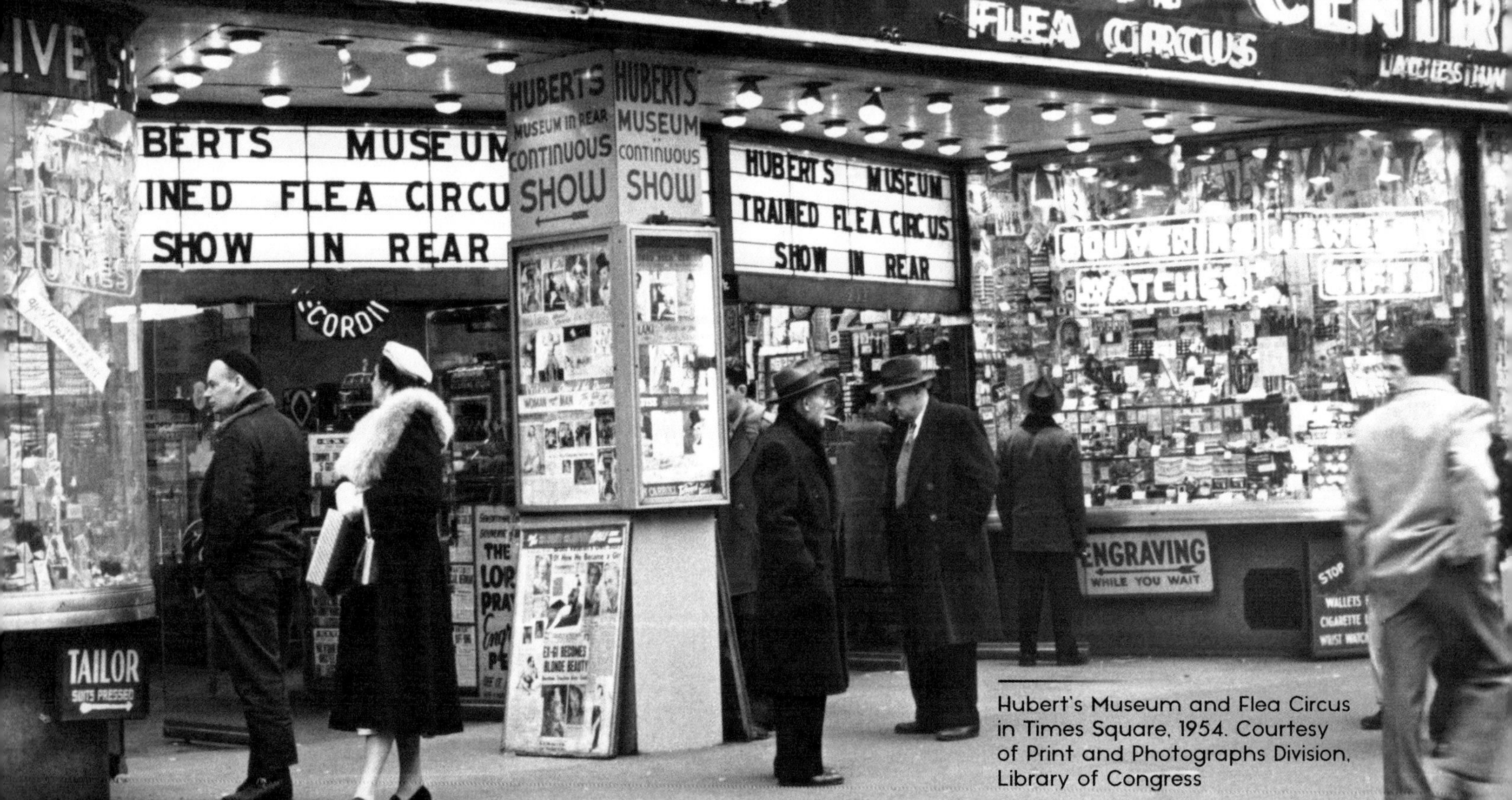

Hubert's Museum and Flea Circus in Times Square, 1954. Courtesy of Print and Photographs Division, Library of Congress

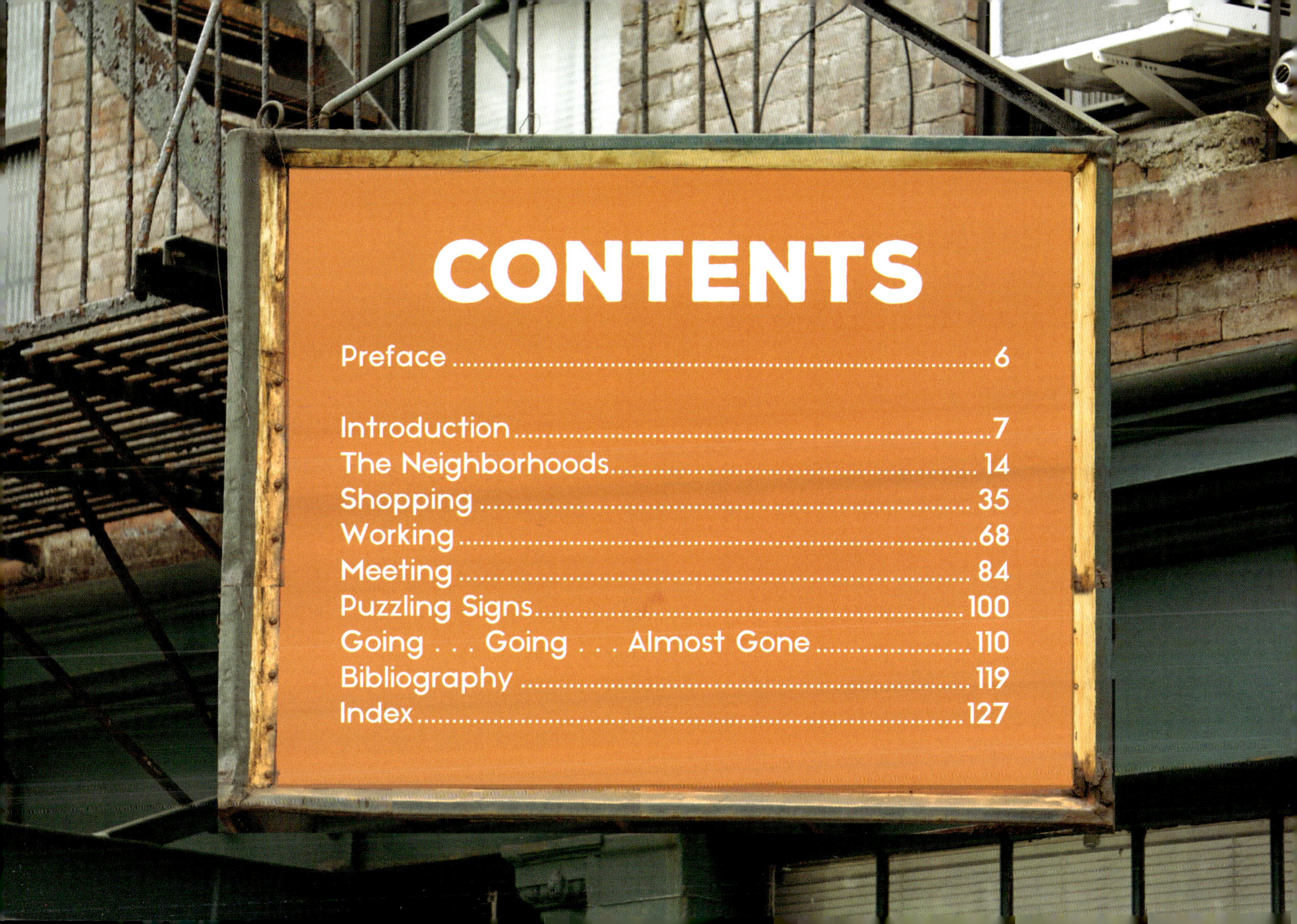

CONTENTS

PREFACE

Measured from Battery Park to the Henry Hudson Bridge, Manhattan is more than 13 miles long, with thousands of buildings. Its skyline makes Manhattan seem like an island of skyscrapers. But a walk through its neighborhoods reveals brownstones, row houses, and tenements, many built before World War II. Their walls provide a canvas for ghost signs: surviving ads for businesses that vanished decades ago.

New York's original inhabitants were the Lenape, Indigenous people who lived for centuries on the island they called Mannahatta. It was a land of dense hardwood forests, freshwater creeks, and abundant wildlife. Henry Hudson sailed into New York's Lower Bay for the Dutch East India Company in 1609. European colonies expanded northward and pushed the Lenape out of their homeland. Because New York's oldest buildings are in Lower Manhattan, my first book, ***Ghost Signs: Clues to Downtown New York's Past***, examined the signs south of Fourteenth Street.

Lower Manhattan is a small part of the borough; Midtown and Upper Manhattan encompass dozens of neighborhoods. *Fodor's See It New York City* advises visitors, "No matter where you are in Manhattan, if you are heading north you're going 'uptown' and if you're heading south you're going 'downtown.'"

With that in mind, I've written *Ghost Signs 2: Clues to Uptown New York's Past.* The examined neighborhoods offer the best opportunities to see the city's ghost signs in Midtown and Upper Manhattan. Use this book as a starting point for your exploration; there are many more ghost signs to discover.

My special thanks to my brother, Pete Mastropolo, for his postproduction work on the images, and to my wife, Beverly, whose skill as a sign-spotter made this book possible.

I'd also like to thank the supporters of my first book: Lincoln Anderson, Dana Arschin, Jen Carlson, Esther Crain, Dean Karayanis, Tod Swormstedt, and Michelle Young, as well as my friends on social media who have shared their discoveries.

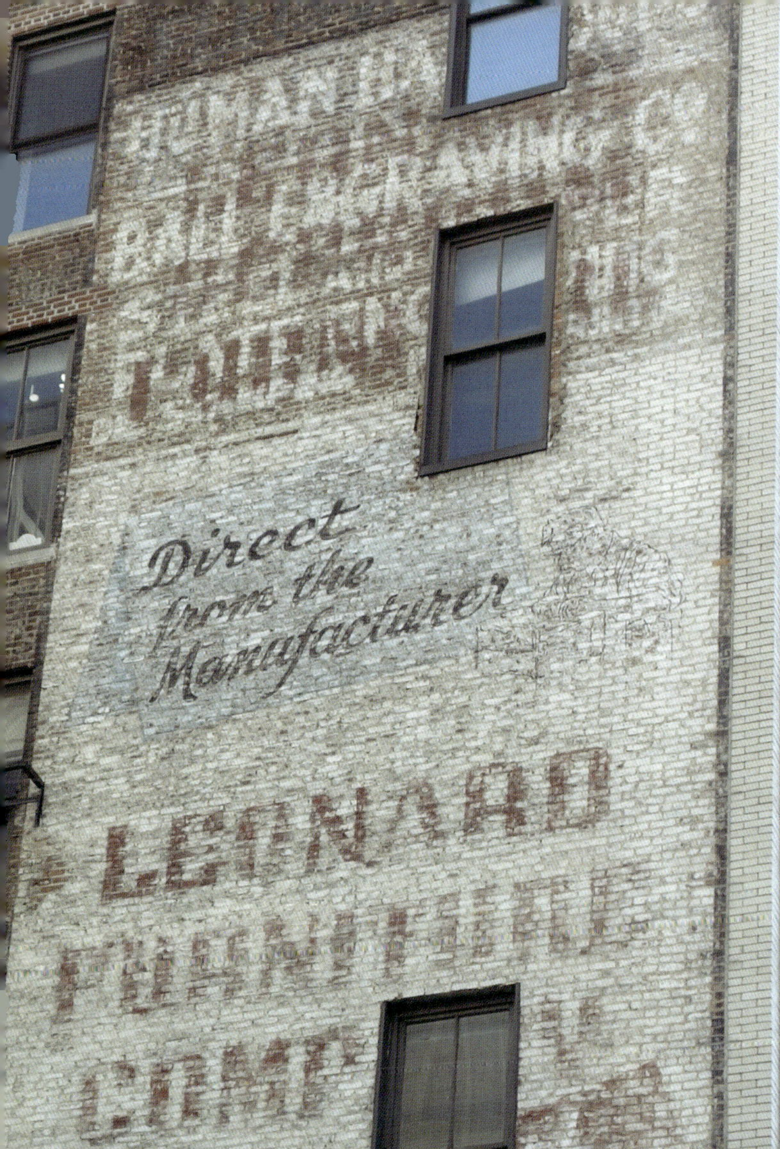

INTRODUCTION

A stroll through any neighborhood in Manhattan provides a history lesson on the economic and social fabric of the past. Hiding in plain sight are faded ads that have improbably survived wind, rain, snow, and the wrecking ball to provide a glimpse of life decades ago. Clues to our jobs, schools, stores, restaurants, and theaters are hidden in the signs.

The oldest ghost signs are painted on brick walls. Sign painters, called "walldogs" because they worked like dogs, used lead paint that leached into the brick. Lead paint was banned in 1978, but its use ensured the longevity of the vintage signs.

117 East Twenty-Fourth Street

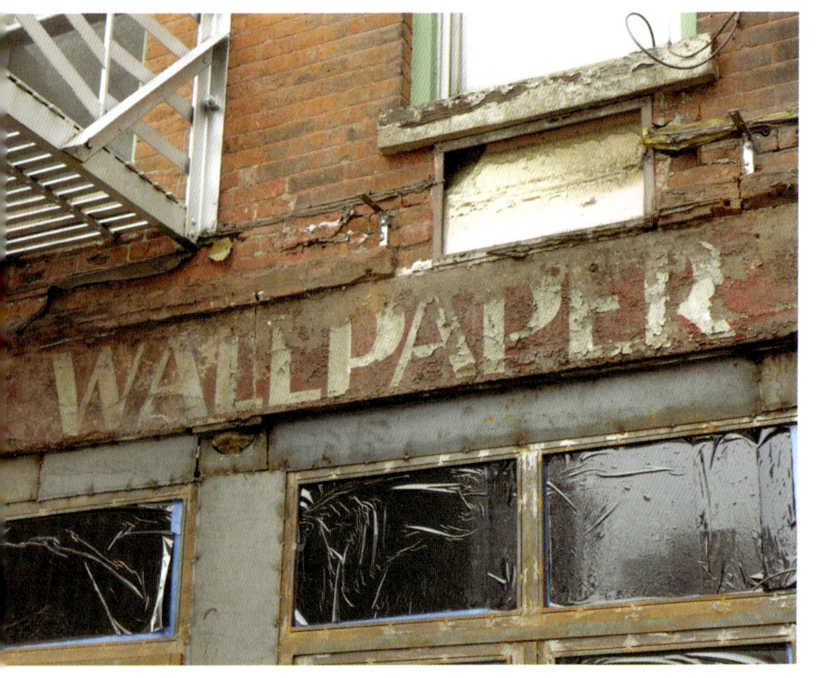

609 Second Avenue

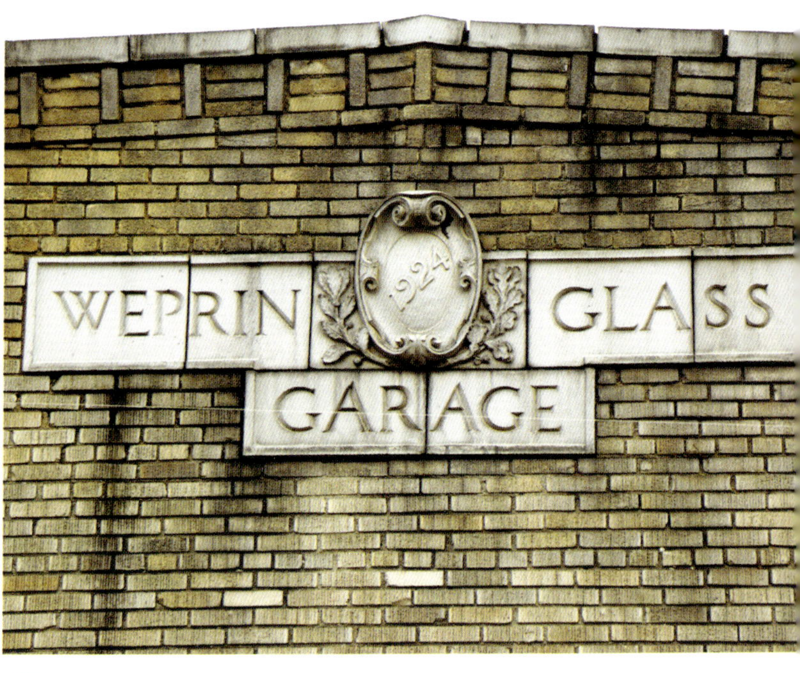

2013 Third Avenue

Signs painted on wood are also among the oldest. This sign was revealed during demolition in 2016.

Vintage signs are engraved in stone.

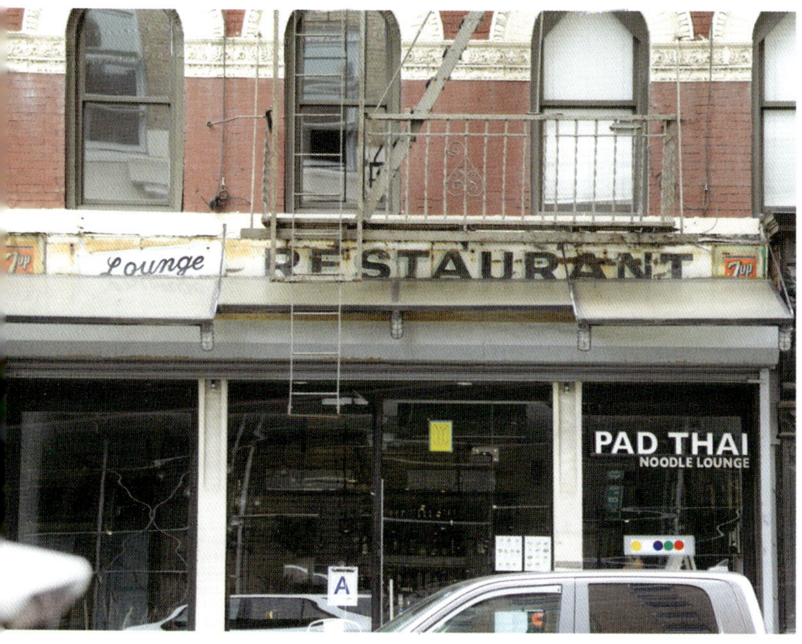

114 Eighth Avenue

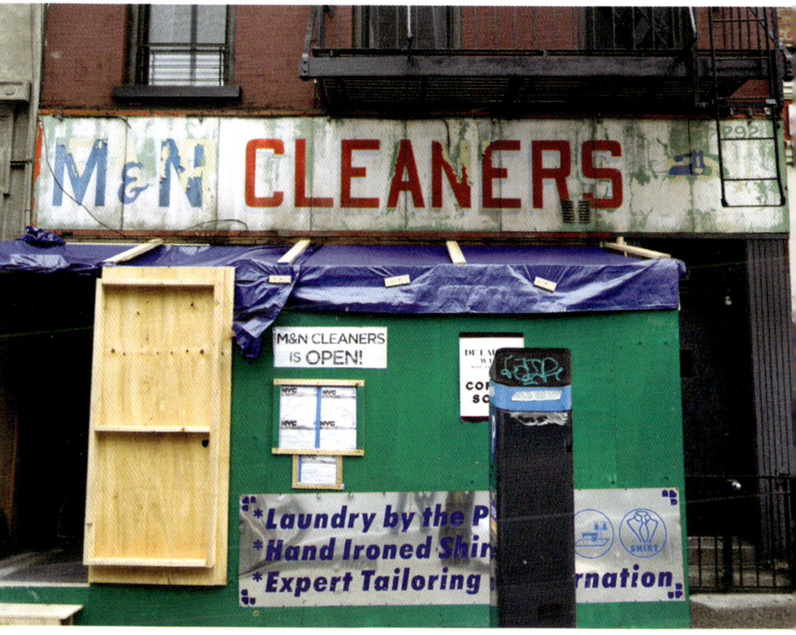

292 Eighth Avenue

Many soft-drink companies provided "privilege" signs, branded with their logos, for free to small grocery and convenience stores. Manufactured with steel, the signs became popular in the 1930s.

Renovations expose ghost signs, if only for a brief time.

The advertised products offer clues to the age of the signs. Crown Coat Front operated in Union Square from 1947 to about 1958. Coat fronts are the linings, once made of haircloth, felt, and canvas, that were sewn into the fronts of coats to stiffen or retain the garment's shape.

105 East Sixteenth Street

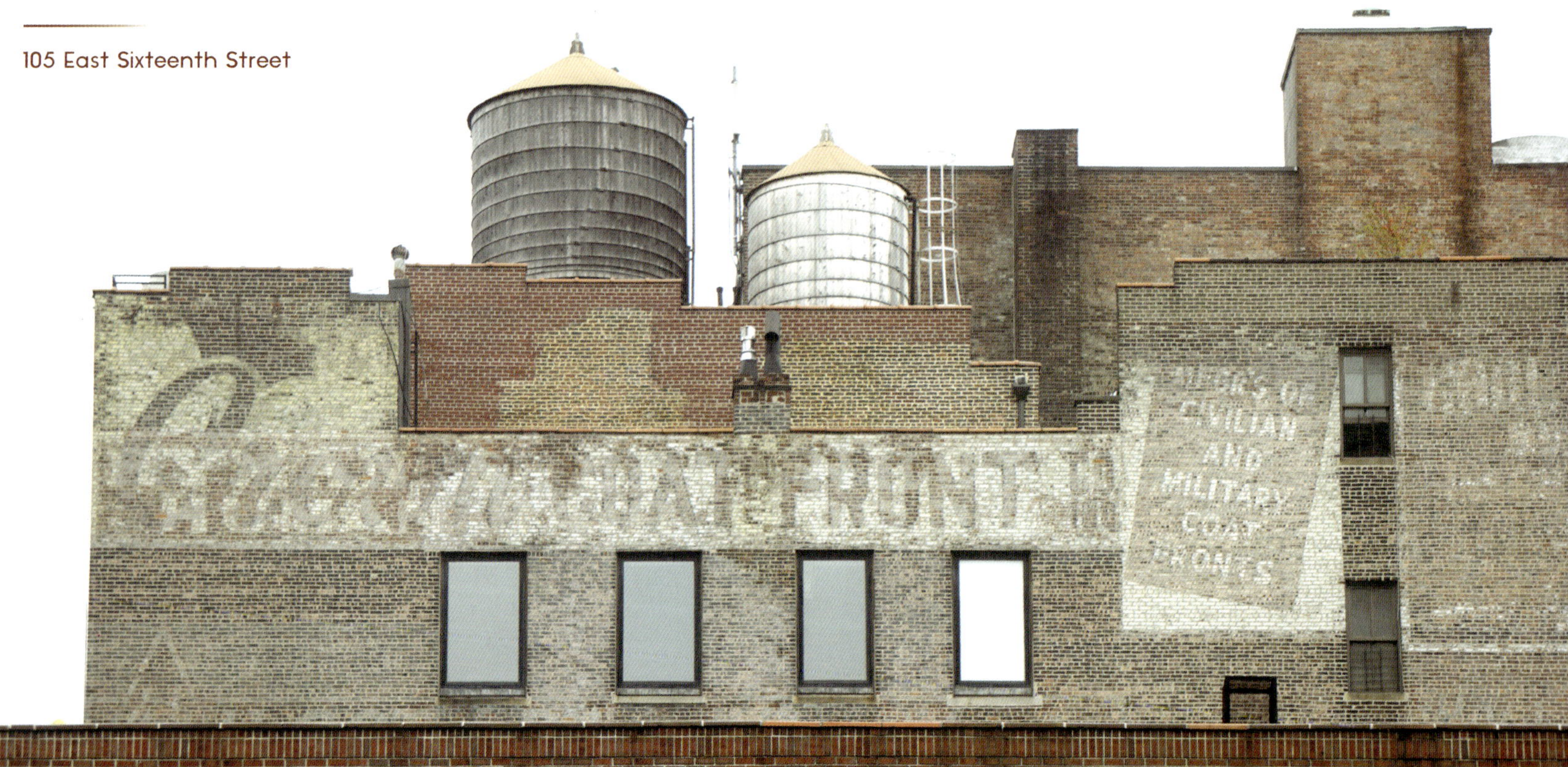

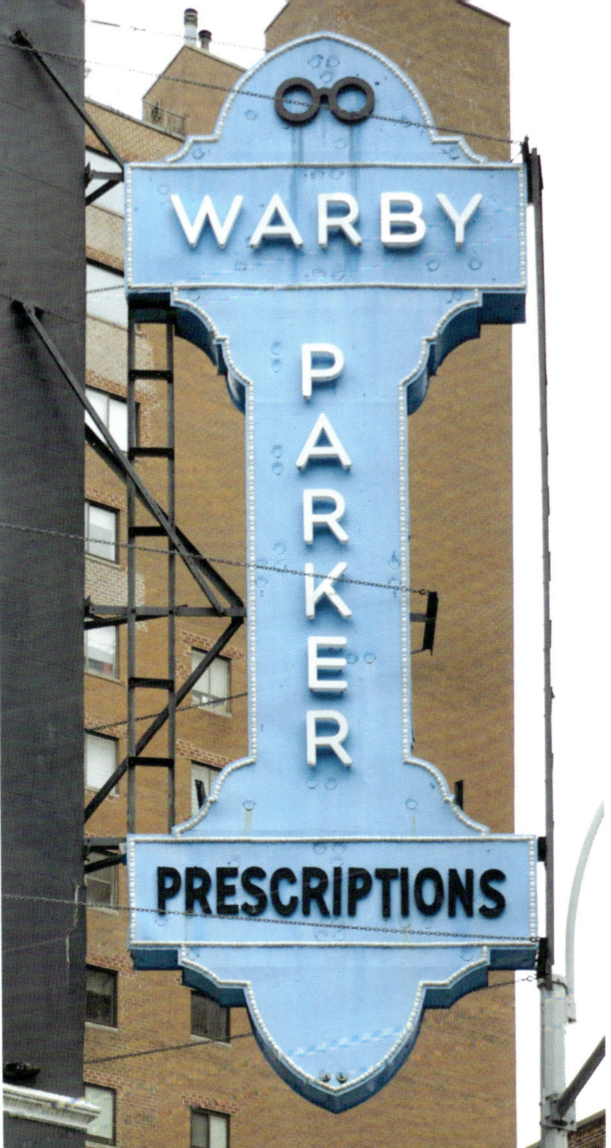

Some businesses repurpose vintage signs. When Lascoff Drugs left its Upper East Side location after more than a century, eyewear retailer Warby Parker added its name and eyeglass frames to the sign—but kept the word "prescriptions."

1209 Lexington Avenue

New construction can create puzzling signs, like this one for Albert Weiss Jewelry.

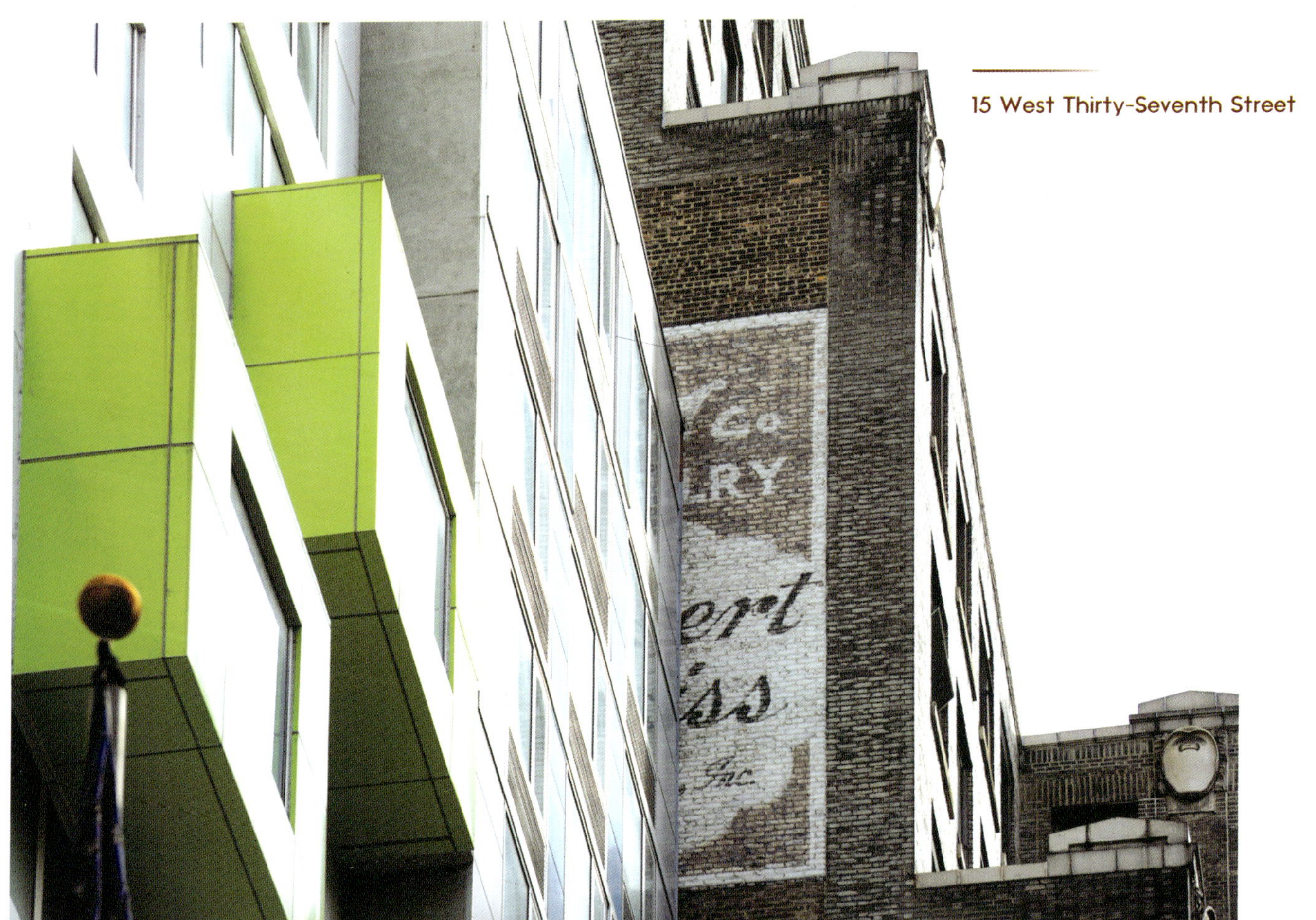

15 West Thirty-Seventh Street

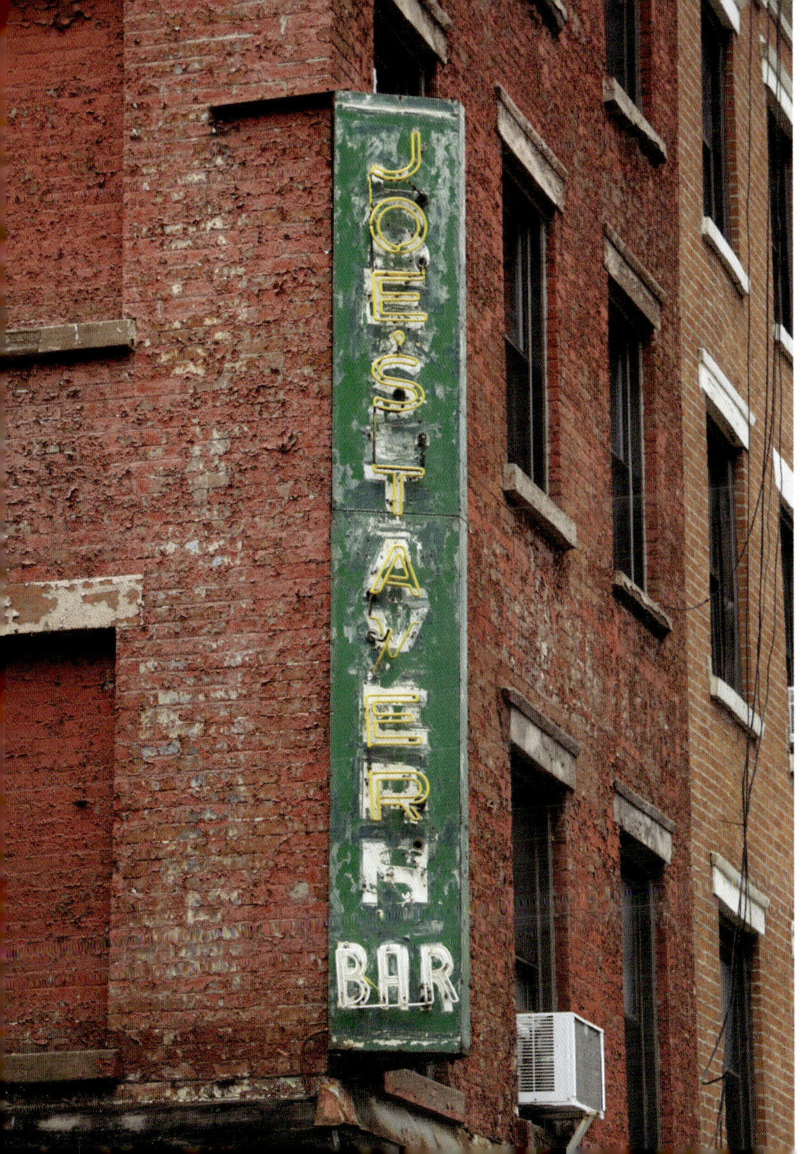

Neon, introduced in the US in 1923, changed signage forever. Cheaper plastic signs and vinyl banners attached to the sides of buildings helped spell the end of the city's ghost signs.

258 Tenth Avenue

THE NEIGHBORHOODS

Union Square was the site of the first , abor Day celebration in 1882. It was originally named Union Place, the intersection, or union, of Bloomingdale Road (now Broadway) and Bowery Road (now Fourth Avenue). Union Square Park has become a gathering spot for protests and activist rallies. The neighborhood's boundaries are Fourteenth to Seventeenth Street and Fourth Avenue to University Place.

In the early 1800s, the **Rialto**, Manhattan's first commercial theater district, was centered on Union Square and Fourteenth Street before moving uptown. By the 1900s Union Square became a wholesaling district of lofts and office buildings. In the 1920s the S. Klein and Ohrbach's department stores attracted shoppers. Union Square Park was renovated in 1985, adding a central lawn, new lighting, and two subway kiosks.

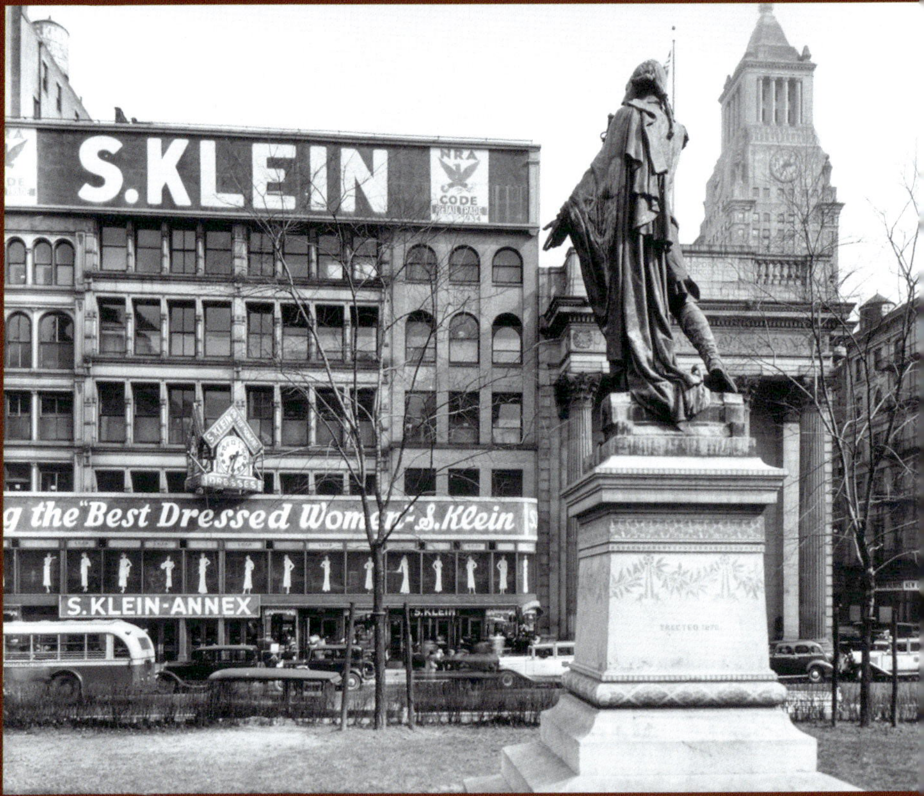

Union Square, 1936. *Courtesy of the Miriam and Ira D. Wallach Division of Art, Prints and Photographs: Photography Collection, New York Public Library.*

Union Square includes Irving Place, which runs from Fourteenth Street to Gramercy Park South. Irving Place was named in the 1830s for Washington Irving, author of *The Legend of Sleepy Hollow* and *Rip Van Winkle*.

The **Meatpacking District** spans from Horatio to Seventeenth Street and Eighth Avenue to the Hudson River. Markets have been part of the neighborhood since the 1840s. By 1900, slaughterhouses and packing plants dominated the area. A handful of meatpacking companies remain in what has become a mecca of boutiques and bars.

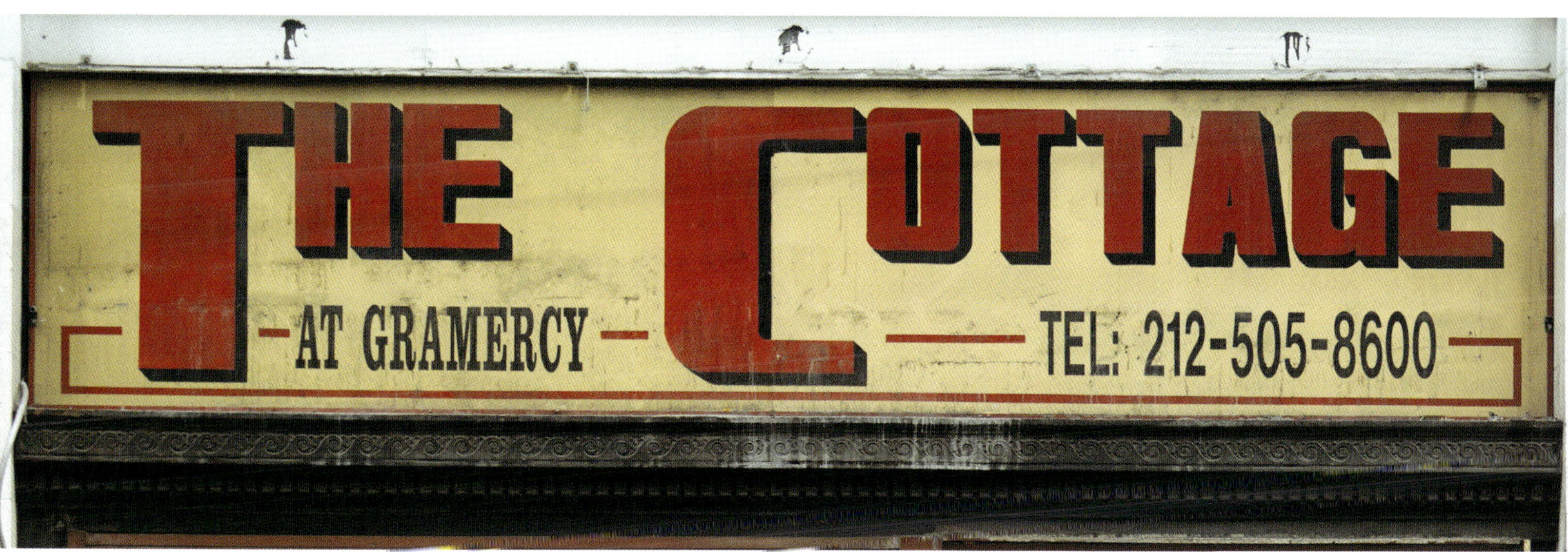

29 Irving Place

In 1831 developer Samuel B. Ruggles purchased 22 acres of swamp to create **Gramercy**. The tony neighborhood runs from Fourteenth to Twenty-Third Street and Third Avenue to Park Avenue South.

Ruggles envisioned a green space at its center, called Gramercy Square. He drained and filled the swamp and sold parcels of land that surrounded it. The 2-acre square was renamed Gramercy Park, which is accessible only to residents of the surrounding buildings.

Chelsea runs from Fourteenth to about Thirtieth Street and from Sixth Avenue to the Hudson River. The theater district moved uptown to Chelsea by 1869. Film studios flourished in the early twentieth century. Chelsea is one of the centers of the city's art world, with more than two hundred art galleries, museums, and performance spaces.

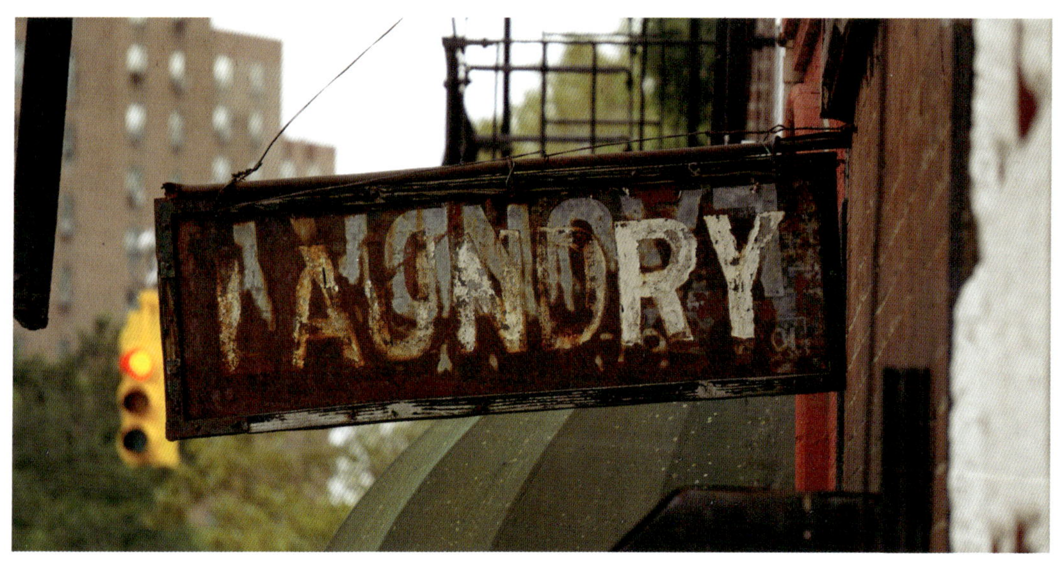

352 East Twentieth Street

The High Line, which delivered millions of tons of meat, dairy, and produce by rail from 1933 until the 1980s, runs through Chelsea. The line opened as a public park in 2009. The elevated greenway provides a view of the Spears warehouse ghost sign.

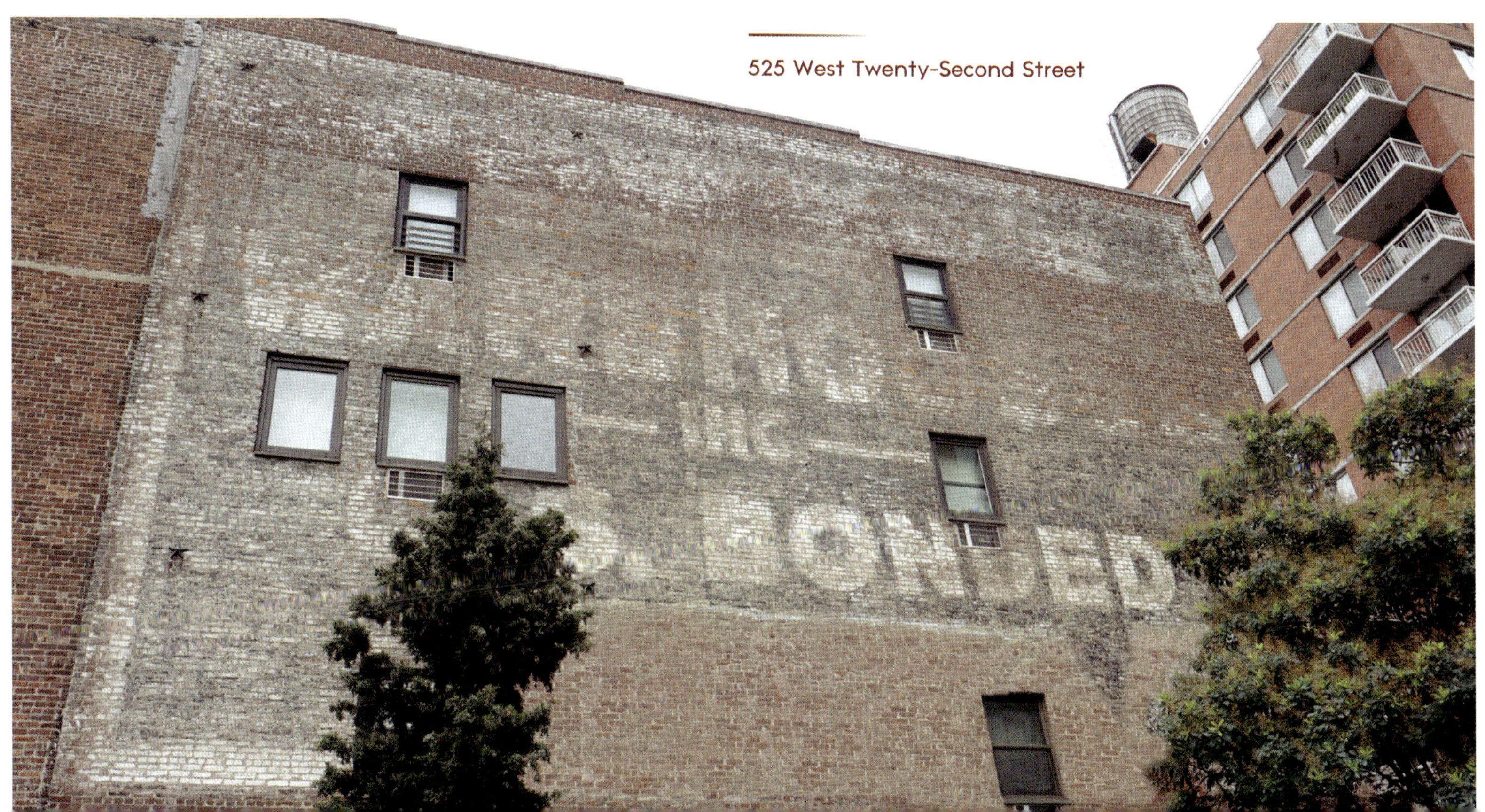

525 West Twenty-Second Street

Around the turn of the twentieth century, high-fashion shops such as Lord & Taylor and Siegel-Cooper catered to women along the Ladies' Mile, generally Fifteenth to Twenty-Fourth Street and Park Avenue South to Sixth Avenue.

The **Flatiron District** is named for the Flatiron Building, one of the most photographed buildings in New York. Named for its resemblance to a clothes iron, its shape is dictated by the wedge-shaped intersection of Fifth Avenue and Broadway. The district's boundaries are roughly Fourteenth to Thirtieth Street and Park Avenue South to Sixth Avenue.

After the Great Depression, the area became the Toy District as toy and novelty shops replaced the department stores that had moved uptown. As the toy business moved overseas, photography studios and camera stores reinvented the neighborhood as the Photo District. By 1985 the area became more residential and was renamed the Flatiron District. Internet-related companies and tech startups have made the area part of the city's **Silicon Alley**.

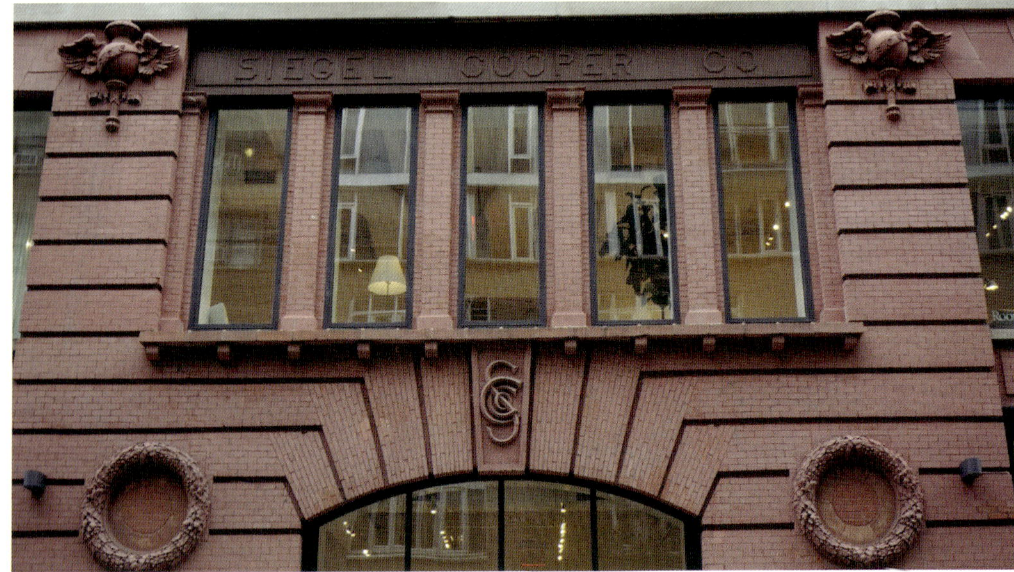

249 West Seventeenth Street

NoMad is a portmanteau, or blend of words, for North of Madison Square Park. The area was mostly open farmland and pasture in the early nineteenth century. Madison Square Park, named for President James Madison, served as a campground and drill field for Union soldiers during the Civil War. NoMad's boundaries are Twenty-Fifth to about Thirty-Fourth Street and Lexington to Sixth Avenue.

The **Rose Hill** neighborhood generally runs from Twenty-Fifth to Thirty-Second Street and Third to Madison Avenue. The area was part of Rose Hill Farm before the American Revolution. Many New Yorkers, unfamiliar with the name, think of Rose Hill as part of NoMad.

Tin Pan Alley, on Twenty-Eighth Street between Fifth and Sixth Avenue, was a gathering place for music publishers and songwriters in the late nineteenth and early twentieth centuries.

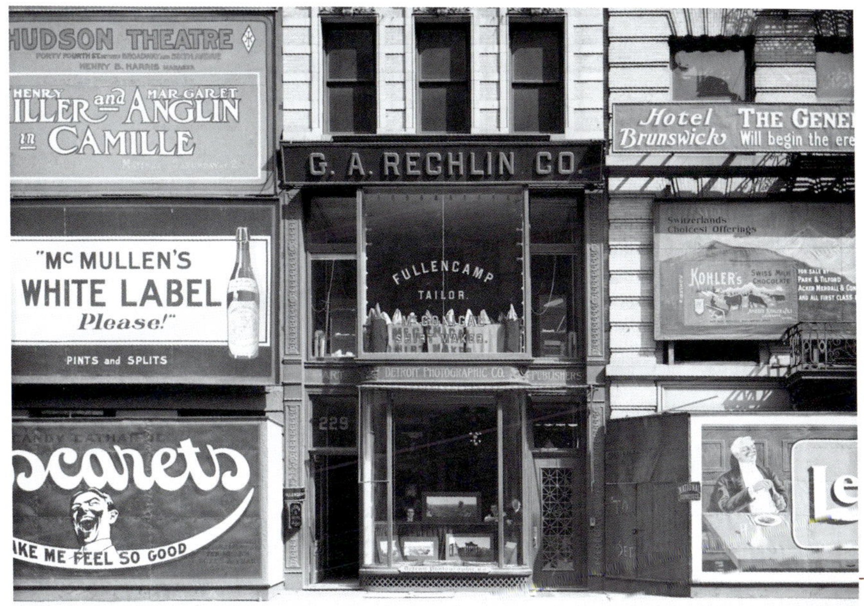

Detroit Photographic, 229 Fifth Avenue, ca. 1900–1905. *Courtesy of the Detroit Publishing Company photograph collection, Library of Congress*

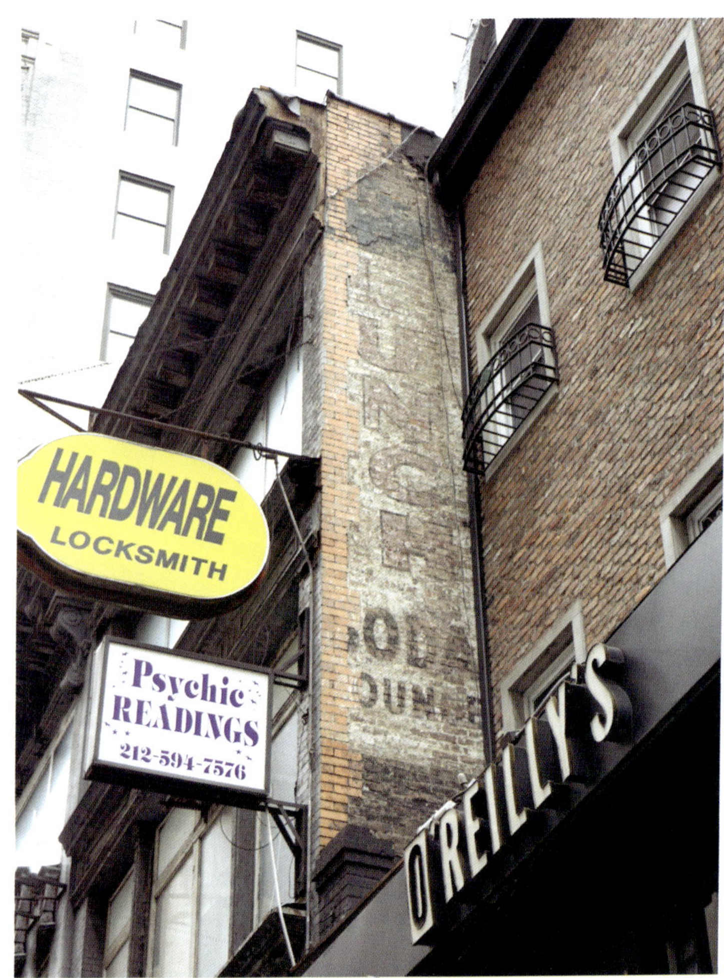

After the Civil War, America's garment industry expanded on the Lower East Side with the invention of the sewing machine and the influx of immigrants with sewing and tailoring skills. When manufacturing in residential buildings was outlawed at the start of the twentieth century, clothing businesses moved uptown to the commercial loft buildings in the Tenderloin, the red-light district that stretched north from Twenty-Fourth Street.

23 West Thirty-Fifth Street

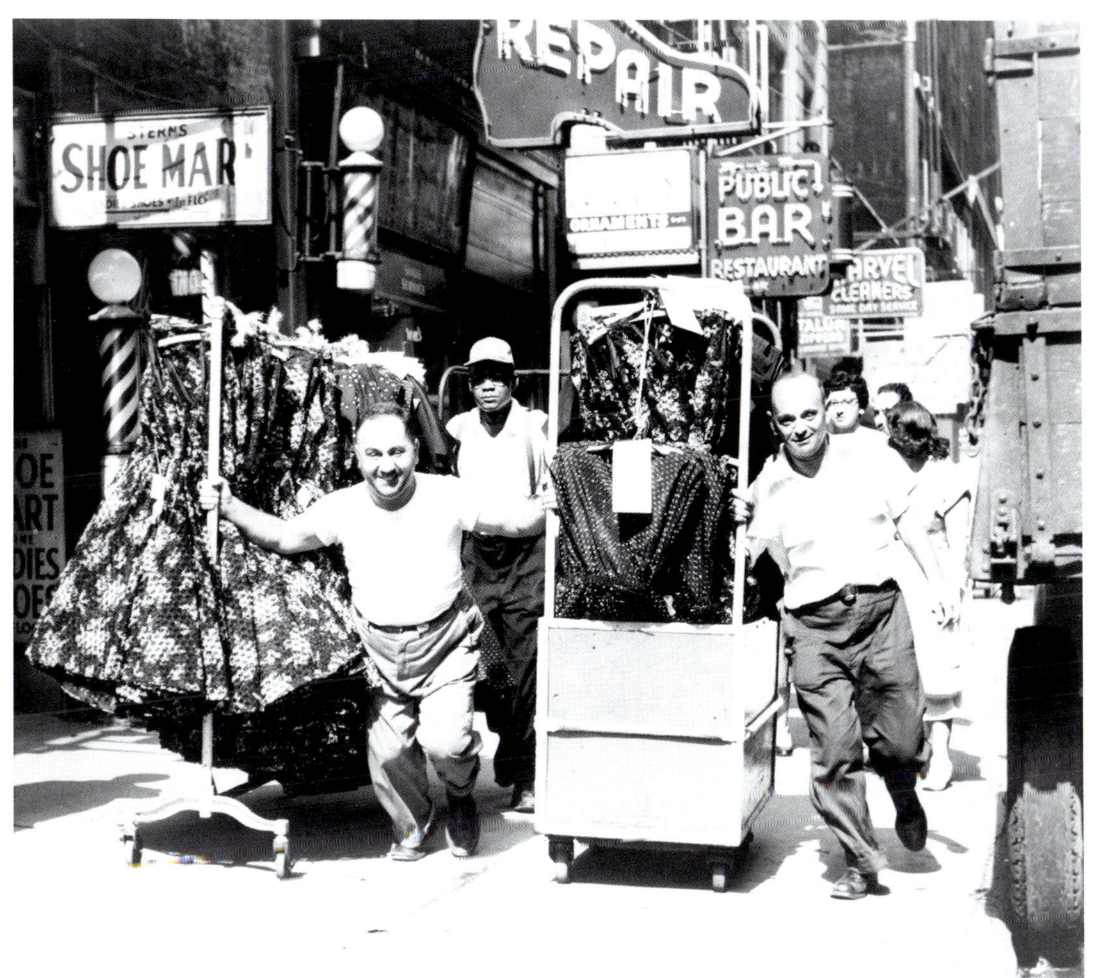

In the 1920s the Garment District bustled with clothing manufacturers, designers, and merchandisers. "Push boys" competed with pedestrians for space, rolling racks of garments through the streets. By the late 1930s, the Garment District ran from Twenty-Fifth to Forty-Second Street and Sixth to Ninth Avenue.

Men Pulling Racks of Clothing on Busy Sidewalk in Garment District, photo by Al Ravenna, 1955. *Courtesy of New York World-Telegram & Sun Newspaper Photograph Collection, Library of Congress*

Furriers were concentrated between Twenty-Fifth and Thirtieth Street in the Fur District.

38 West Twenty-Sixth Street

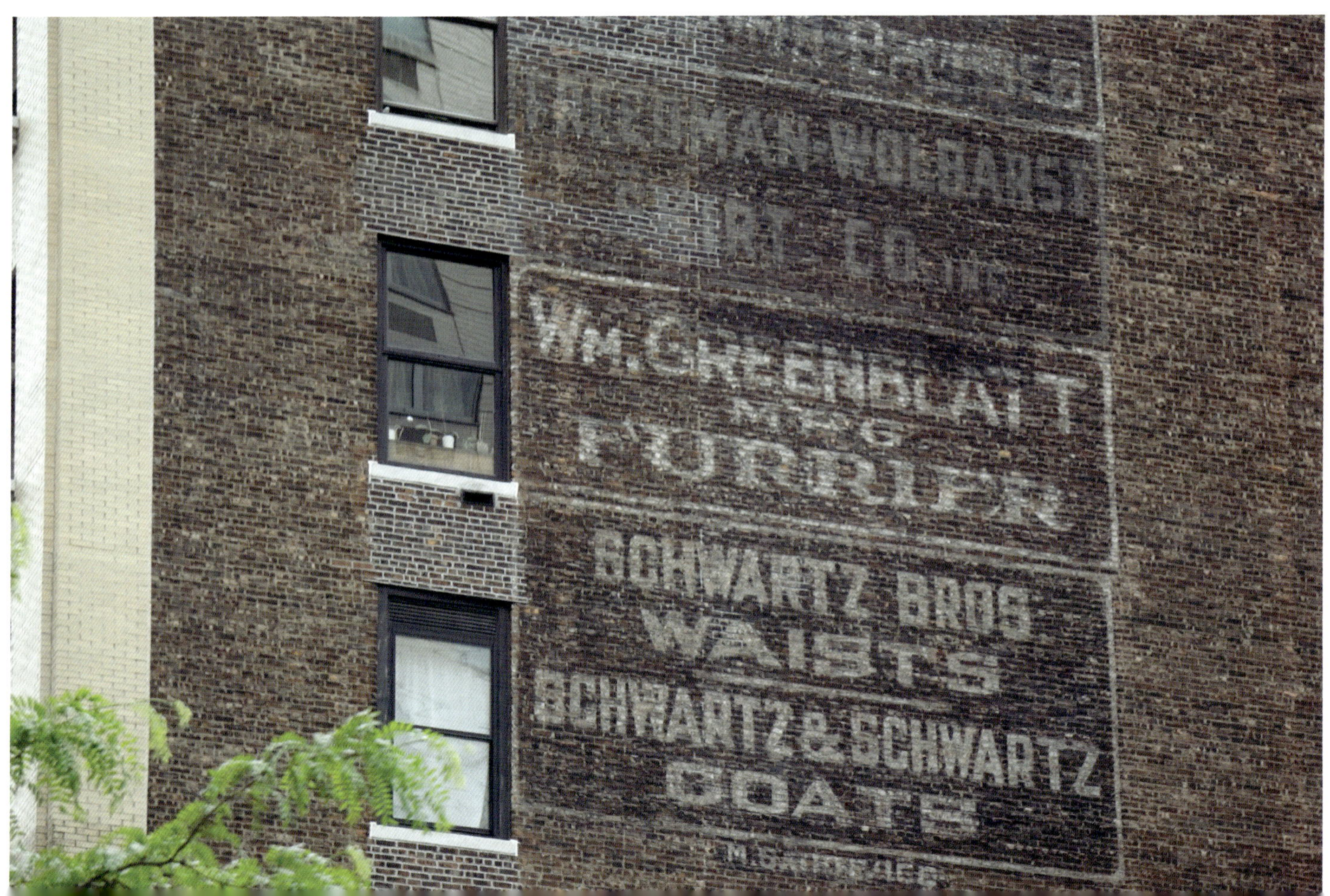

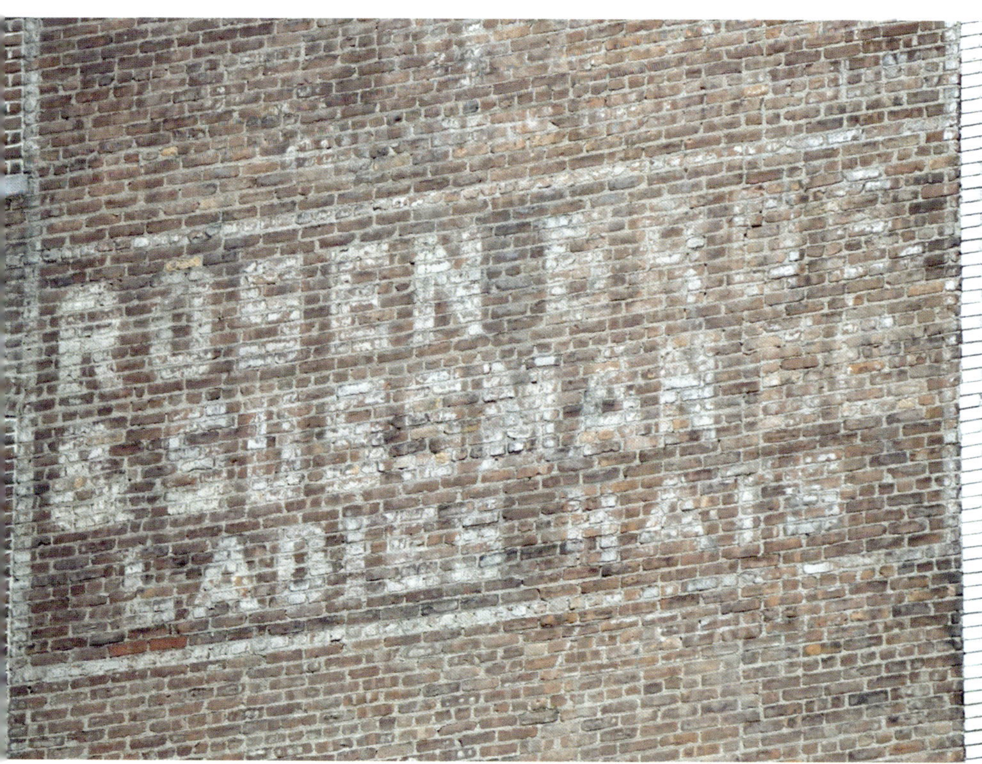

64 West Thirty-Ninth Street

Wholesale hat sellers and manufacturers occupied the Millinery District below Fortieth Street.

As clothing manufacturing moved overseas, the Garment District declined. However, many famous designers have maintained their showrooms and warehouses in what is now the **Fashion District**. Shops selling fabric, accessories, buttons, beads, and lace line the neighborhood, stretching from about Thirty-Fourth to Forty-Second Street, between Sixth and Ninth Avenue.

In the 1700s Kip's Bay was an inlet of the East River that was later filled in. The bay extended from what is now Thirty-Second to Thirty-Seventh Street. British troops fought George Washington's army at Kip's Bay during the American Revolution.

Kips Bay, without the apostrophe, is a neighborhood of medical centers, brownstones, and bars. Its boundaries are roughly Twenty-Third to Thirty-Eighth Street and the East River to Lexington Avenue. South Asian restaurants line Lexington Avenue in an area known as **Curry Hill**, a pun on neighboring Murray Hill.

A steep glacial till, or mound of gravel and boulders, once stretched from Lexington Avenue to Broadway, rising from Thirty-Fourth Street and declining toward Forty-Second Street. Robert Murray, a Quaker merchant, rented land from the city in the mid-1700s and built a large house and farm here known as Murray Hill. The hill began to be leveled in the early 1800s to permit access to trains.

Murray Hill's boundaries are generally Thirty-Fourth to Fortieth Street and Third to Fifth Avenue. Many of the mansions built by the end of the nineteenth century remain. The B. Altman department store opened in 1906, followed by Arnold Constable and Bergdorf Goodman. The neighborhood includes missions and consulates to the United Nations.

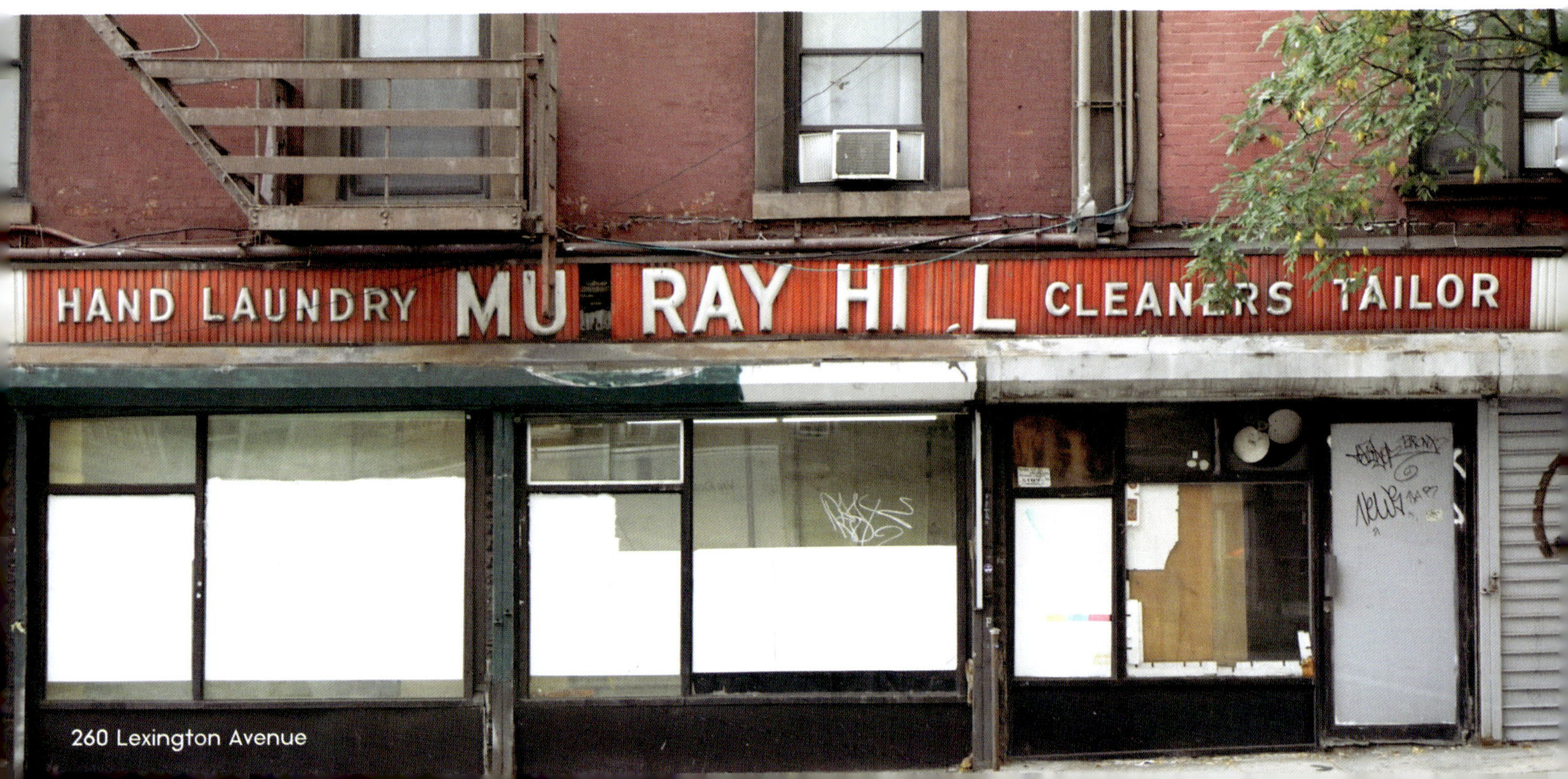

260 Lexington Avenue

Turtle Bay was a cove of the East River in the 1600s that offered shipbuilders shelter from the harsh elements. Turtle Bay's name is a corruption of the Dutch word ***deutal***, or bent blade, which referred to the shape of the bay. The inlet was filled in by the end of the Civil War. Slaughterhouses, breweries, cattle pens, and railroad yards made the neighborhood one of the most polluted in the city.

Turtle Bay's blight was cleared by 1952 for the construction of the United Nations headquarters. The removal of the Second and Third Avenue elevated trains allowed the construction of office buildings and condominiums. Turtle Bay ranges from about Forty-Third to Fifty-Third Street and the East River to Lexington Avenue.

Koreatown is centered on Thirty-Second Street between Madison Avenue and the intersection of Sixth Avenue and Broadway. Its restaurants, grocery stores, bookstores, beauty salons, and nightclubs draw visitors from nearby Herald Square and the Garment District. Korean businesses began to sprout here in the late 1970s with the establishment of Koryo Books and a few restaurants. The block has been designated **Korea Way**.

Herald Square, between Thirty-Fourth and Thirty-Fifth Street and Sixth Avenue and Broadway, was named for the headquarters of the *New York Herald* newspaper. To its south is **Greeley Square**, named for Horace Greeley, publisher of the rival *New York Tribune*.

Herald Square has been a retail destination since Macy's department store moved here from downtown in the early twentieth century; Gimbels and B. Altman soon followed. In 1984 the building that housed Gimbels became the Manhattan Mall. In 1999 Herald and Greeley Square were transformed into small parks, with chairs, tables, umbrellas, and food kiosks.

The **Theater District** was born at the turn of the twentieth century, when playhouses began to move uptown from Union Square and Madison Square. The Theater District extends from Fortieth to Fifty-Fourth Street and Sixth to Eighth Avenue. At its heart is **Times Square**, formed by the intersection of Seventh Avenue, Forty-Second Street, and Broadway. The neighborhood also includes movie theaters, restaurants, hotels, and television studios.

Originally called Longacre Square, Times Square was renamed when the *New York Times* moved its headquarters here in 1904. That year the first electrical ad was installed on the side of a bank on Forty-Sixth Street. The city requires that Times Square building owners display illuminated signs. Massive neon and high-definition , ED screens, some the size of a football field, compete for wall space.

The Camel Cigarettes sign that blew smoke rings from 1941 to 1966 was one of the most memorable. Steam behind the sign simulated smoke that was blown over Broadway.

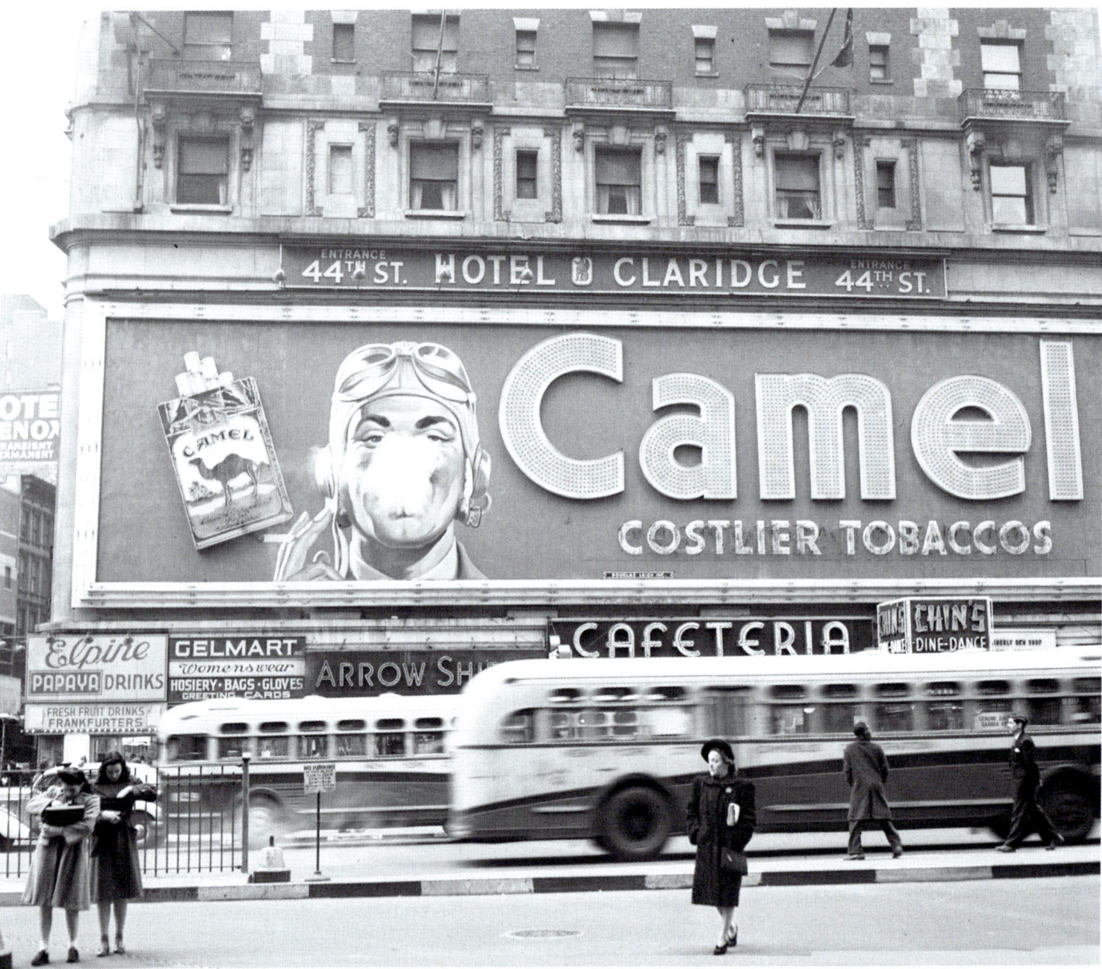

Camel cigarettes advertisement in Times Square, 1943. *Courtesy of the Farm Security Administration, Office of War Information Photograph Collection, Library of Congress*

Hell's Kitchen runs from Thirty-Fourth to Fifty-Ninth Street and Eighth Avenue to the Hudson River. In the 1700s the area was open farmland and suburban villas. The construction of the Hudson River Railroad on Eleventh Avenue, completed in 1849, brought Irish immigrants who worked on the nearby docks and railroad. Youth gangs terrorized the neighborhood after the Civil War, earning Hell's Kitchen its name. Organized crime prospered here during Prohibition, when shipping warehouses were used as bootleg distilleries.

The city cracked down on crime beginning in the 1980s, as the neighborhood became gentrified. Real estate developers hoped to soften the district's reputation by renaming it **Clinton**, a reference to DeWitt Clinton Park, and **Midtown West**.

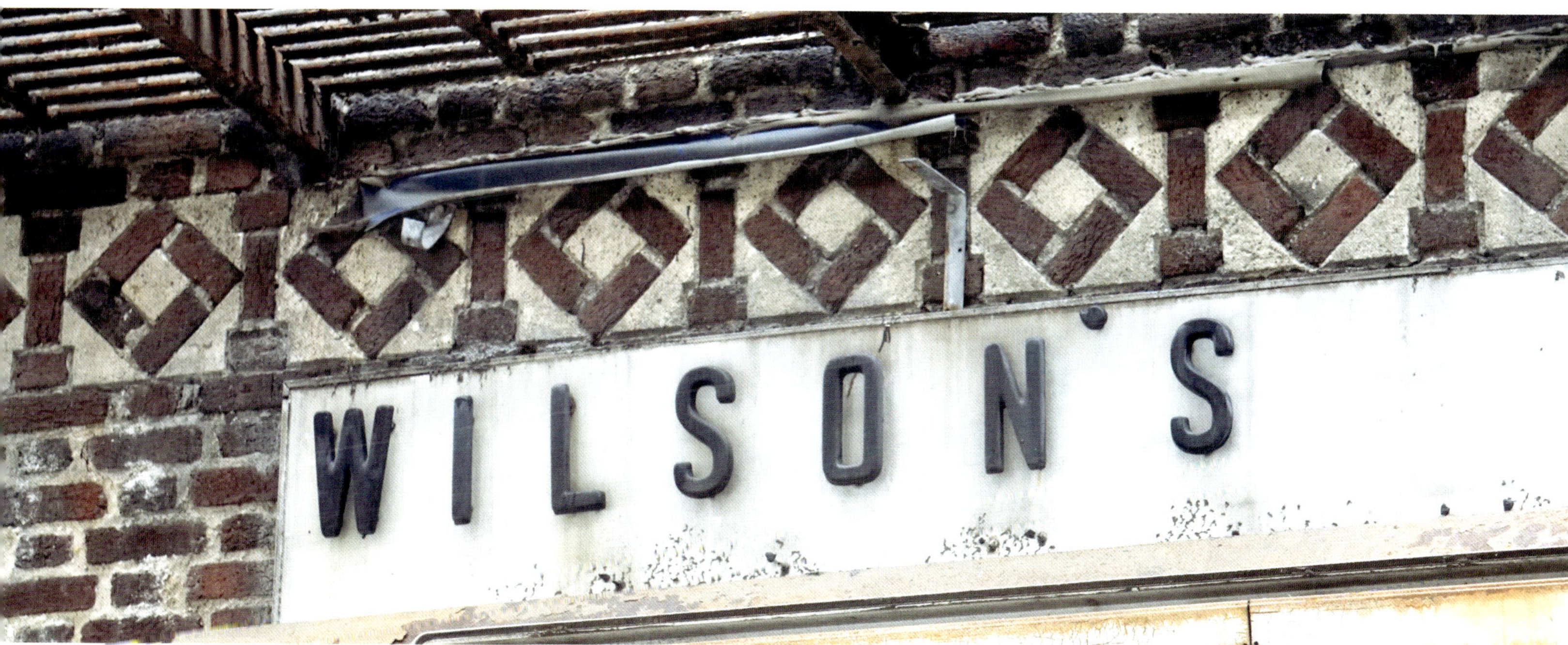

842 Seventh Avenue

The **Diamond District** is located on Forty-Seventh Street from Fifth to Sixth Avenue. Originally based downtown, the jewelry trade began to relocate here in 1941. More than two thousand dealers in diamonds and jewelry operate in booths in the district's exchanges.

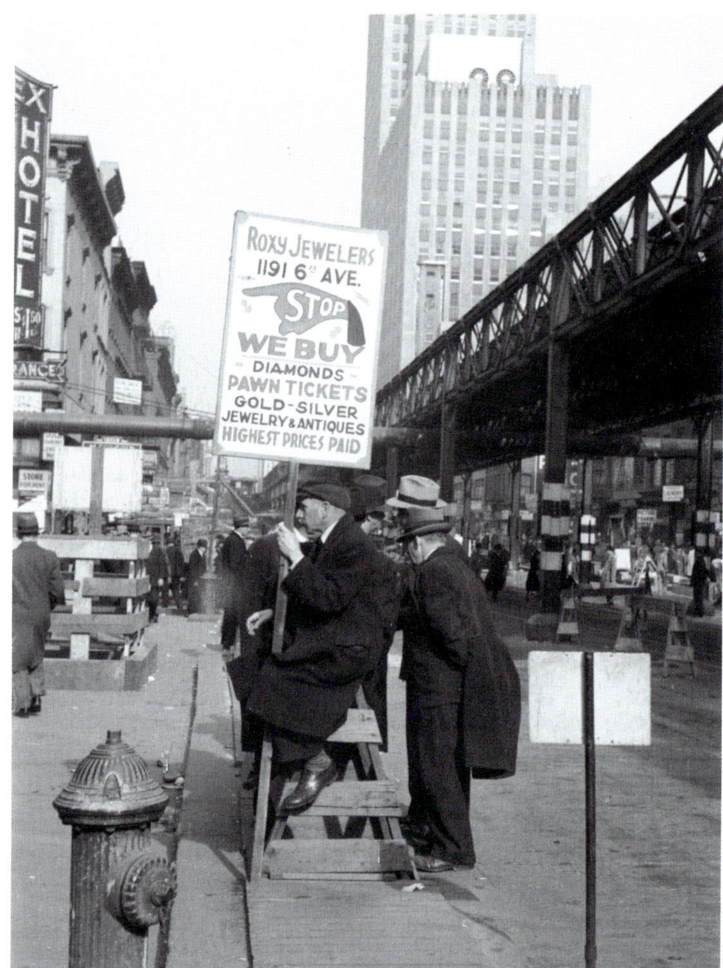

Sign man on Sixth Avenue in Diamond District, 1937. *Courtesy of the Farm Security Administration, Office of War Information Photograph Collection, Library of Congress*

The **Upper East Side** runs from Fifty-Ninth to Ninety-Sixth Street and from the East River to Fifth Avenue. After World War II the neighborhood was called the Silk Stocking District to reflect its affluent residents along Fifth and Park Avenue. The Upper East Side remains one of the city's most exclusive neighborhoods and comprises Lenox Hill, Carnegie Hill, and Yorkville. Museum Mile, which extends up Fifth Avenue, includes the Museum of the City of New York, the Solomon R. Guggenheim Museum, the Metropolitan Museum of Art, and El Museo del Barrio.

Lenox Hill extends from Sixtieth to Seventy-Seventh Street and Lexington to Fifth Avenue. The neighborhood is named for James Lenox, a merchant who owned farmland here in the nineteenth century.

As the New York and Harlem Railroad and elevated trains reached the Upper East Side in the 1800s, breweries and piano factories were built along Fourth Avenue, renamed Park Avenue in the late 1800s. Wealthy brewers George Ehret and Jacob Ruppert and industrialist Andrew Carnegie built mansions in what became **Carnegie Hill**. Its boundaries are Eighty-Sixth to Ninety-Sixth Street and Lexington to Fifth Avenue.

A small village grew around the Eighty-Sixth Street railroad station, which became **Yorkville**. German immigrants moved from the Lower East Side to Yorkville beginning in 1880. Irish, Czech, Slovak, Hungarian, and Lebanese immigrants arrived over time. Its boundaries are from Seventy-Ninth to Ninety-Sixth Street and the East River to Third Avenue. The neighborhood lost much of its German identity by 1930, when most German New Yorkers lived in Queens.

The **Upper West Side** is a largely residential neighborhood of brownstones and luxury apartment buildings that runs from 59th to 110th Street and Central Park West to the Hudson River. Dutch settlers in the seventeenth century established the **Bloomingdale District** in the area above Ninety-Sixth Street from Amsterdam Avenue to the Hudson River. The neighborhood's Anglicized name may derive from Bloemendaal, a town in the Netherlands' tulip region. The Bloomingdale District is often called **Manhattan Valley**, owing to the gentle slope of the land from 96th to 110th Street.

San Juan Hill, an African American neighborhood of tenements, jazz clubs, and Black churches, was razed in the 1960s to build the Lincoln Center for the Performing Arts. San Juan Hill ranged from Fifty-Ninth to Sixty-Fifth Street and Amsterdam to West End Avenue.

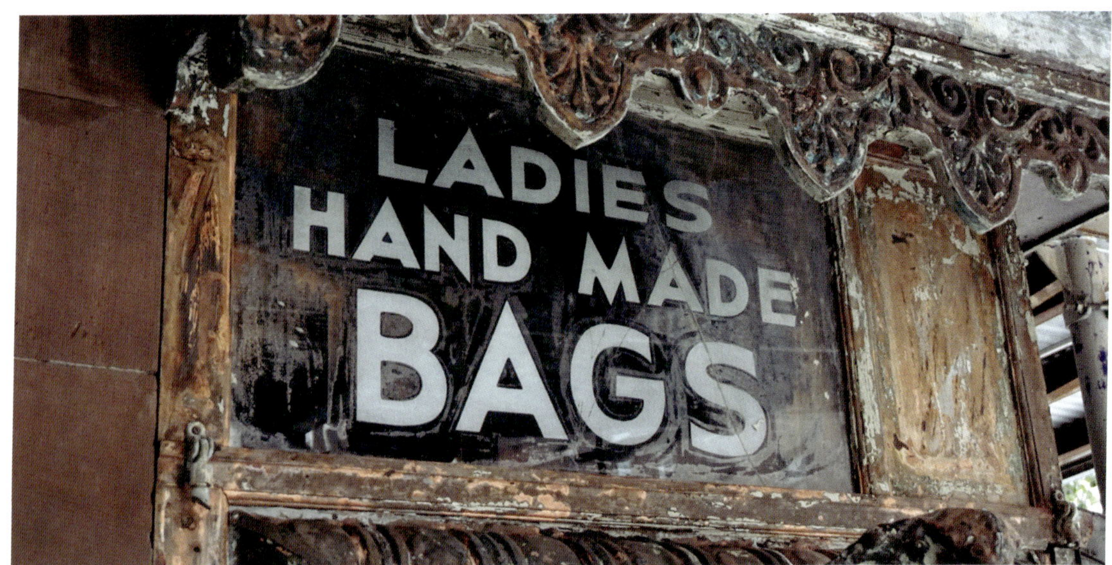

1024 Lexington Avenue

While **Harlem** is known as the center of African American culture in New York and perhaps the entire country, the neighborhood has been home to many ethnic groups. Native Americans farmed the flatlands before the Dutch established the settlement of New Haarlem, after the Dutch city of Haarlem, in 1660. After the Civil War, Italian and Jewish immigrants moved here.

By the early twentieth century, Blacks arrived as part of the Great Migration to escape the Jim Crow South and find better jobs. Puerto Rican and , atin American migration began after World War I. African Americans began to leave Harlem after World War II for the outer boroughs, in a trend that has continued. Gentrification began in the early 1990s. The influx of new businesses on 125th Street, Harlem's "Main Stem," helped revitalize the neighborhood.

Harlem encompasses much of northern Manhattan. Its general boundaries are 96th to 155th Street across the width of Manhattan. Three distinct neighborhoods have evolved: East, Central, and West Harlem.

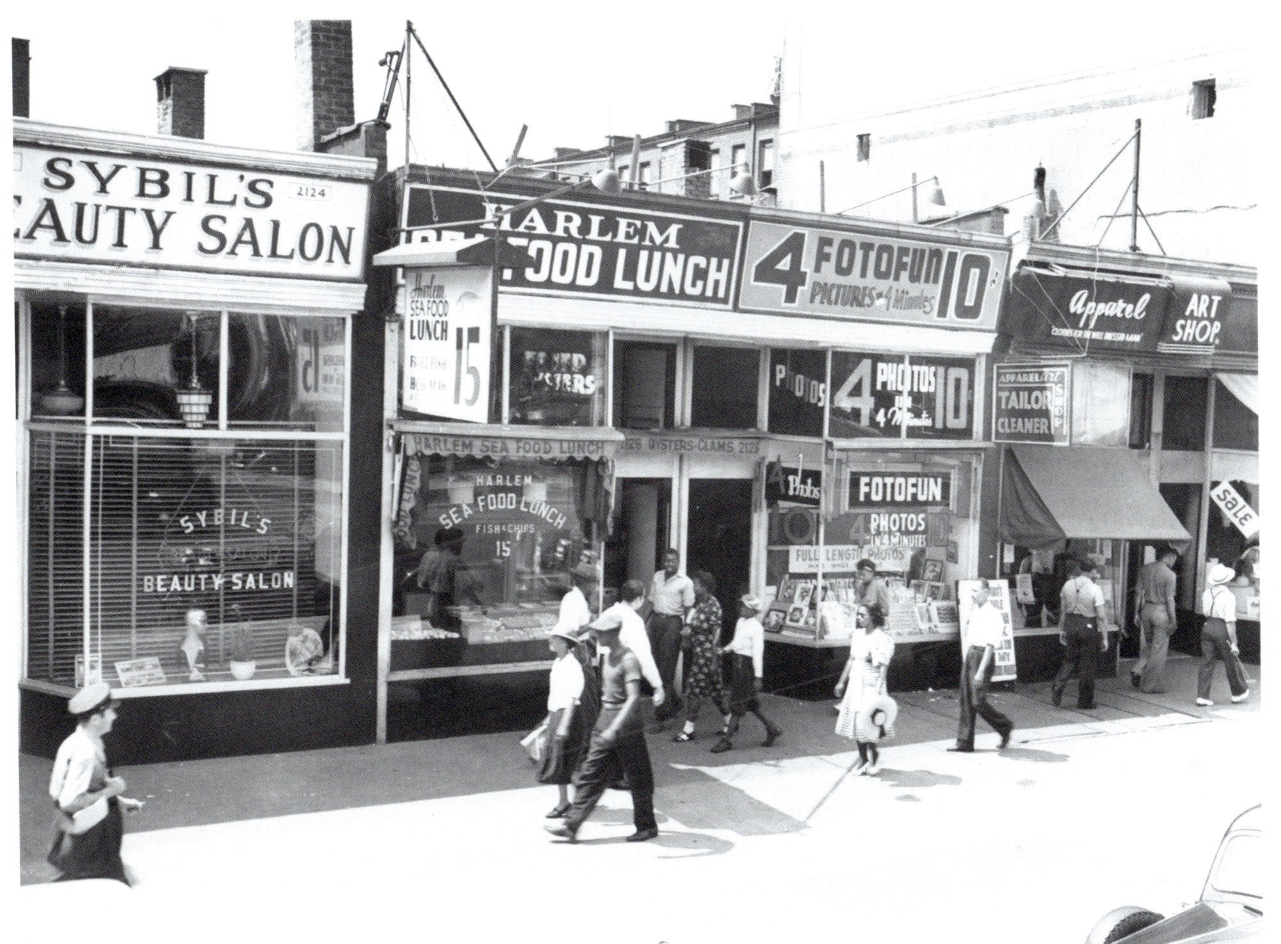

Harlem storefronts, 1939. *Courtesy of Schomburg Center for Research in Black Culture, Photographs and Prints Division, New York Public Library Digital Collections*

East Harlem is a predominantly Latinx community, called Spanish Harlem or El Barrio (the Neighborhood). Bodegas, restaurants, and botanicas, which sell folk medicine and religious items, line its streets. Storefronts house Catholic and evangelistic Protestant churches.

East Harlem runs from 96th to about 142nd Street and from the East River and Harlem River to Fifth Avenue. German, Irish, Scandinavian, and eastern European Jewish immigrants moved here in the early 1900s. By the 1930s, more than 100,000 southern Italian and Sicilian immigrants lived in Italian Harlem, Manhattan's first , ittle Italy neighborhood.

East Harlem suffered from poverty, drug abuse, and a high crime rate in the 1960s and 1970s. New, market-rate housing has been built in the twenty-first century as the neighborhood has become more culturally diverse.

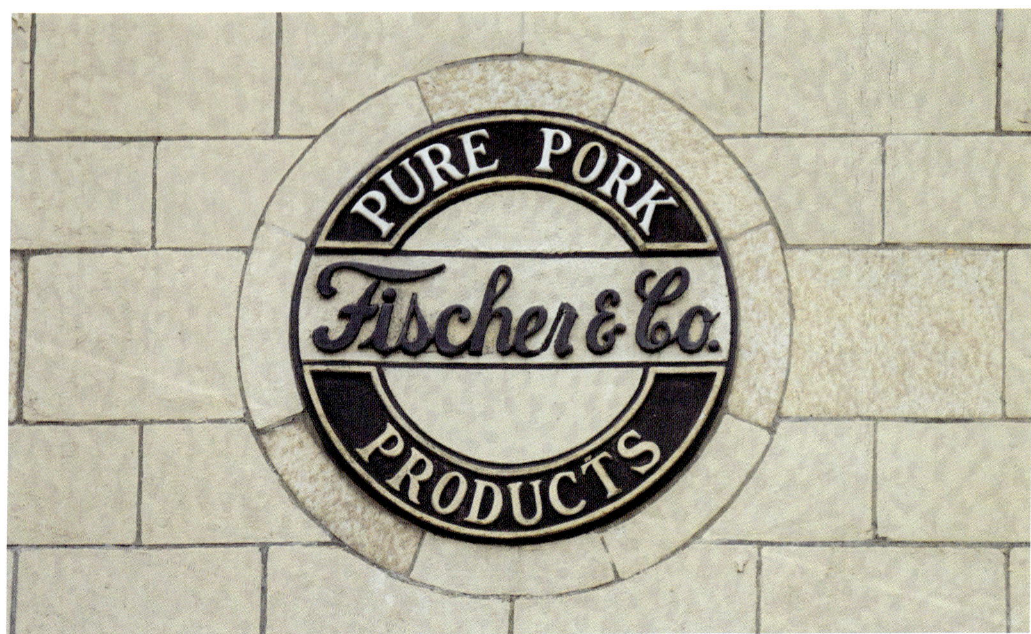

2291 Second Avenue

Central Harlem runs from 110th to 155th Street and Park to St. Nicholas Avenue. In the 1880s Central Harlem was envisioned as an upper- and middle-class neighborhood for white residents. Whites resisted living here, and buildings remained empty until 1919, when middle-class Black families moved into townhouses along Strivers' Row on 138th and 139th Street.

The Harlem Renaissance of the 1920s was born here, a fertile period for African American artists, writers, actors, and musicians. During the Harlem Renaissance, some of America's greatest jazz musicians, poets, artists, and writers emerged from the nightclubs, theaters, and dance halls of Central Harlem. The period ended in the early 1930s, when the neighborhood was devastated by the job losses of the Great Depression.

West Harlem comprises three neighborhoods: Morningside Heights, Manhattanville, and Hamilton Heights.

Morningside Heights is a primarily residential neighborhood on a high plateau between Morningside and Riverside Park. Its boundaries are from 110th to 125th Street and from Morningside to Riverside Drive. Its main thoroughfare is Broadway. Columbia University owns much of Morningside Heights, which contains a variety of academic and religious institutions. The Cathedral of St. John the Divine and Grant's Tomb are located here.

Development began in the early 1900s, when the first subway line was built, linking Morningside Heights with Lower Manhattan. It was a neighborhood of white middle-class families until the Great Depression, when whites left the neighborhood for the suburbs. They were replaced by African American and Puerto Rican families. Gentrification began in the 1980s after a period of decline.

Manhattanville runs from 122nd to 135th Street and from Adam Clayton Powell Jr. Boulevard to Riverside Drive. The village of Manhattanville was established in 1806 and populated by wealthy merchants, mostly Quakers. Manhattanville's proximity to the Hudson River made it an important port for freight bound for Upper Manhattan. Latin American immigrants moved here in the twentieth century. Columbia University has expanded into Manhattanville, which houses many of its students and faculty.

Hamilton Heights is named after Founding Father Alexander Hamilton, who lived the last two years of his life on his estate here, when it was mostly farmland. The area is now part of the Hamilton Grange National Memorial.

Hamilton Heights spans from 135th to 155th Street and Edgecombe and St. Nicholas Avenue to Riverside Drive. Like Morningside Heights, its spacious brownstones and row houses were left empty after the white flight of the 1930s. The neighborhood became home to a large Black professional class.

In the 1920s, wealthy African Americans moved to the **Sugar Hill** neighborhood, which runs from 145th to 155th Street and Edgecombe to Amsterdam Avenue. Its name is reflective of the "sweet life" of its residents during the Harlem Renaissance, including Duke Ellington, W. E. B. Du Bois, Thurgood Marshall, and Cab Calloway.

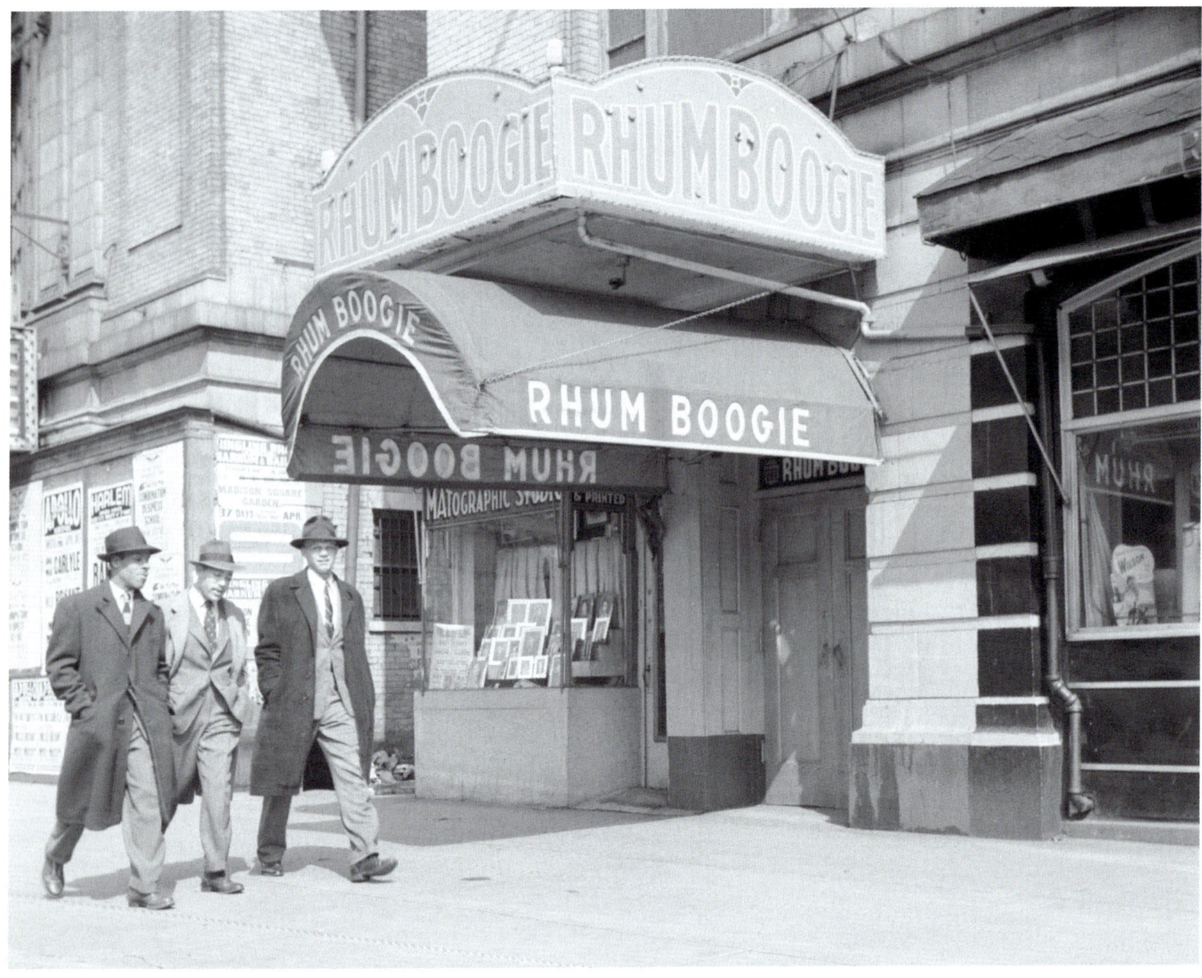

Rhum Boogie Club, 2223 Seventh Avenue, Harlem, 1943. *Courtesy of the Farm Security Administration, Office of War Information Photograph Collection, Library of Congress*

SHOPPING

OMEGA OIL

Omega Oil was a liniment that promised to cure everything from weak backs and lumbago to sunburn and sweaty feet. The company moved to New York from Boston at the beginning of the twentieth century and spent decades advertising its dubious curative properties in newspapers and on walls across the country.

Omega pioneered the use of endorsements by professional athletes. A 1934 *New York Daily News* ad featured boxer John L. Sullivan, who states, "You can put me down as saying that Omega Oil is fine stuff to rub on the body and limbs. Its green color suits me, too."

Omega Oil was acquired by Colgate-Palmolive-Peet in 1931 and disappeared sometime after 1957 when it was accused of false advertising by the Federal Trade Commission.

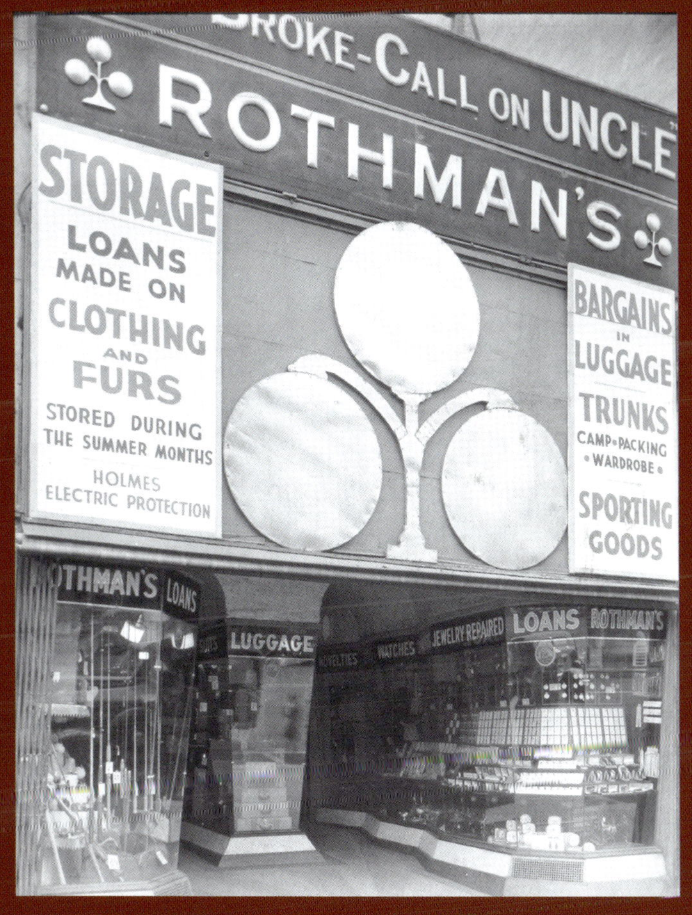

Rothman's Pawn Shop, 149 Eighth Avenue, 1938. *Courtesy of the Miriam and Ira D. Wallach Division of Art, Prints and Photographs: Photography Collection, New York Public Library.*

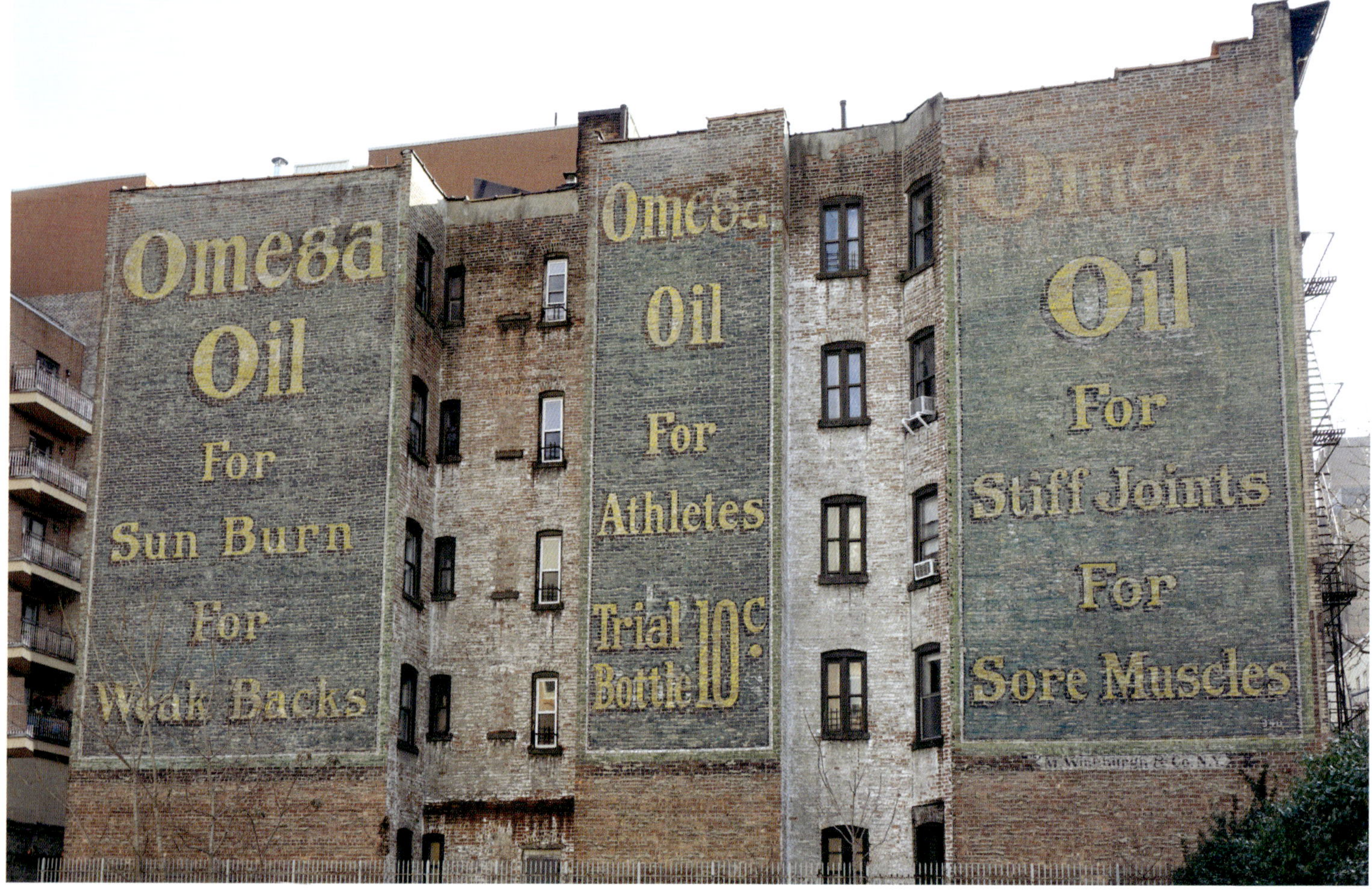

287 West 147th Street

METROPOLITAN WINE & LIQUOR

"If the up-up price of wine has discouraged its use at your table, except on occasion, our budget discovery should be heartening news," advised the *New York Herald Tribune* in 1948. "The Longo brothers, Jack, Joe and Chris, have a store at 474 Ninth Avenue, selling a line of dry reds for as little as 54 cents a fifth or $1.96 for a gallon."

The Longo Brothers were Italian immigrants who opened Metropolitan Wine & Liquor in 1933. Their name and the year they opened the shop are displayed across the roofline. A faded and defaced sign for Metropolitan remains on the north side of the building. Metropolitan operated in Hell's Kitchen until 1998.

474 Ninth Avenue

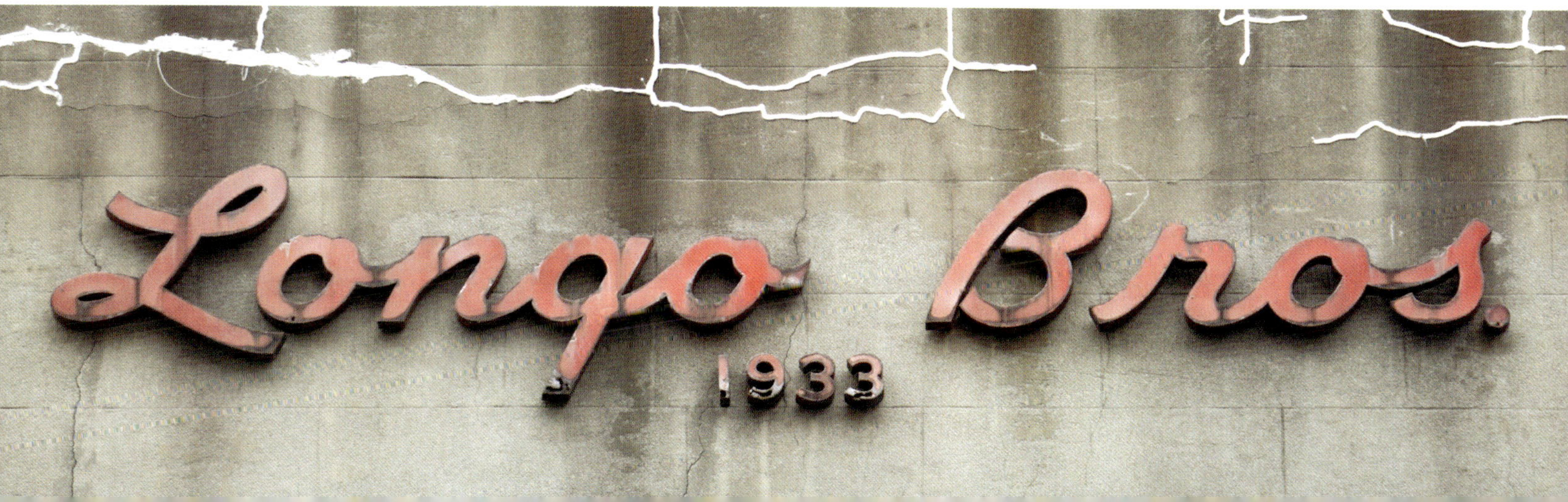

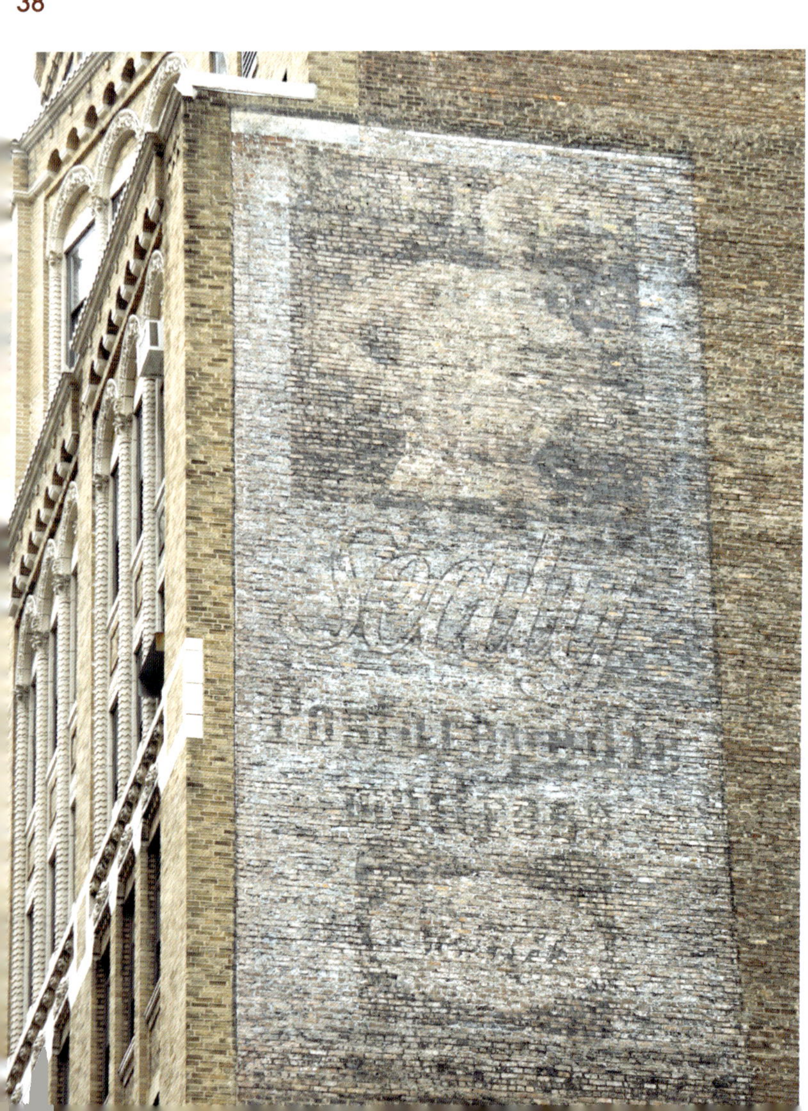

SEALY

In 1881, cotton gin builder Daniel Hayes began to make cotton-filled mattresses for his neighbors in Sealy, Texas. In 1889 Hayes invented a machine that compressed cotton for his mattresses. He licensed the device to other mattress manufacturers with the name "Mattresses from Sealy." The brand's popularity grew and Sealy became one of the largest mattress manufacturers in the world.

In 1950, Sealy's Posturepedic mattress debuted and became one of Sealy's main brands. Its sign tops a stack that includes Doehler Metal Furniture and Manning-Bowman.

128 East Thirty-Second Street

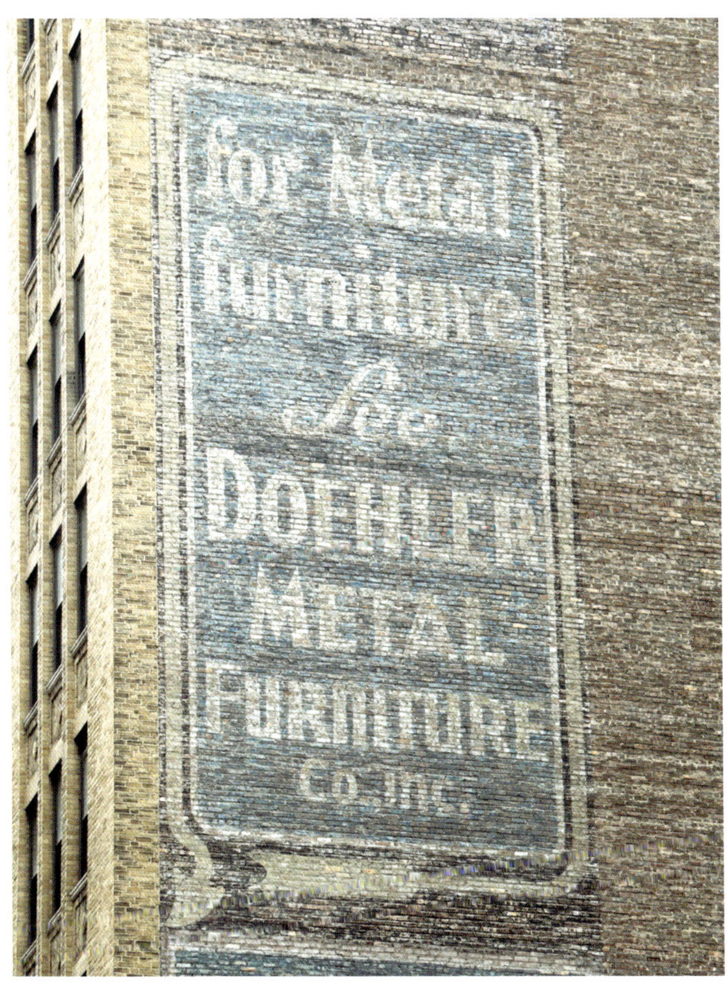

DOEHLER FURNITURE

Doehler Die Casting was founded in Brooklyn in 1907 by German immigrant Herman Doehler. Die casting is a method of producing metal parts by forcing molten metal into a mold made of two pieces of steel, or dies. By 1942 Doehler was considered the largest die caster in the world.

The company established Doehler Furniture, which moved into this building in 1933. Doehler Furniture did a brisk business during and after World War II, selling tables, chairs, desks, and lockers. The company remained here until about 1990.

128 East Thirty-Second Street

MANNING-BOWMAN

Manning-Bowman was founded in Meriden, Connecticut, in 1832, a manufacturer of ceramic and metal giftware. Its sign reads, "Manning-Bowman Means Best—Electric Appliances, Smart Gifts." In the early 1900s, the company expanded its line to include chafing dishes, coffee percolators, and copper tableware. By 1915 Manning-Bowman added electrical appliances: irons, toasters, waffle makers, and, later, electric clocks.

Portions of the company began to be sold off before World War II, and its Meriden plant closed about 1951. Manning-Bowman operated an office and showroom here from about 1945 to 1975. Its art deco tableware and giftware remain popular with antique collectors.

128 East Thirty-Second Street

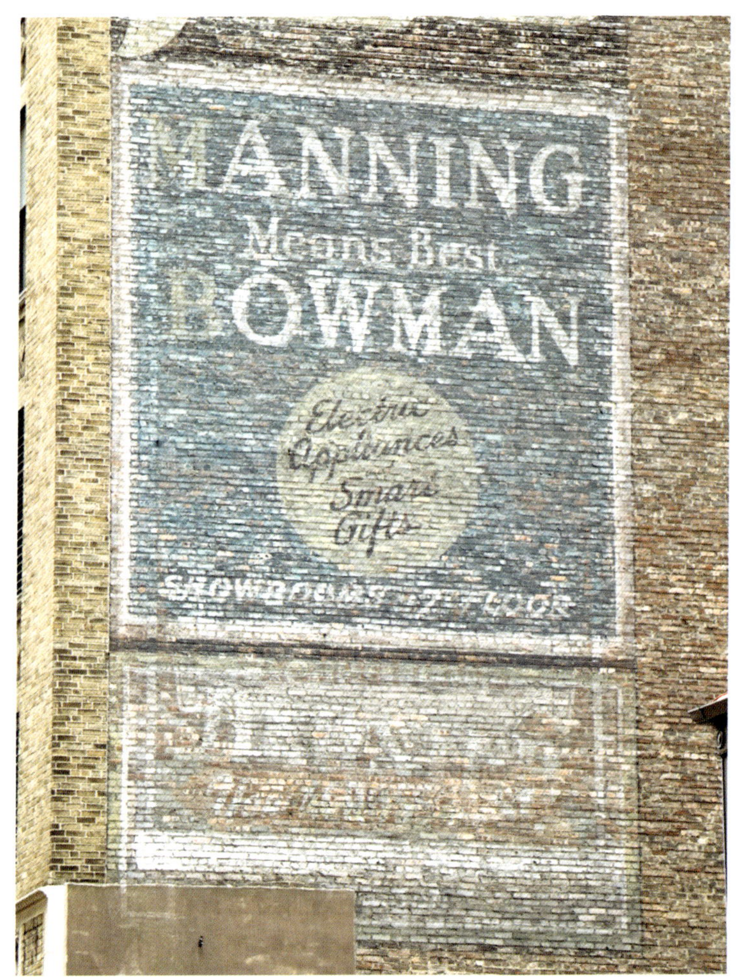

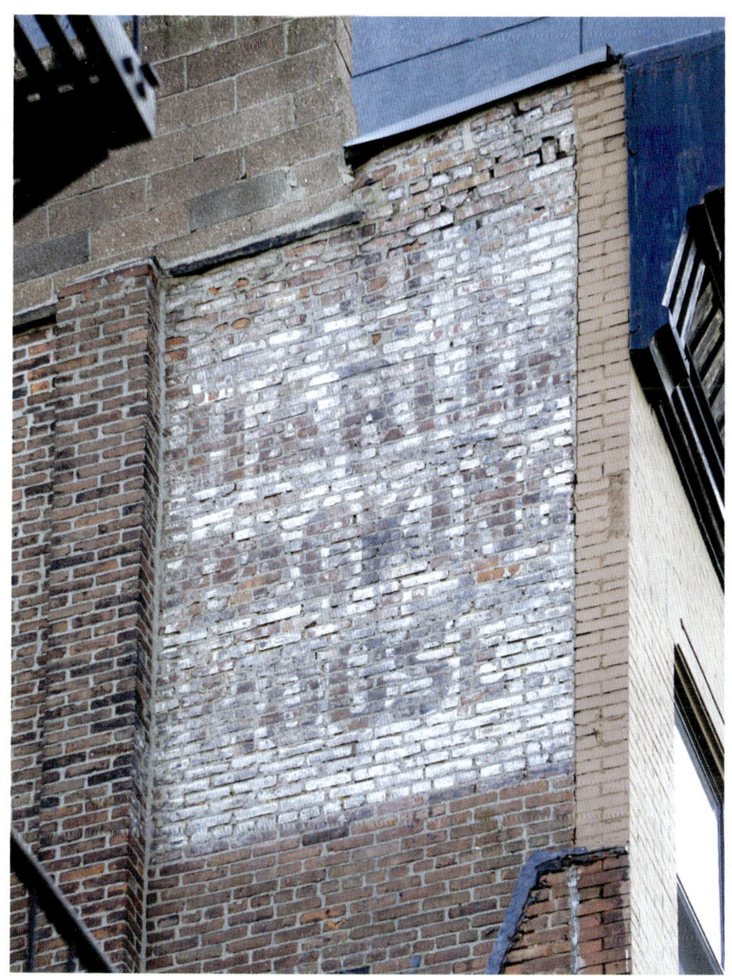

RICHARD WEBBER HARLEM PACKING HOUSE

In the late nineteenth century, Richard Webber operated one of the largest meatpacking businesses in the US. His complex of buildings in Harlem included a slaughterhouse and a retail store advertised as "The Food Department Store." Its 1895 Romanesque Revival building received landmark status in 2017.

Webber sold meat, fish, poultry, and vegetables at the store and offered delivery to New Jersey: "We can serve you at your Country Home with the same good results as at your City Residence," read a 1910 ad in the *Hackensack* (NJ) *Record*. Webber died in 1908; his company operated in Harlem until 1928.

2191 Third Avenue

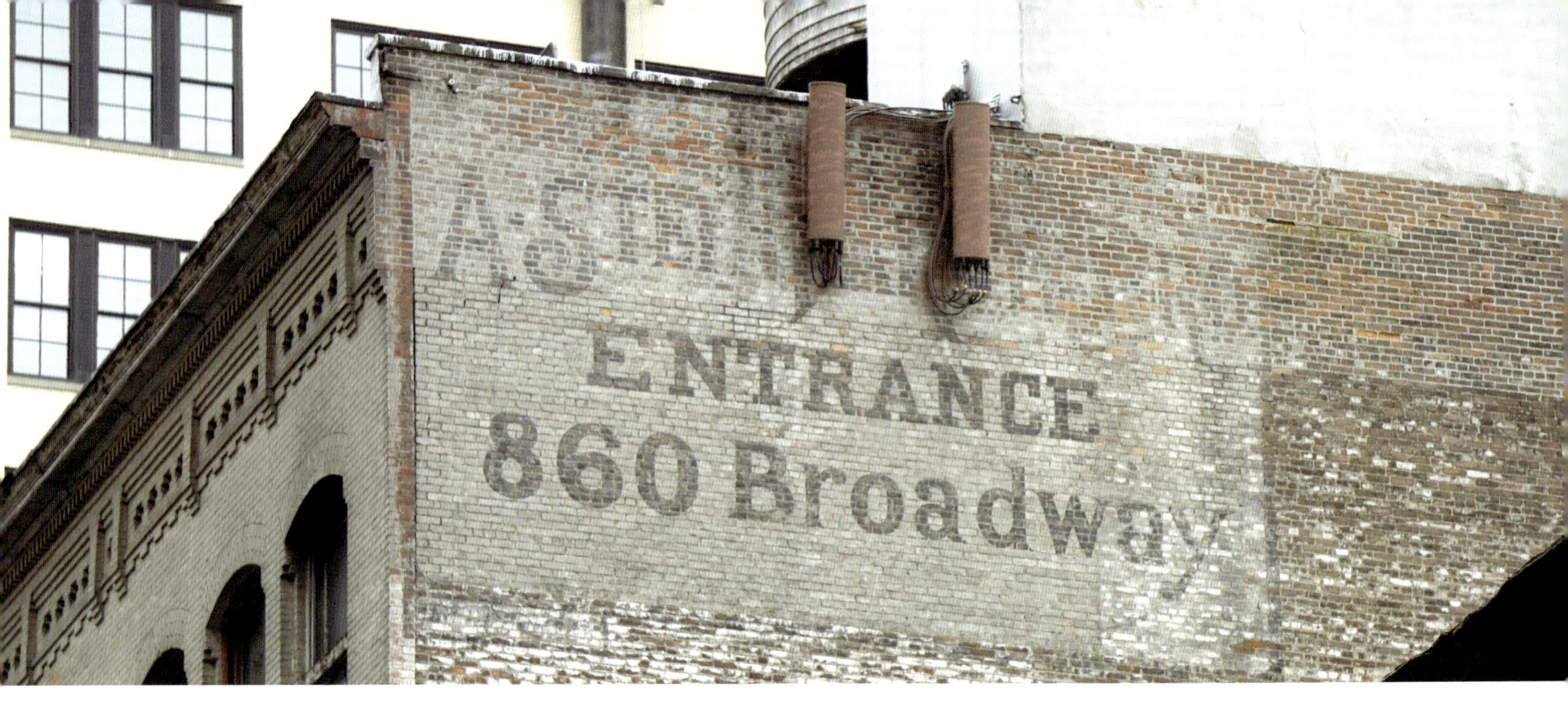

860 Broadway

A. STEINHARDT

Brothers Abraham and Edward Steinhardt founded their notions and small-wares import business in Lower Manhattan in 1873. As the company expanded, it moved to larger locations. Steinhardt added fans, purses, holiday goods, dolls, and novelties by 1912, when it moved to Union Square. The company went out of business in 1929.

BAZAR FRANCAIS

In the 1890s, Charles R. Ruegger sold imported French kitchenware under the Bazar Francais brand from his shop downtown. By the 1930s Bazar Francais moved to Chelsea, where it sold home furnishings, earthenware, and copper and iron pots imported from France and manufactured in its factory.

By 1969, Bazar Francais was considered the first gourmet store, "known the world over," its ads claimed, "for exemplary copper and kitchenware." Bazar Francais closed in 1975.

668 Sixth Avenue

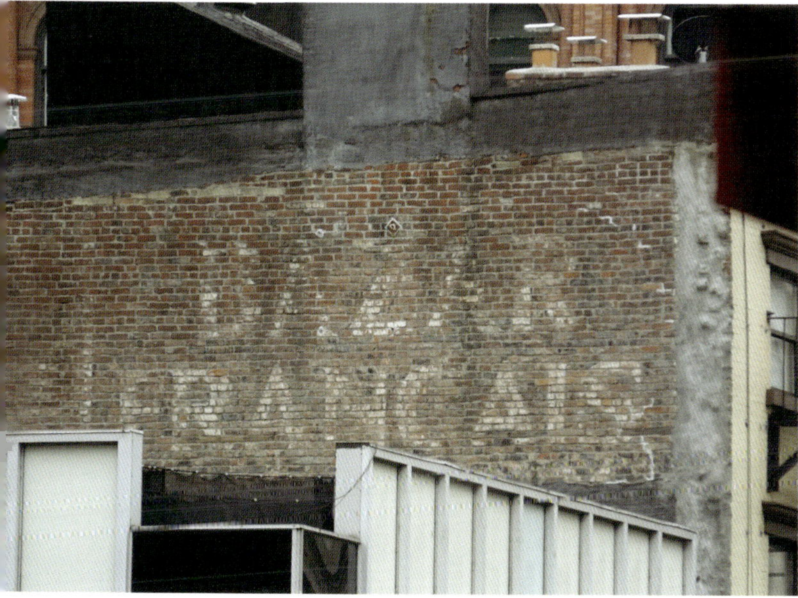

666 Sixth Avenue

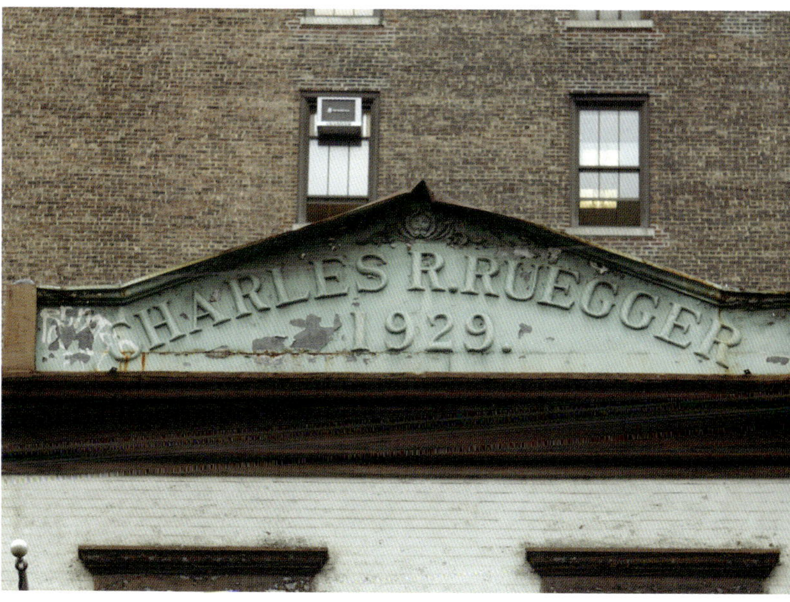

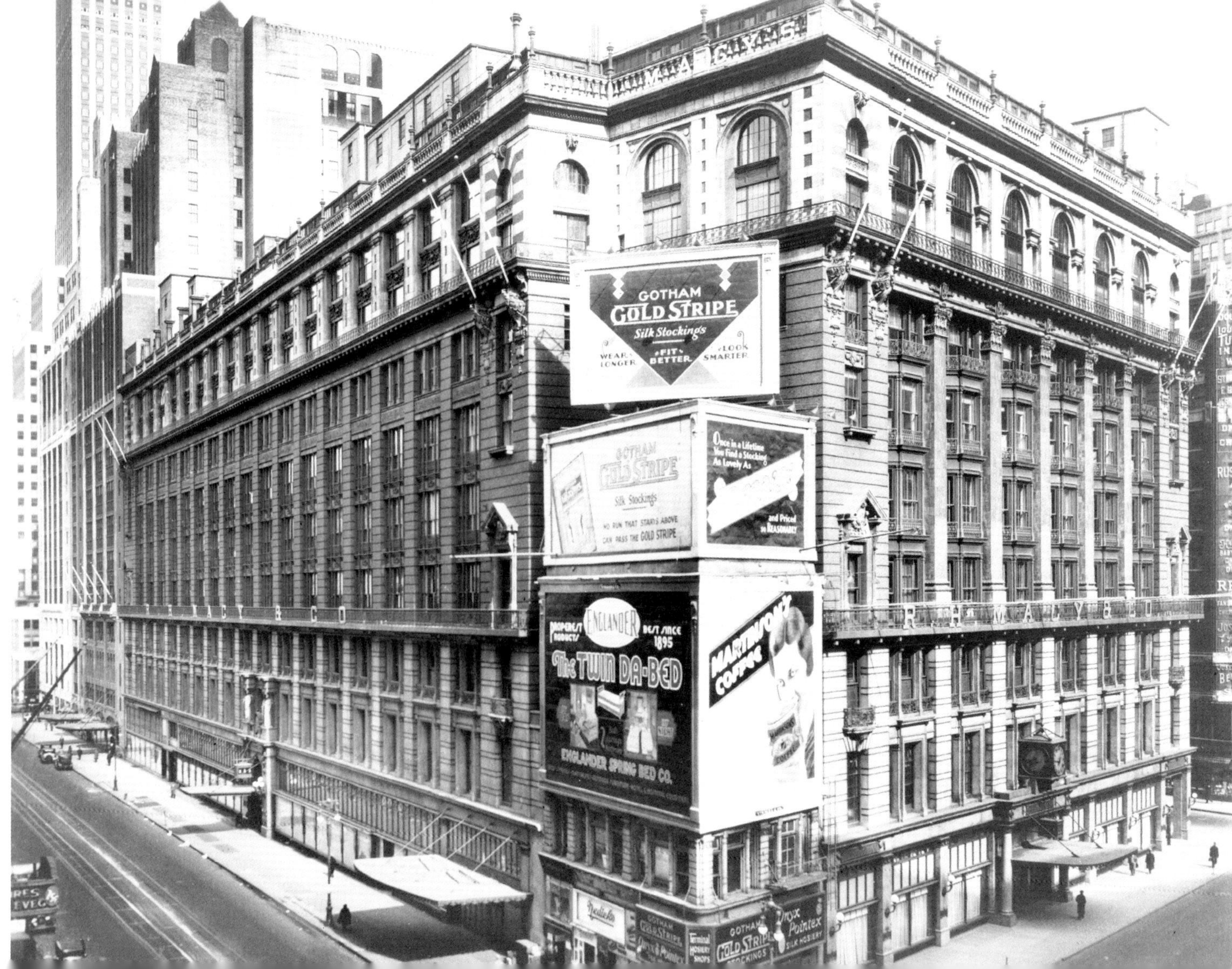
GOTHAM
GOLD STRIPE
Silk Stockings
WEAR LONGER
FIT BETTER
LOOK SMARTER
GOTHAM
GOLD STRIPE
Silk Stockings
NO RUN THAT STARTS ABOVE CAN PASS THE GOLD STRIPE
Once in a Lifetime You Find a Stocking As Lovely As
and Priced so Reasonably
PROPEREST PRODUCTS
ENGLANDER
BEST SINCE 1895
The TWIN DA-BED
ENGLANDER SPRING BED CO.
MARTINSON'S COFFEE
R. H. MACY & CO.
GOTHAM GOLD STRIPE STOCKINGS
Pointex SILK HOSIERY

Opposite: Macy's, 151 West Thirty-Fourth Street, Herald Square, 1931. *Courtesy of Prints and Photographs Division, Library of Congress*

MACY'S

Macy's sold fancy dry goods—textiles and ready-to-wear clothes—when it opened downtown in 1858. Macy's moved to Herald Square in 1902. The store expanded in three stages from Broadway to Seventh Avenue. When it was completed in 1924, it was the largest store in the world.

A vintage Macy's sign still exists, but it is no longer visible from the sidewalk. Sharp-eyed visitors to the Empire State Building's 86th Floor Observation Deck can spot the faded sign.

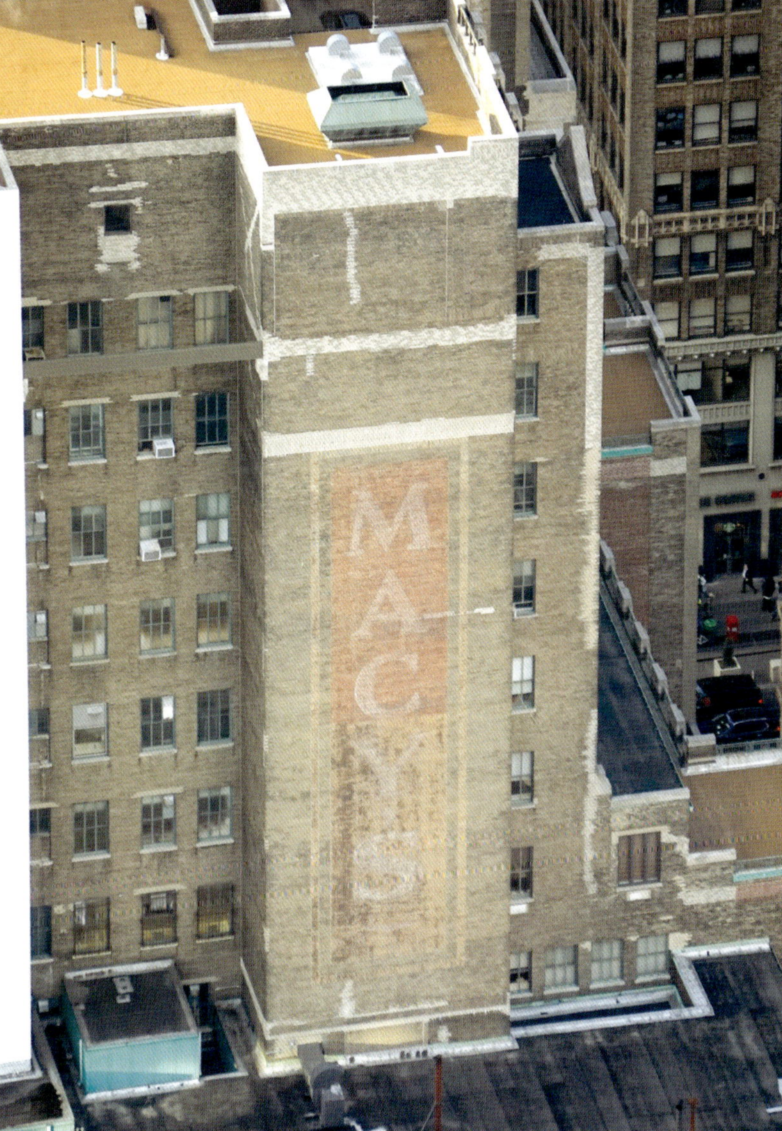

166 West Thirty-Fifth Street

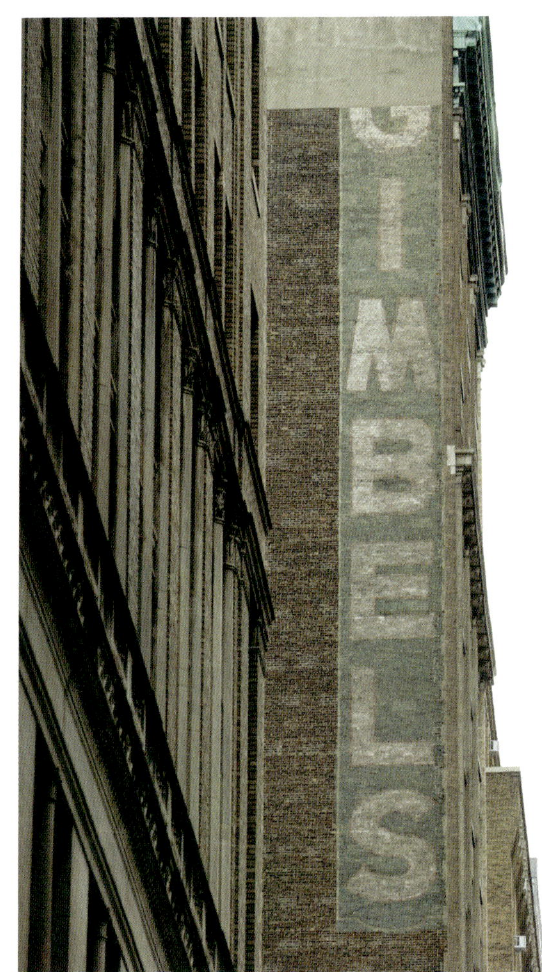

GIMBELS

When Gimbels opened in 1910 a block south of Macy's, it soon became the retailer's chief competitor. The saying "Does Gimbels tell Macy's?" became popular, meaning competitors would never share business information. Customers often confused the two stores, but Macy's remained more upscale. Gimbels was conveniently located above the subway. It was the first store in New York to feature a "bargain basement" with low-cost items. Gimbels closed its doors in 1986, but its ghost sign remains on the store's warehouse.

119 West Thirty-First Street

BLOOMINGDALE'S

Joseph and Lyman Bloomingdale opened their East Side Bazaar on the Lower East Side in 1872, selling a wide variety of European fashions. It became one of the first department stores. The Bloomingdale brothers moved to Fifty-Ninth Street and Lexington Avenue in 1872, later expanding to cover the entire block.

In the early 1900s, Bloomingdale's posted their slogan "All Cars Transfer to Bloomingdale's" on delivery wagons, beach umbrellas, and wall signs visible to passengers on elevated trains.

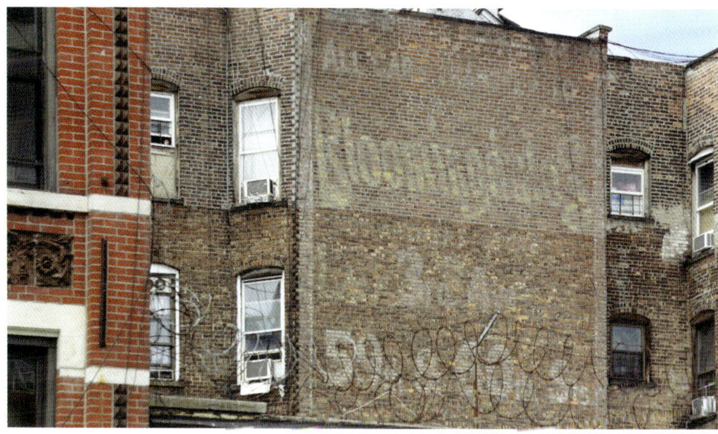

124 East 116th Street

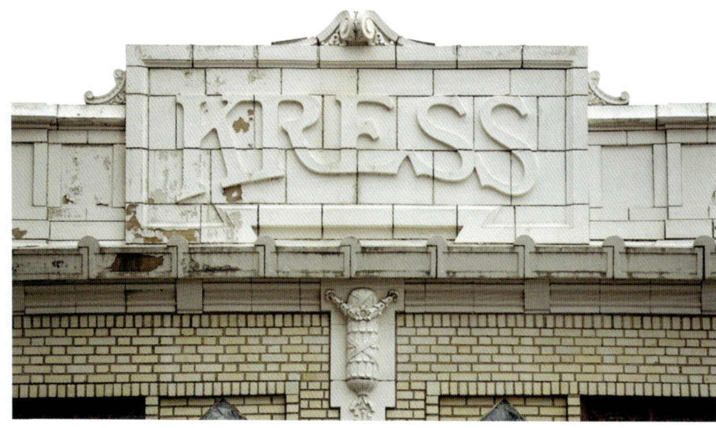

1915 Third Avenue

KRESS

Samuel H. Kress launched the first of a chain of 5-10-25 Cent Stores in 1896. Kress would grow to include 264 stores. Kress stores were noted for their elaborate architecture and became prominent local landmarks.

Genesco, a footwear retailer, acquired Kress in 1964 and began closing its stores in 1980. The stores that remained were sold to McCrory in 1981; most operated as Kress stores until McCrory went out of business in 2001.

MCCRORY

Woolworth, Kresge, and McCrory were among the first discount variety stores in the US. At its height, McCrory operated 1,300 stores under its own and other names. The chain was founded by John Graham McCrorey, who opened his first store in Scottdale, Pennsylvania, in 1882. The *New York Times* reported that McCrorey "was so thrifty he legally changed his name, dropping the 'e,' because he did not want to pay the cost of the extra initial in the gilt letters on his store signs" (Barmash 1987).

McCrory operated a five-and-dime store on the ground floor of this , adies' Mile building when it was built in 1911, a few years before the name change. A 1912 ad offers "15,000 Different Items for Your Selection—Nothing Over 10 Cents." Products included double boilers, curtain rods, and door panels. The department store remained in Chelsea through the 1930s.

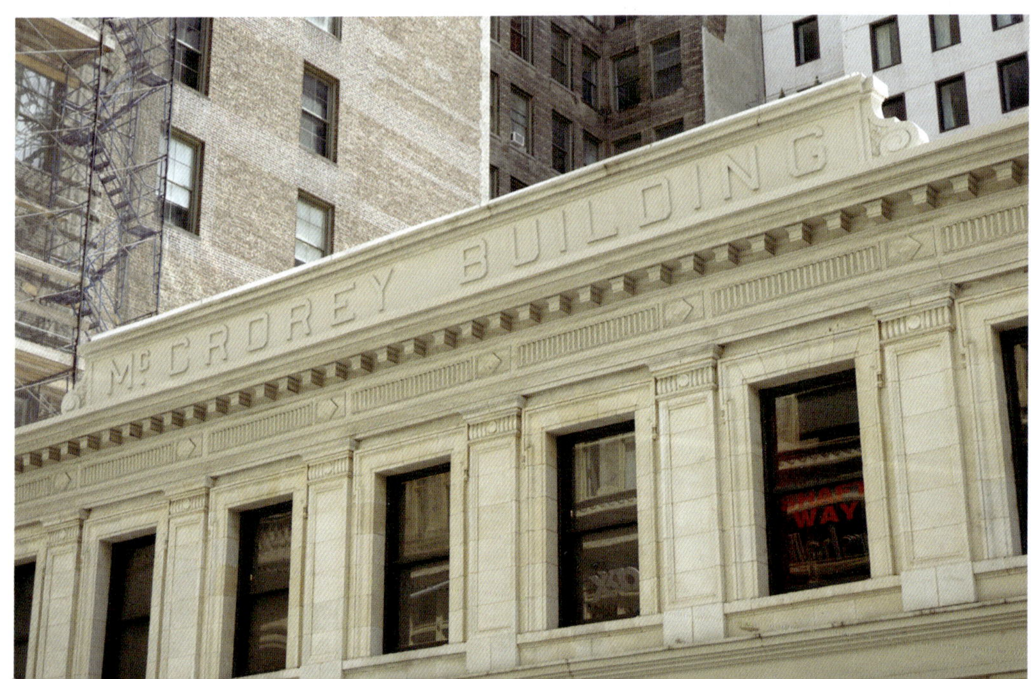

50–58 West Eighteenth Street

BARCLAY CIGARETTES

Barclay cigarettes were introduced by Brown & Williamson in 1966. The brand was relaunched in 1980 as an "ultra-low tar" cigarette. Barclay used a tuxedo-clad man in its ads with the slogan "The Pleasure Is Back." Barclay claimed its cigarettes were 99 percent tar-free. Barclay was an immediate hit but ran into trouble in 1983, when the Federal Trade Commission stated that Barclay had more tar than it advertised.

After litigation in 1998, new restrictions were placed on tobacco companies that banned ads such as this Hell's Kitchen sign, which became easy to miss when a tall building was erected across from it. In 2006, Brown & Williamson sold the Barclay brand to R. J. Reynolds. Barclay was renamed Kent and marketed in other countries.

840 Eighth Avenue

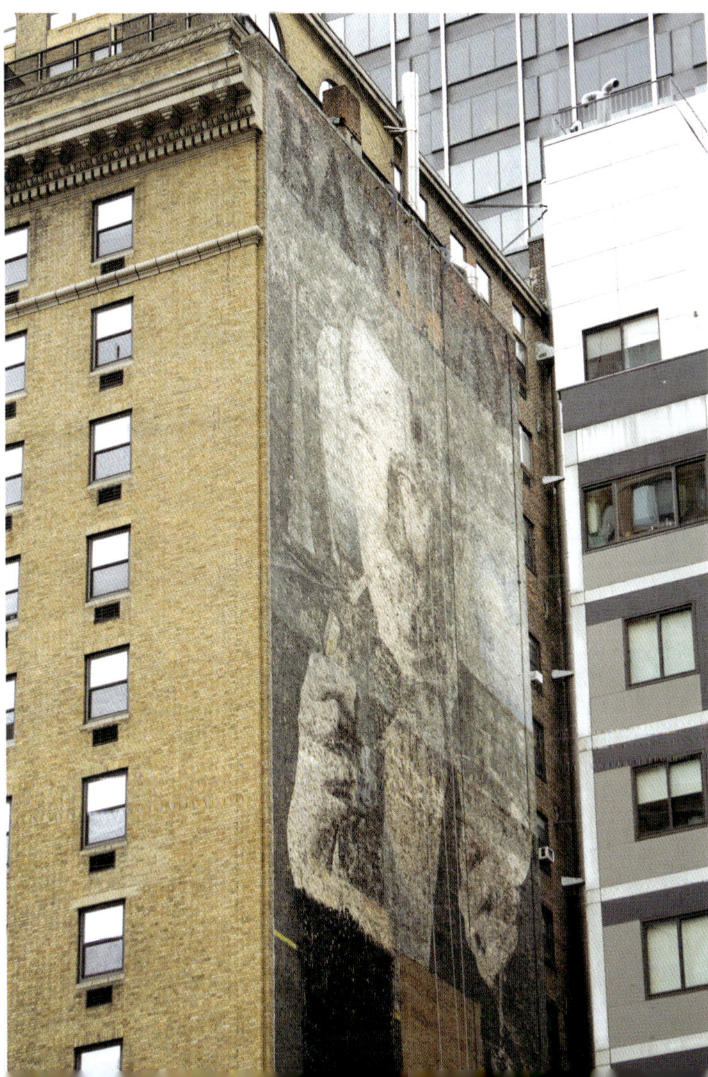

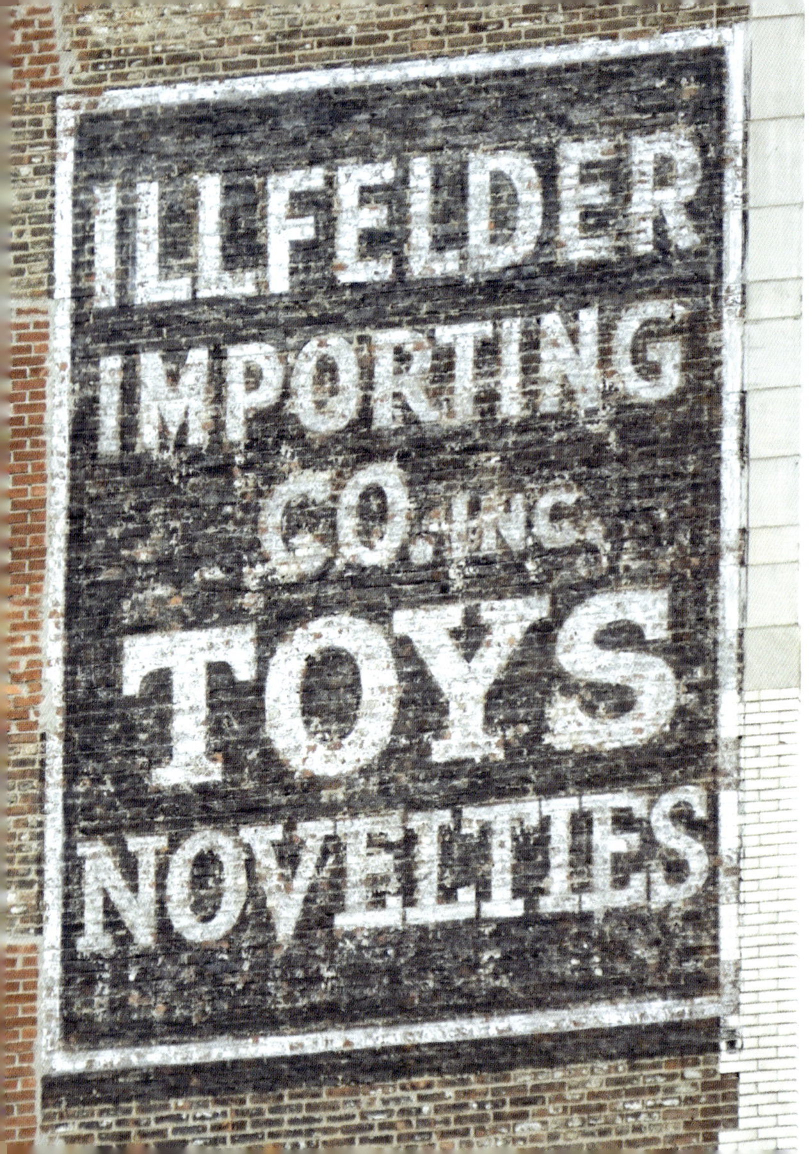

ILLFELDER

The Illfelder family operated a pencil factory in Bavaria when they opened a New York branch in 1861. The company evolved into an importer of toys, notably dolls, by the turn of the twentieth century. Illfelder moved from Lower Manhattan to this Toy District building in 1938. The company left the building about 1968.

131 East Twenty-Third Street

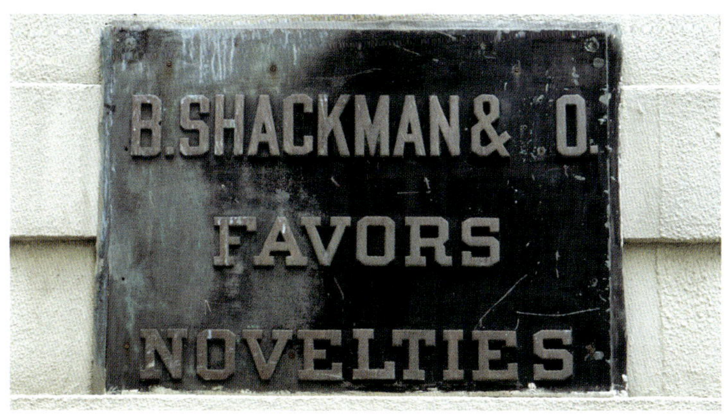

85 Fifth Avenue

B. SHACKMAN

Bertha Shackman launched her "favors and novelties" business in 1898, selling inexpensive toys, gifts, and souvenirs. B. Shackman moved its headquarters a few times in the early twentieth century, spending two decades at 906–908 Broadway before moving to the Toy District. In the 1970s, B. Shackman operated a mail-order business from the back of the store. "Up front, there is a thriving retail trade," the *New York Times* noted, "with one side of the store devoted to an immense collection of miniature furnishings and the other side to the sort of games, toys, puzzles, and novelties that seem to have vanished years ago" (Van Gelder 1976).

LOUIS MATTIA

"I love lamps," Louis Mattia told the *New York Times*. "I'm crazy about them" (Brewer 1990). Mattia operated his lamp and chandelier repair shop in Turtle Bay from 1960 to 1995. Mattia also manufactured lamps out of unusual items that included fire extinguishers, Chinese ginger jars, and, for one doctor, a human skull. Mattia's sign was revealed when an awning was removed during renovation. The ghost sign displays the old PL(aza) telephone exchange. All-number calling began in 1958, and most areas adopted it by the mid-1960s.

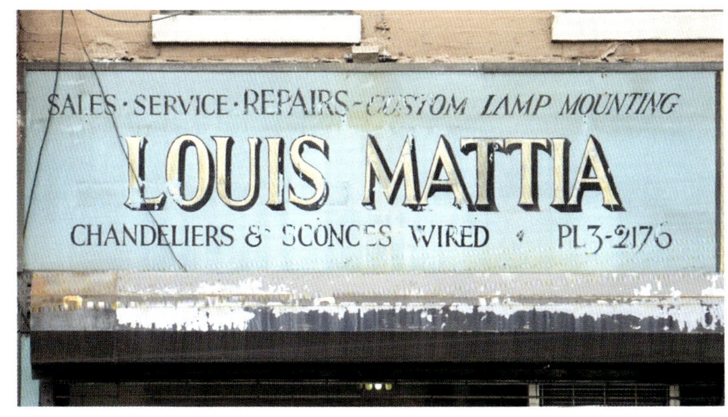

980 Second Avenue

WEBER & HEILBRONER

Weber & Heilbroner, "furnishers to men who know," was a chain of men's clothing stores founded by Milton Weber and Louis Heilbroner in 1902. Its sign on the Marbridge Building in Herald Square reads, "Stein-Bloch Clothes, in the New York Manner." The haberdashers moved here about 1923. This location was one of the last to operate when Weber & Heilbroner went out of business in the late 1970s.

950 Sixth Avenue

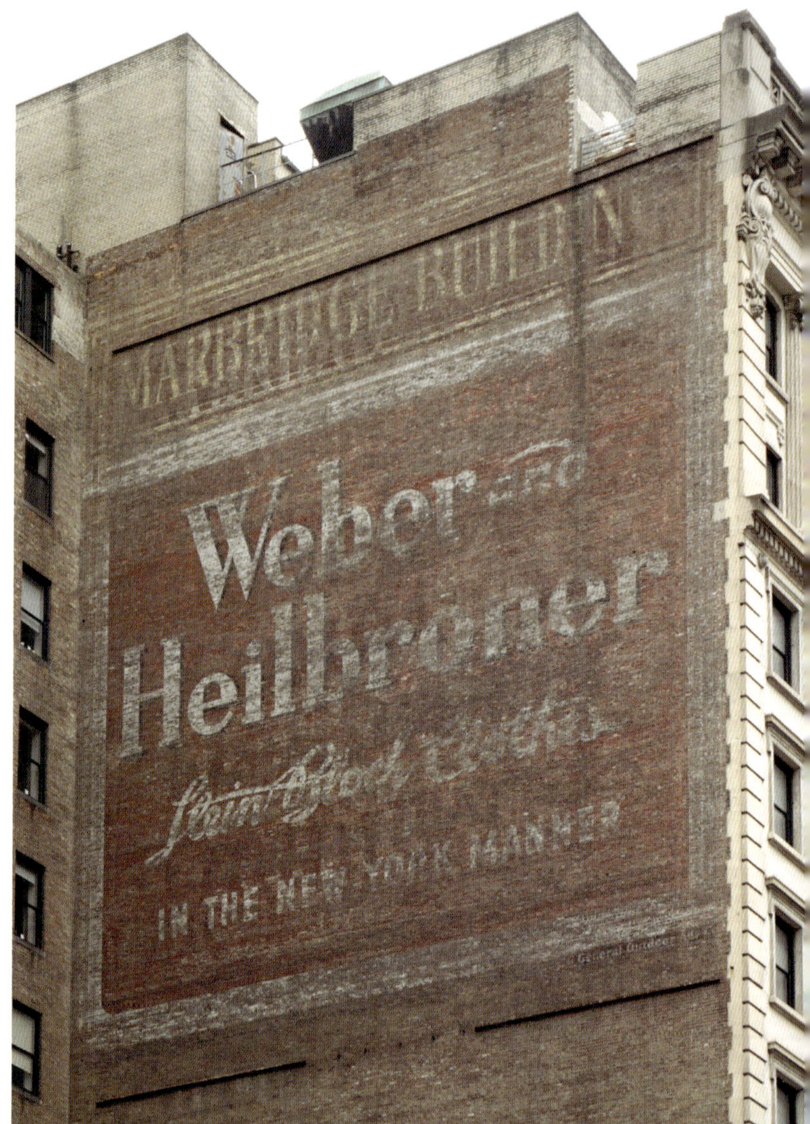

MISS WEBER MILLINERY

The faded sign on the Ladies' Mile advertises the millinery shop of Ida L. Weber. Below the shop's name and building number is the instruction "Take Elevator." Electric elevators were a relatively new invention when the hatmaker operated here from 1911 to 1913. Weber later moved to Thirty-Ninth Street in the Millinery District.

48 West Twenty-Second Street

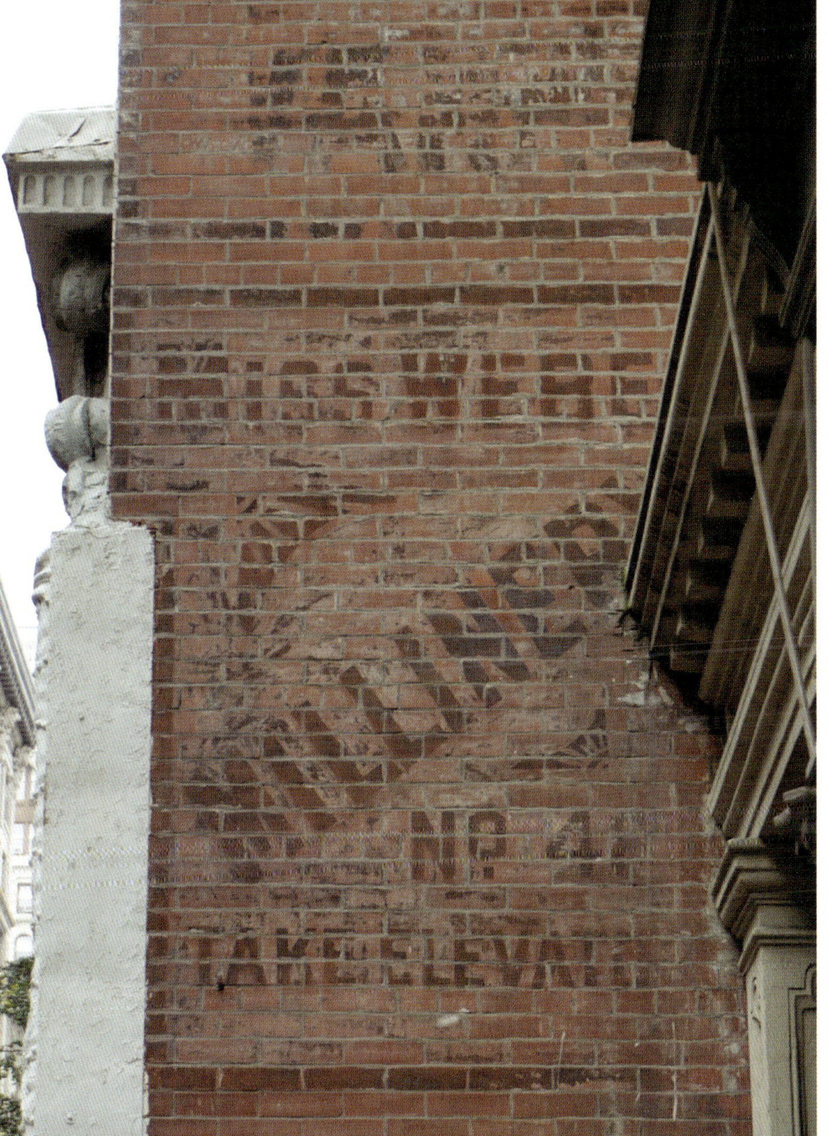

D'AIUTO

D'Aiuto boasted that it sold "the Best Cheesecake in America." Luca and Anna D'Aiuto, Italian immigrants, opened their first bakery in 1924. By the 1970s, when their son Mario took over, D'Aiuto had five stores, including its flagship in the Garment District. Mario created the Baby Watson brand of cheesecake, featuring his baby picture. "We knew we had a good cheesecake," D'Aiuto told the *New York Daily News*, "but we needed a name that wasn't as ethnic. Watson sounded good and everybody loves babies" (Hamlin 1980). Business declined, and by 2012 only the original shop remained. The business was sold that year but never recovered its past popularity.

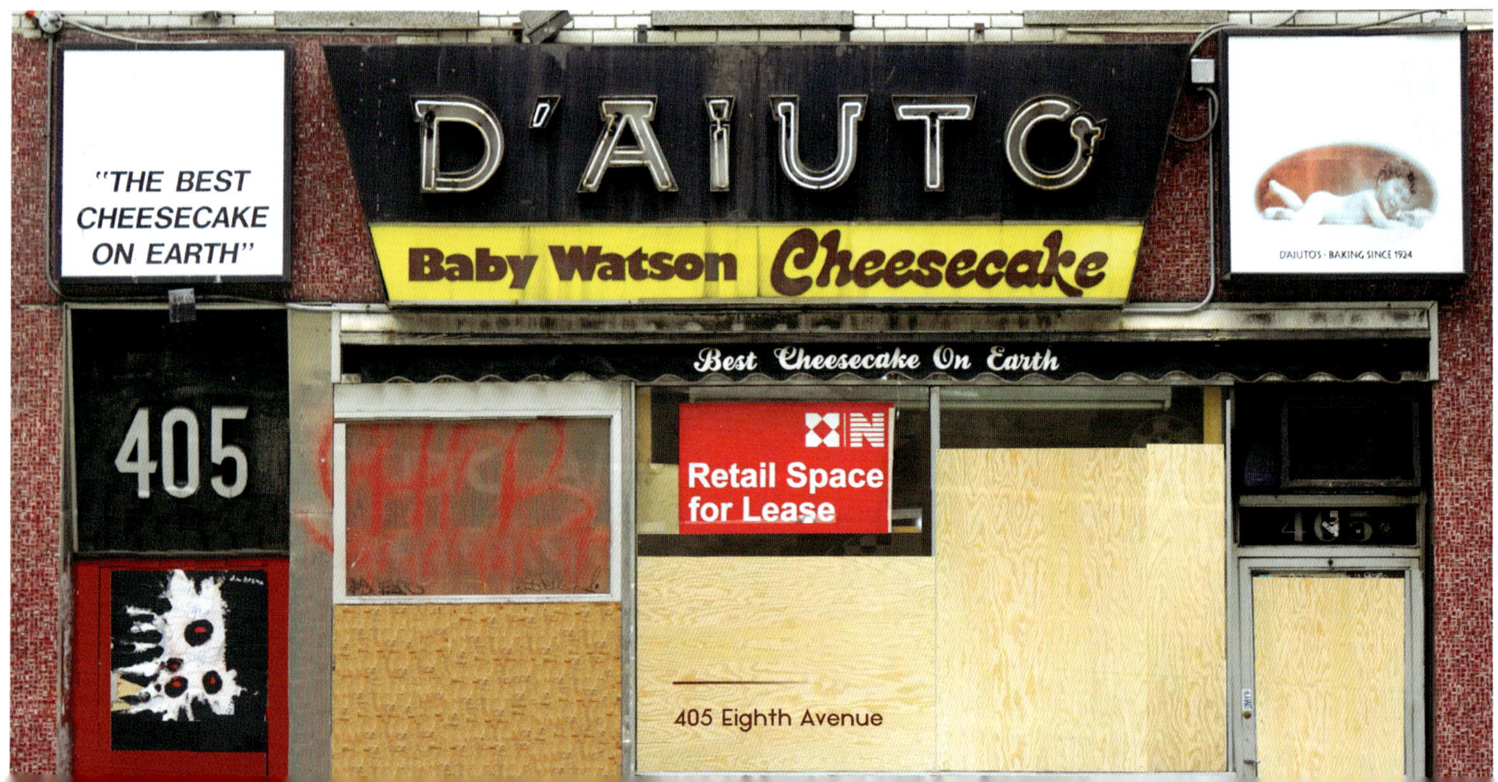

405 Eighth Avenue

GRIFFON SHEARS

Griffon Cutlery Works sold nail files, tweezers, scissors, and manicure sets. Griffon moved into its Chelsea offices in 1920, where a faint depiction of its popular pinking shears can still be seen. "The Griffon shears pinks as it cuts, gives a ravel-proof finish zig-zag edge to almost any fabric," read a 1947 *New York Daily News* ad. "Griffon has been one of the country's top scissors makers since 1888; all their years of experience went into these precision shears."

As inexpensive ready-made clothing became available in the mid-twentieth century, the popularity of home sewing declined and Griffon left Chelsea in the mid-1960s.

151 West Nineteenth Street

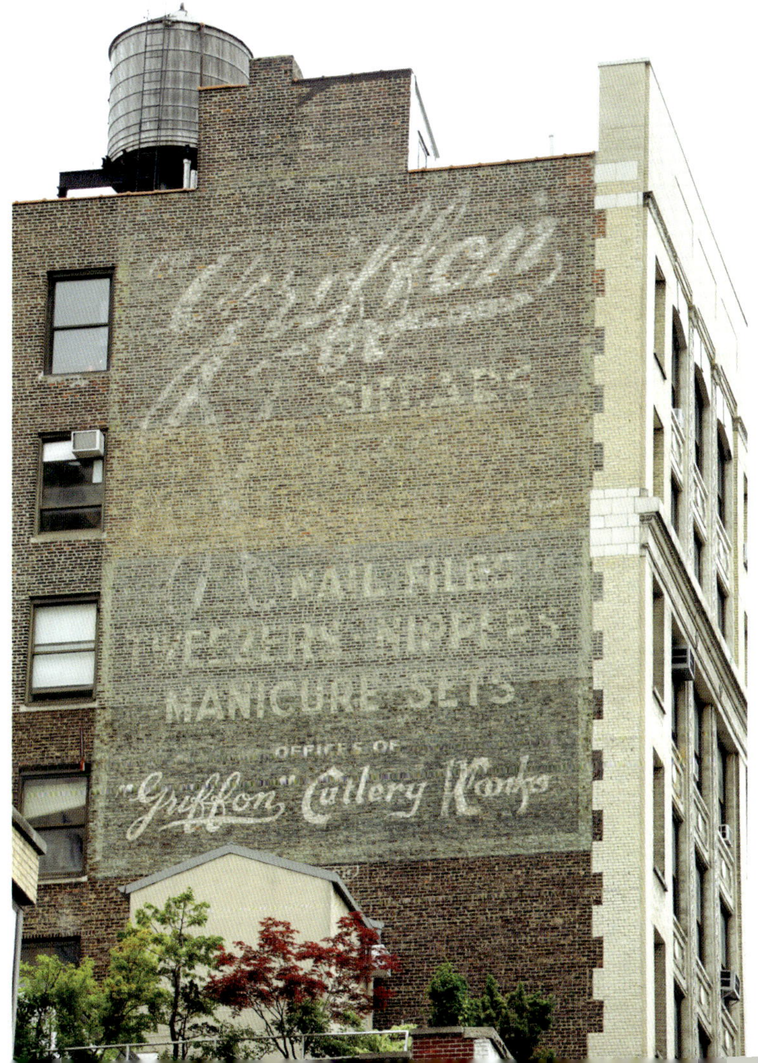

HARRIET HUBBARD

Harriet Hubbard Ayer was a Victorian-era socialite forced to reinvent herself when she was left destitute after her husband's business collapsed. Divorced in 1882, Ayer moved to New York and in 1886 founded Recamier, a beauty cream and perfume company at 25 Union Square. One story goes that on a trip to Paris, Ayer encountered a chemist who had created the formula for a face cream used by famous French socialite Juliette Recamier. Ayer purchased the formula and used it to create Recamier Toilet Cream, which claimed, "It will remove tan and sunburn, pimples, red spots or blotches, and make your face and hands as smooth, as white, and as soft as an infant's."

Dogged by scandals and unscrupulous family members, Ayer lost the company and was committed to a mental asylum for fourteen months. On her release, Ayer wrote a popular beauty column for the *New York World*. A new company with the Hubbard name formed in 1903 and moved to Kips Bay in 1911, where it remained until about 1950. E. J. Audi Fine Furniture & Rugs shares the wall with Harriet Hubbard's sign.

317 East Thirty-Fourth Street

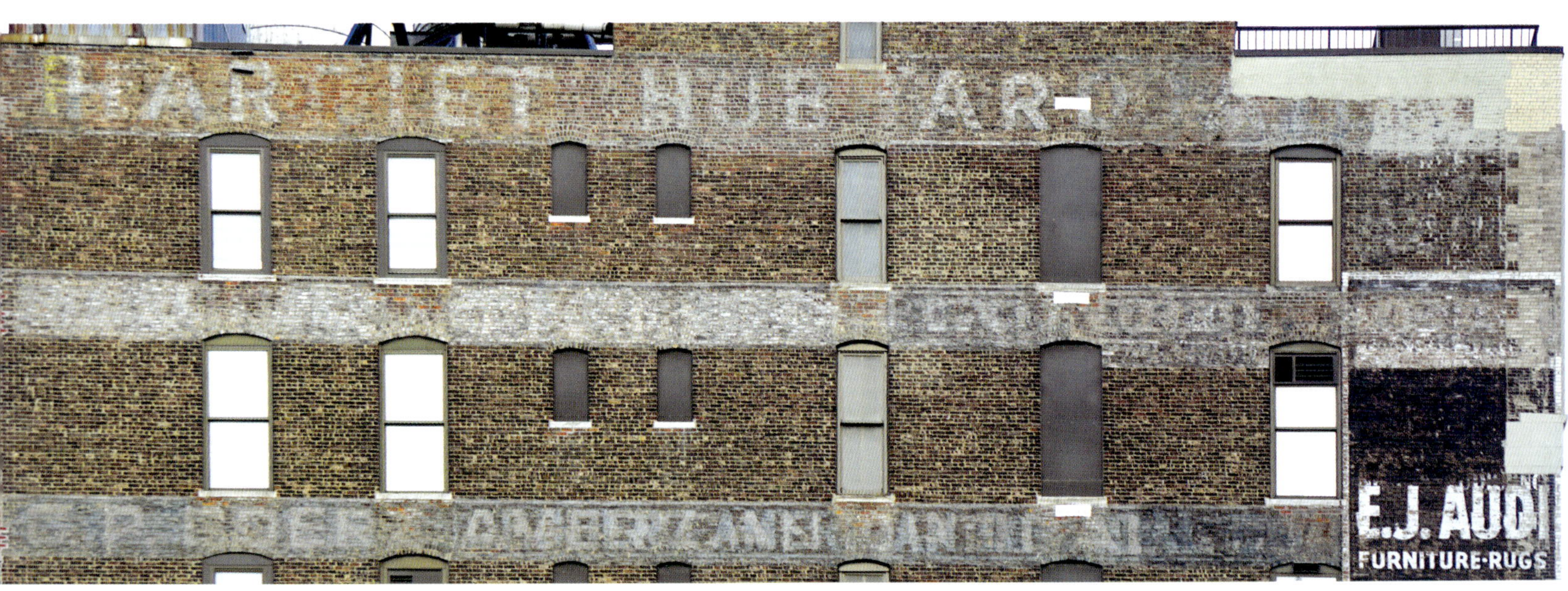

J. M. HORTON ICE CREAM

James Madison Horton founded J. M. Horton Ice Cream in 1870. By 1916, Horton supplied more than half the city's ice cream, producing more than 3 million gallons of the dessert each year. Horton operated six stores in Manhattan and two in Brooklyn. Its ads called the company the "largest manufacturers of ice cream in the world."

The Horton store on the Upper West Side opened in 1890. Its triangular pediment high above the street displays the company name, designed to be read by passengers on the Ninth Avenue elevated train. The store closed in 1908, and by 1930 the company was acquired by Borden.

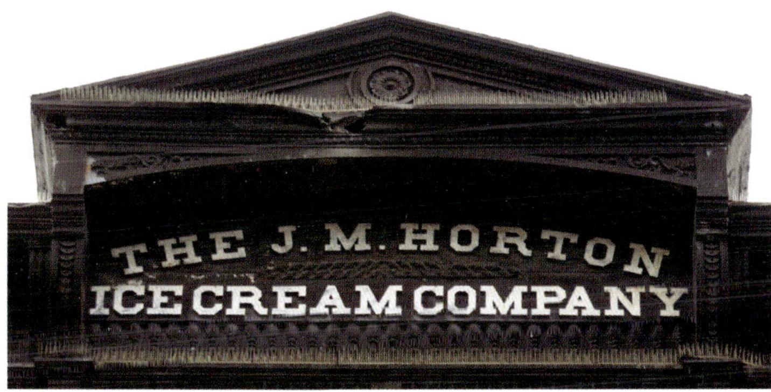

302 Columbus Avenue

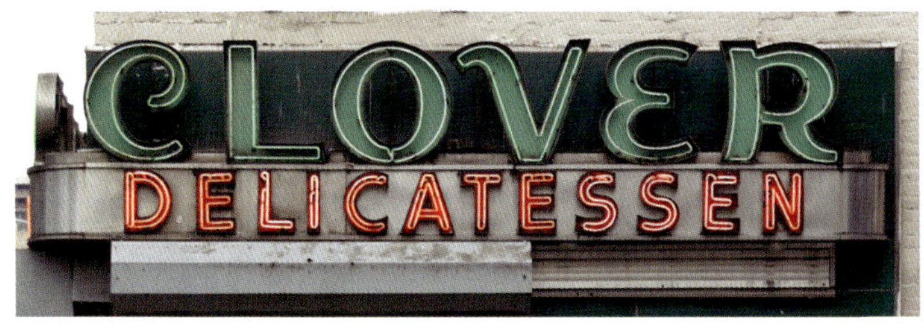

621 Second Avenue

CLOVER DELICATESSEN

Clover Delicatessen opened in 1948 and was operated by three generations of the Cuttita family until it closed in August 2020. Its glorious neon signs, on both sides of the corner of Thirty-Fourth Street and Second Avenue, brightened Kips Bay for a period after it closed.

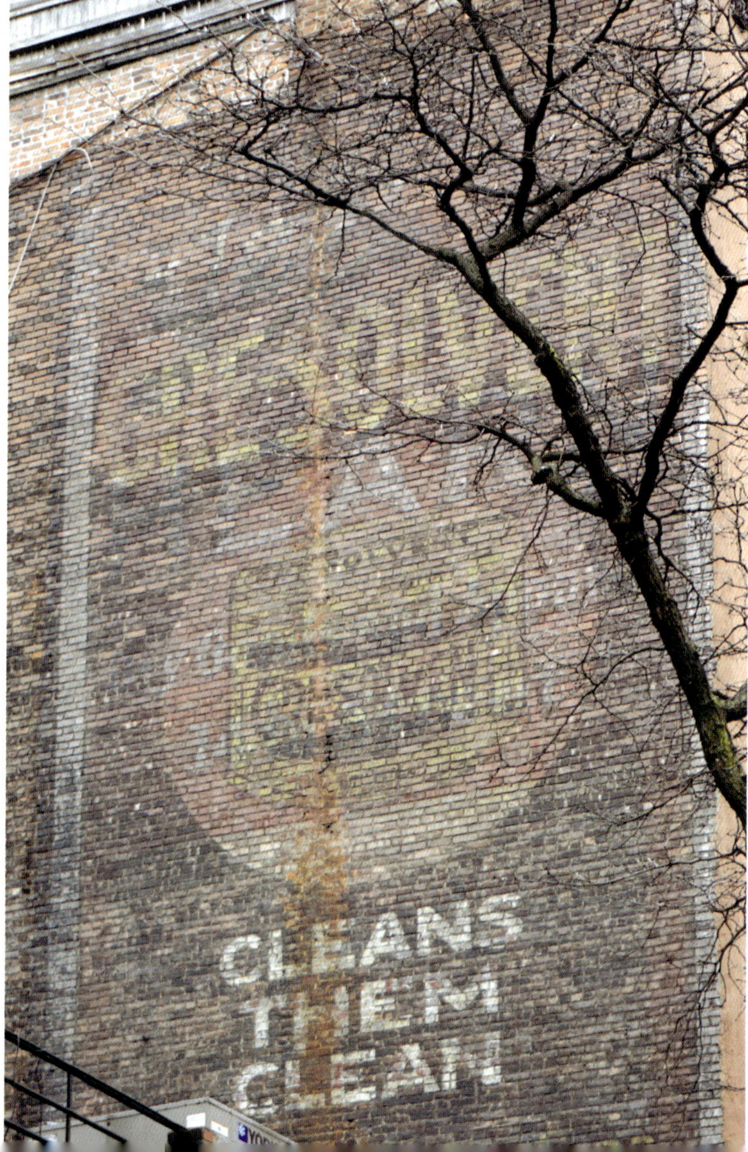

GRE-SOLVENT

"The disagreeable feature of dirty hands and severe scrubbing of the same can easily be avoided by using Gre-Solvent, which instantly removes stains of machinery and machine oil, without the least trouble," read a 1903 story in *American Inventor*. Gre-Solvent was sold by the Utility Co. in Hell's Kitchen and remained in business until 1972.

363 West Fifty-First Street

A. S. BECK

"Fifteen years ago, A. S. Beck opened his first shoe store—on an idea," read a 1925 ad in the *New York Daily News*. "He believed that if he were to put more style and more value than was customary for the price into the shoes he sold, the men and women of New York would be quick to recognize his efforts."

From that first store, Alexander Samuel Beck, a Hungarian immigrant, grew A. S. Beck into a chain of thirteen stores. Beck sold the business, and its name, in 1920. A. S. Beck moved into the Herald Square building across from Macy's in 1936. The store, with its art deco signage, was the last of the chain to close in 1982.

I. MILLER

Israel Miller opened his first store at 1554 Broadway in 1911, making shoes for the actors and dancers who worked in the Times Square theater district. As his business grew, the building and adjoining 1552 Broadway were remodeled in 1926 and became the I. Miller Building: "The Show Folks Shoe Shop Dedicated to Beauty in Footwear."

In 1927, Miller conducted a contest asking voters to choose the most-popular actresses of the day. Statues of the winners—Ethel Barrymore, Marilyn Miller, Mary Pickford, and Rosa Poncelle—were installed in niches on the facade. I. Miller closed in the 1970s.

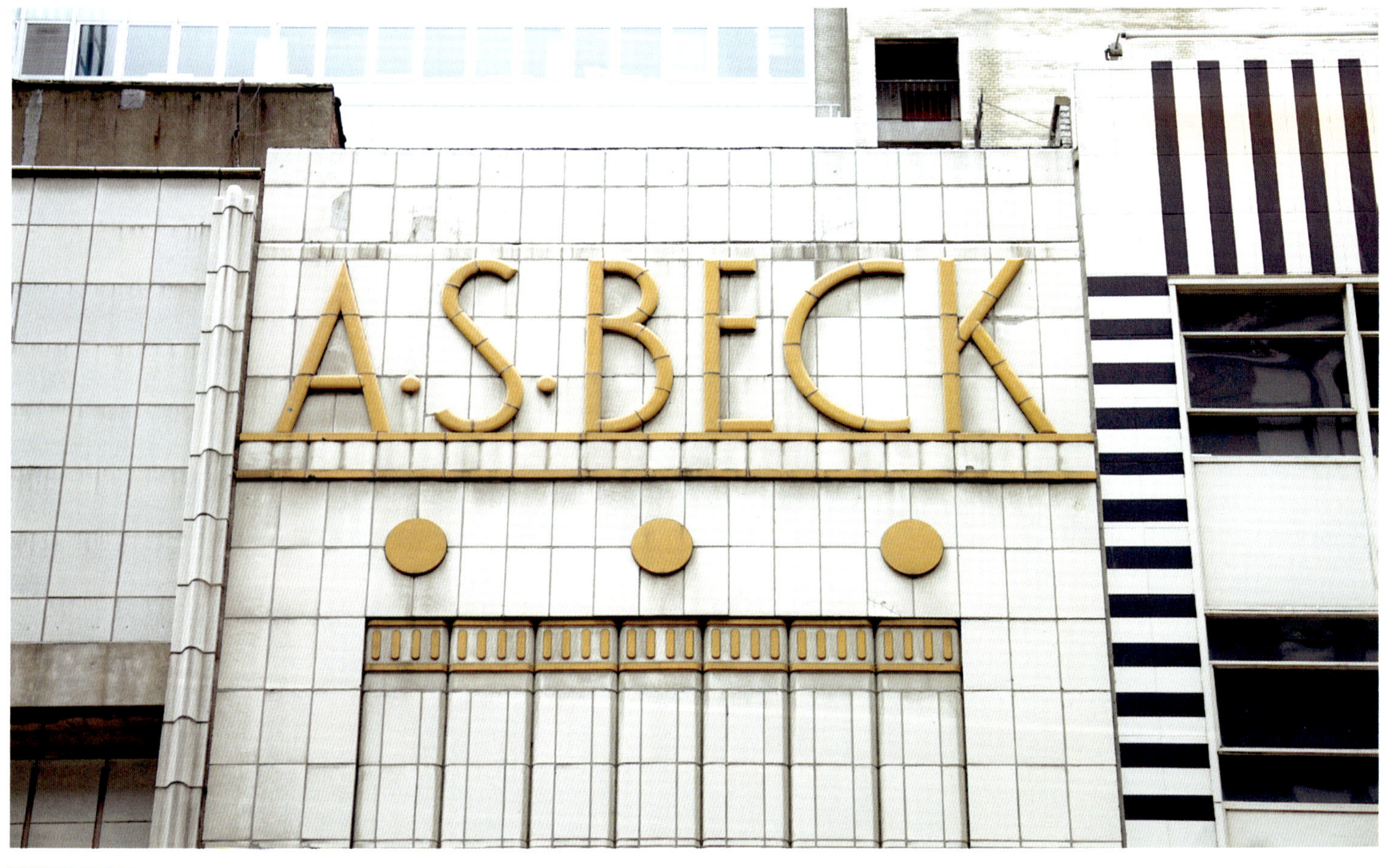

128 West Thirty-Fourth Street

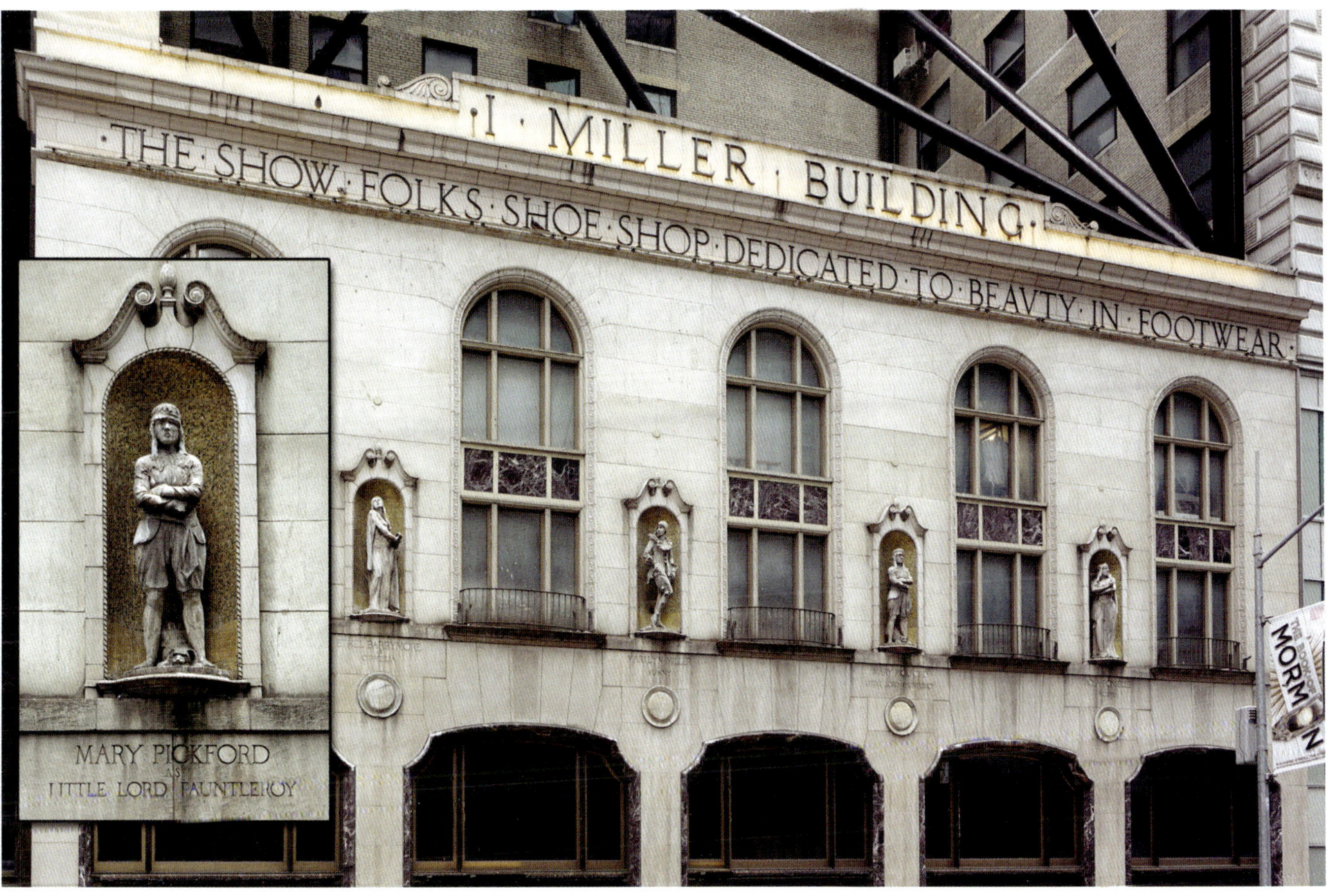

1552 Broadway

LERNER SHOPS

"To carry styles that are at all times in the forefront of fashion—to have them just a little sooner than everyone else—and to keep them always in the pink of freshness—that is the Lerner policy," read a 1922 ad in the *New York Evening World*. Lerner Shops was founded in 1918 by Samuel A. Lerner and Harold M. Lane. The women's-wear stores were soon found "in every important neighborhood in New York," moving into this Garment District building in 1928.

Lerner remained in the building for only two years but left behind two elaborate coats of arms along the roofline. By 1985, Lerner was an 823-store chain and was acquired by the Limited. In 1995, Lerner changed its name to New York & Company.

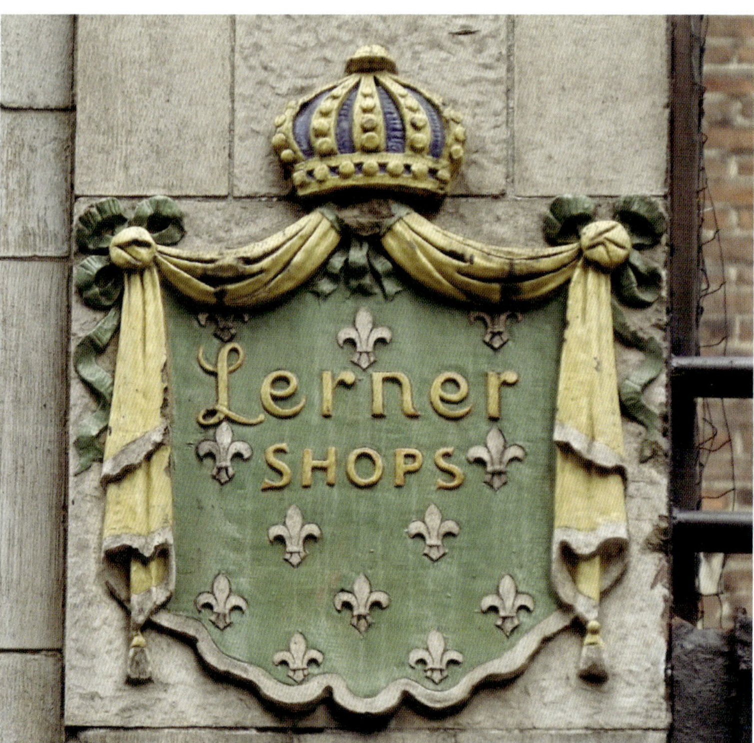

478 Seventh Avenue

GARMENT DISTRICT

BLOGG & LITTAUER

Solomon Blogg and Paul Littauer started their clothing-manufacturing business in Greenwich Village at the turn of the twentieth century. They moved to the Garment District in 1912. Blogg & Littauer described themselves in a 1922 *New York Times* ad as "manufacturers of stylish clothing for stout women."

The company name became part of the 1928 silent film comedy *The Latest from Paris.* Its star, Norma Shearer, plays a saleswoman for the company's constantly quarreling partners. Despite its Hollywood turn, Blogg & Littauer went out of business in the 1930s.

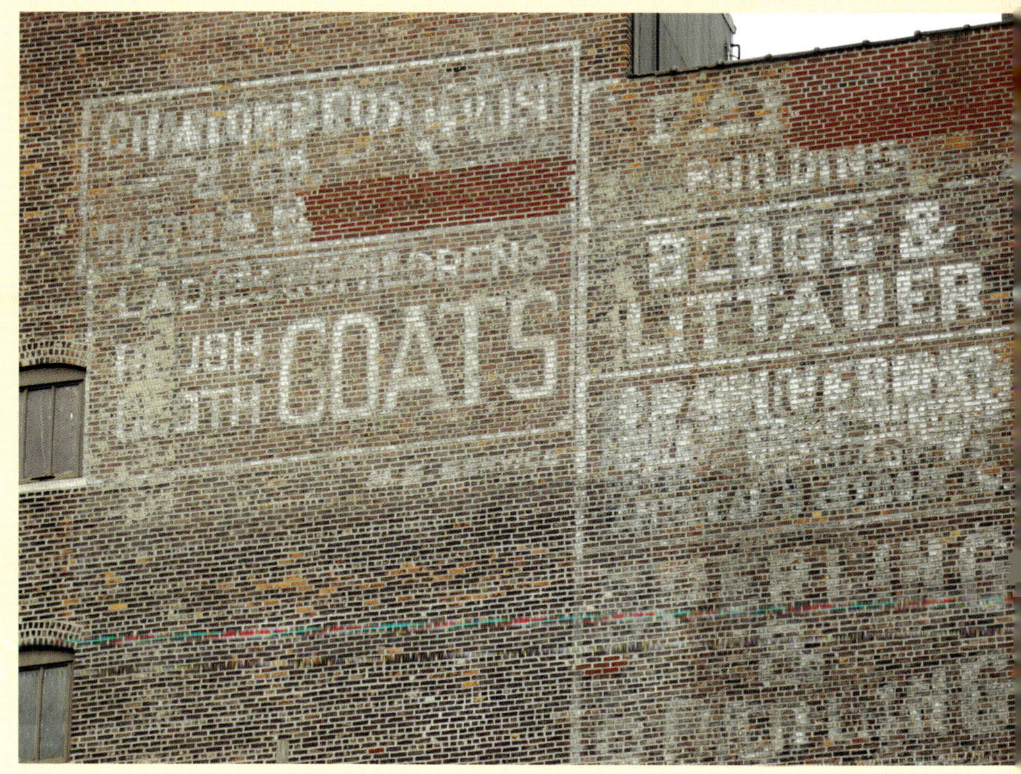

151-163 West Twenty-Sixth Street

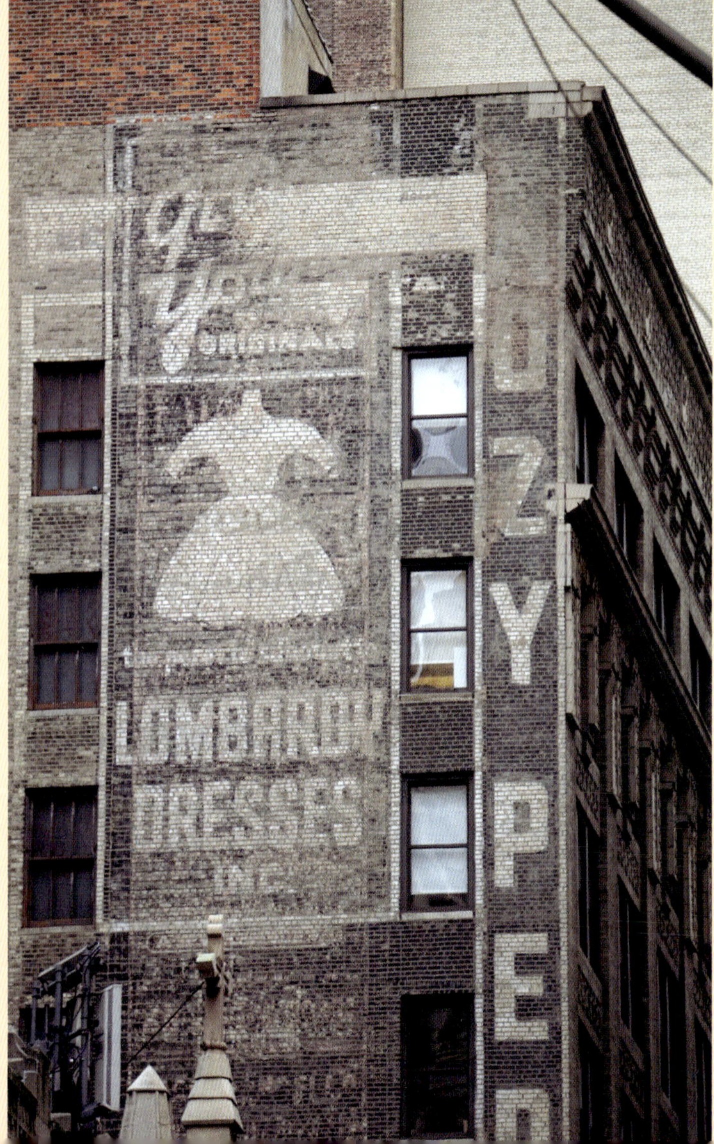

LOMBARDY DRESSES

"Anyone who spends more than $150 for a dress should have her head examined," said Suzy Perette dress designer Victor Costa in the *New York Daily News* (Chapman 1973). Lombardy Dresses, founded by Austrian immigrant Sidney Blauner in 1929, distributed Suzy Perette and Gigi Young dresses. Lombardy moved into this Garment District building in 1939.

MAGID HANDBAGS AND COBLENTZ BAG

Anna I. Magid founded her millinery business in 1901. In the 1930s she added military ornaments, leather goods, and handbags. The company became Magid Handbags soon after it moved to the Garment District in 1937. "A handbag, like a home, is no better than its foundation," read a 1947 *Honolulu Star-Bulletin* story about Louis Coblentz, founder of Coblentz Bag. "A fine handbag, though it employs the finest materials and workmanship, also deserves a fine frame." Coblentz Bag moved here in 1938, where it remained until going out of business about 1980.

---

134 West Thirty-Seventh Street

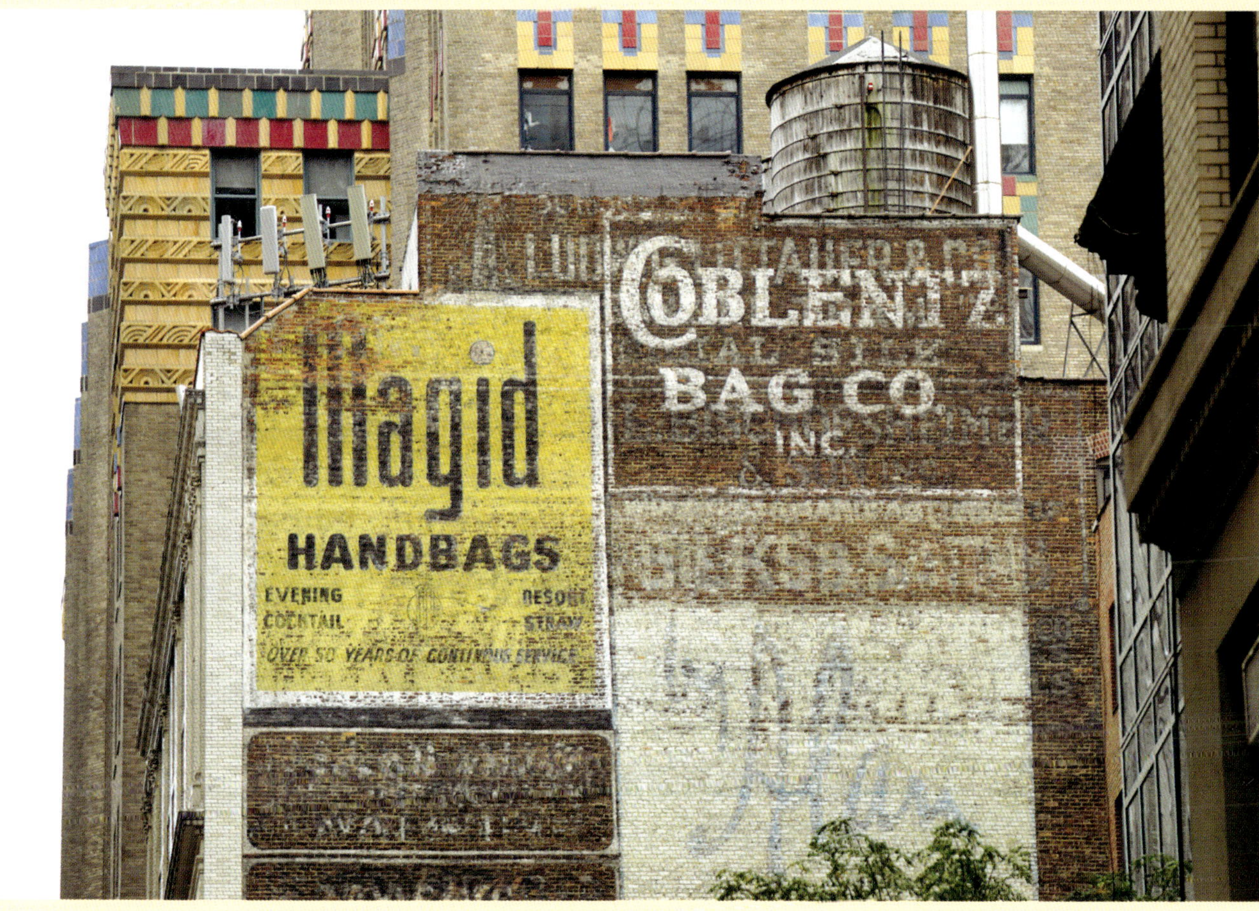

30 East Thirty-Third Street

ROBERT BESTIÉN AND MM HANDBAGS

"Robert Bestién, dark, handsome and not yet thirty (in fact, only twenty-seven) has been in the handbag business since he was virtually a child," noted the (Los Angeles) *Daily Town Talk* in 1972. "He summarily dismissed the conservative older designer the firm had employed for years, and announced to one and all he was forthwith dropping out of the business end and into the designing end" (Gallagher 1972).

Robert Bestién Handbags was here from about 1978 to 1987. Next to its sign is one for MM Handbags, named for company head Morris Moskowitz. "Morris is a perfectionist and insists that every handbag bearing the 'MM' label must leave the house with the same high degree of excellence that is associated with a work of art," noted *Handbags & Accessories* in 1961. MM operated here from 1952 to 1984.

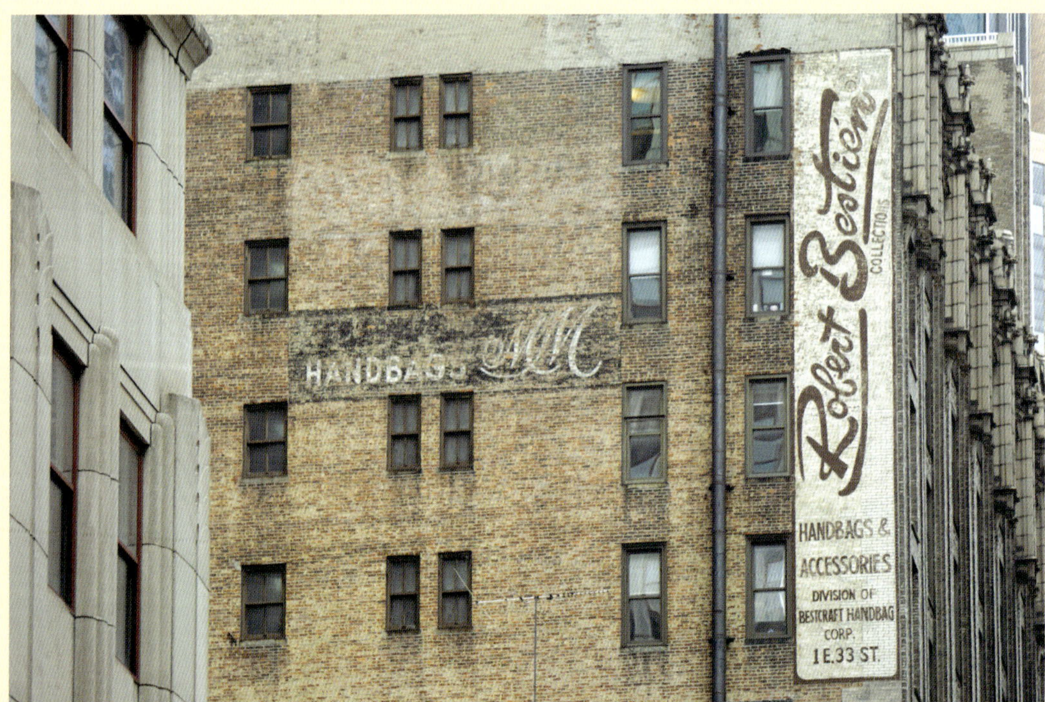

1 East Thirty-Third Street

BAAR & BEARDS

"A woman tires of a dress long before it bores the company it keeps. That is the opinion of Sylvan M. Baar, president of the accessories firm Baar & Beards," noted the *New York Times*. "Mr. Baar believes that a dress can grow old gracefully, without losing the affection of its owner, if it has the proper accessories from the beginning" (McC. 1956).

Baar and designer Milton Beards sold ladies' scarves, embroidered collars, hand-crocheted stoles, and other accessories here until they moved in 1998. "When buying a dress, the variations that are possible should be evaluated," said Baar. "Every change prolongs the life of the dress by keeping it interesting to the wearer."

15 West Thirty-Seventh Street

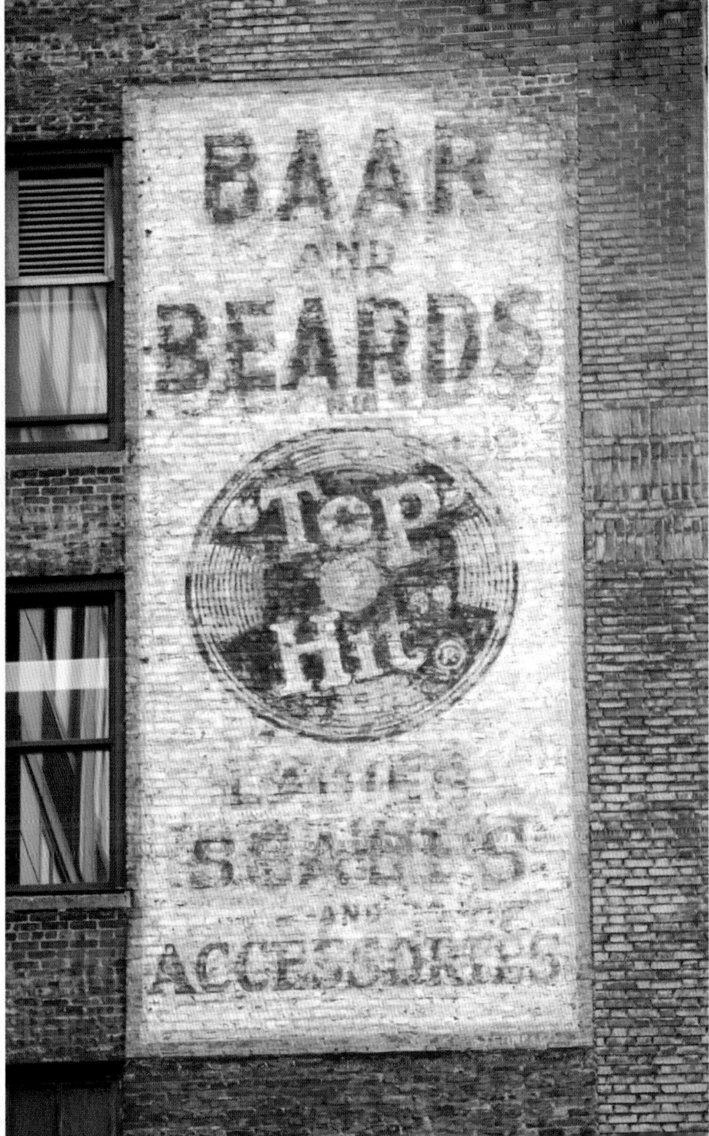

WORKING

GENERAL ELECTRIC

The General Electric Building was built in 1931 for RCA Victor and was renamed when the recording company moved to 30 Rockefeller Plaza in 1933. Above the building's main entrance is a clock with the GE logo. Two disembodied arms above the clock hold bolts of electricity. In 1993 General Electric donated the Turtle Bay building to Columbia University.

570 Lexington Avenue

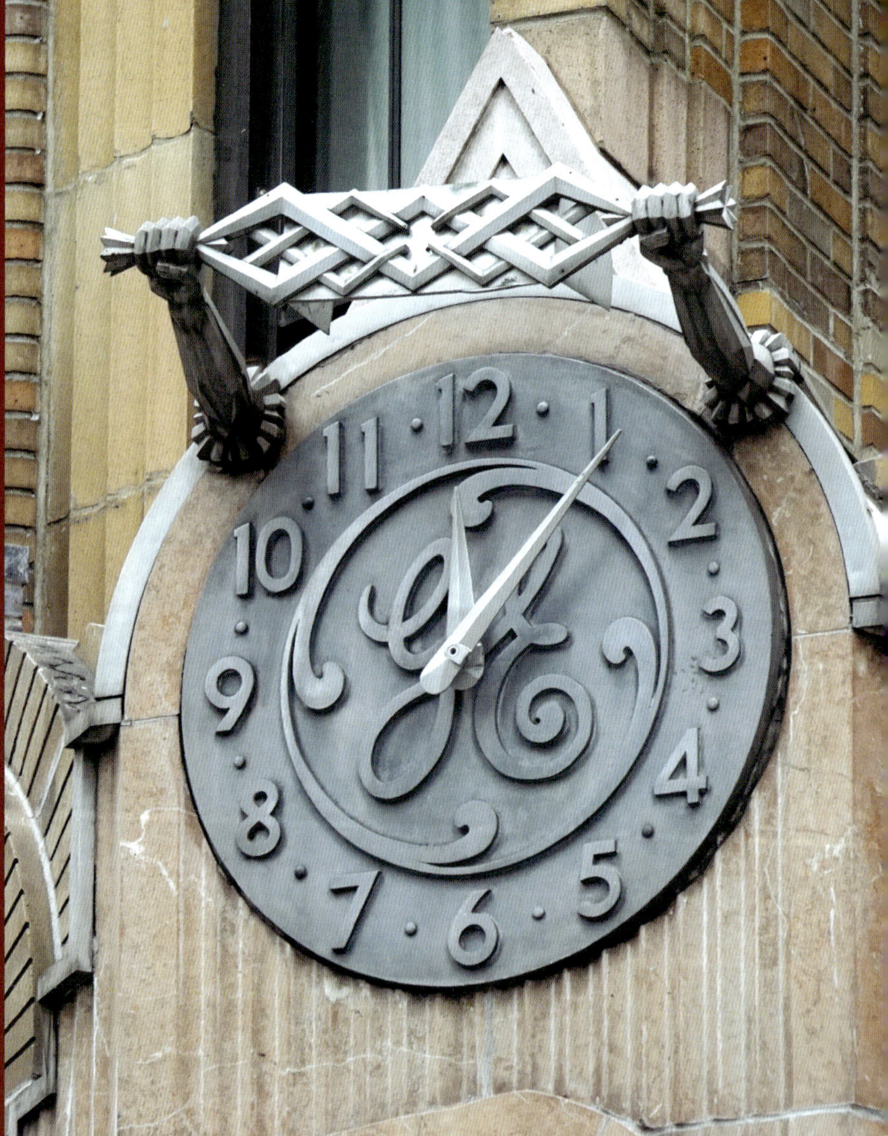

BERLEY

"Max Berley, formerly known as Max Berlowitz, of the real estate firm Berlowitz & Co., has reorganized his business under the name of Berley & Co., Inc., with offices at 1182 Broadway," read the *Real Estate Record and Builders Guide* in 1922. Bob Middleton of Mack Sign painted the sign about 1970.

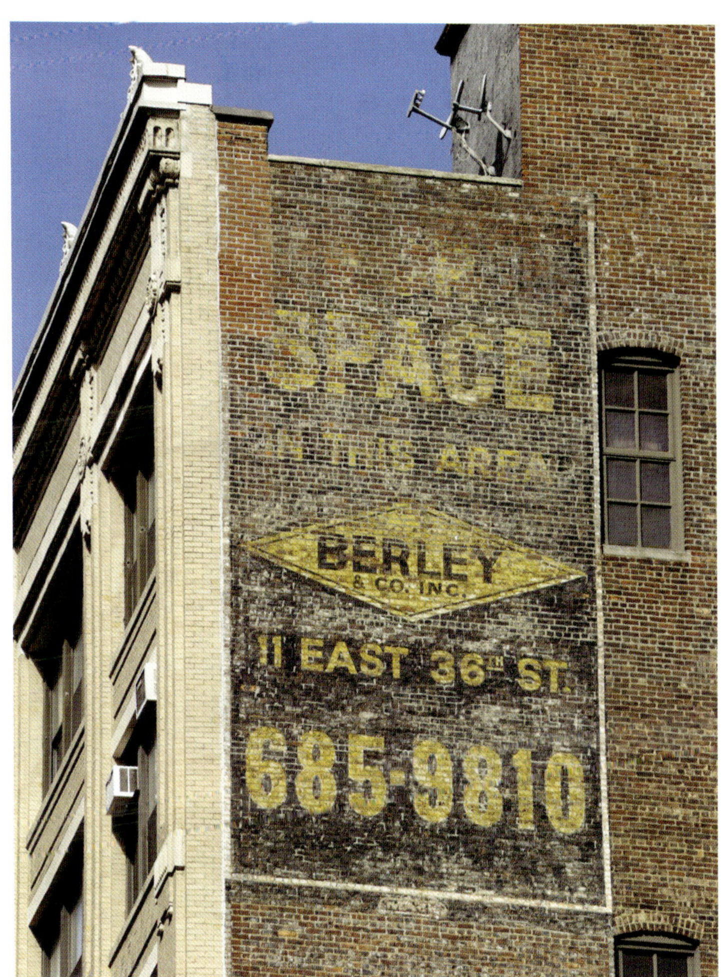

115-121 West Twenty-Ninth Street

LIFE MAGAZINE

Life was a humor magazine when founder John Ames Mitchell moved its operations to Chelsea in 1895. John Carrere and Thomas Hastings designed the building in a Beaux-Arts style the *New York Times* described as "unmistakably French, with a lower section of delicately rusticated limestone, rich ornament at the bracketed cornice and a rounded, double-height mansard with four tall, slender chimneys" (Gray 1995).

Mitchell provided apartments for his writers, artists, and editors above the library and writing rooms; a Prohibition-era speakeasy was discovered during renovations. *Life* staffers remained in the building until 1931. In 1936 Henry Luce transformed *Life* into a general-interest news magazine, which was published until 2007. In 2017 the building's Gilded Age glamour was restored, and it reopened as the Luxe Life Hotel.

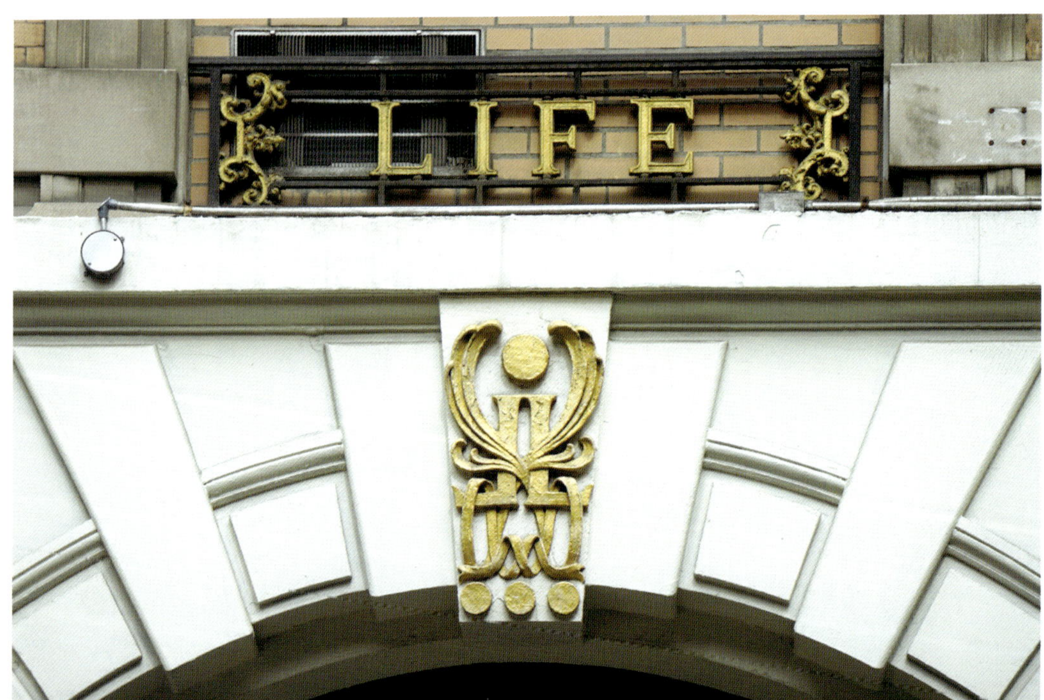

19 West Thirty-First Street

CHARLES SCRIBNER'S SONS

The Scribner bookstore opened in 1913 in a Beaux-Arts building designed by Ernest Flagg. The building served as a bookstore with Scribner's corporate headquarters above. The company's best-known writers, including Ernest Hemingway, Ring Lardner, Thomas Wolfe, and Harper Lee, were often spotted in its aisles. "Virtually every Scribner author came through there," Charles Scribner III told United Press International. "Hemingway used to come in stomping around in his boots—and there are all the legendary stories, like Wolfe sleeping upstairs so he could read our books, Harper Lee working in the store while writing *To Kill a Mockingbird*" (Maxwell 1989).

The lettering of Scribner's wall sign is made of inlaid red brick. The building was granted landmark status in 1982. Rizzoli bought Scribner's in 1984 and closed the store in 1989, when it became too expensive to operate.

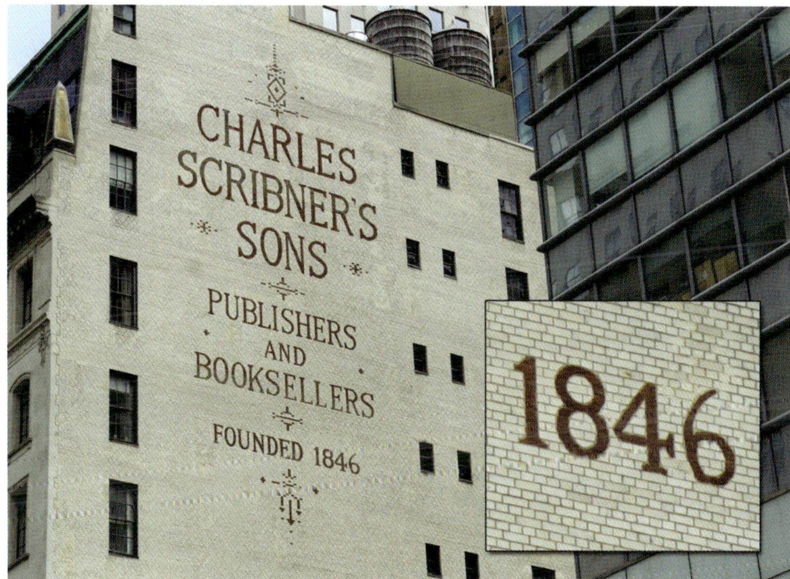

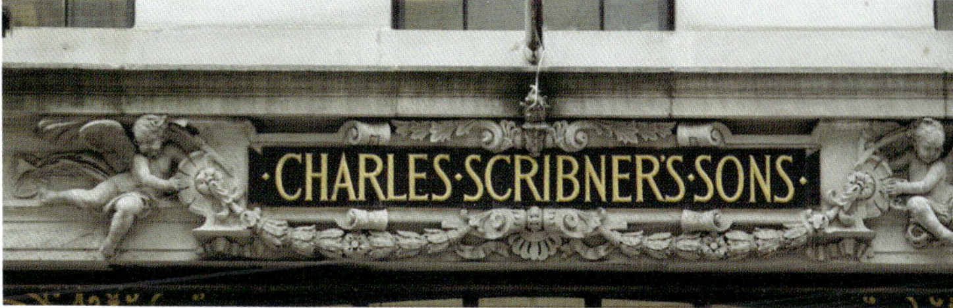

597 Fifth Avenue

SCRIBNER PRESS

The Scribner Press manufactured the thousands of books published by Scribner as well as the printing, binding, and mailing of *Scribner's Magazine*, which described the facility on its opening in 1908: "The equipment of the Scribner Press represents the most recent and improved inventions in the way of labor-saving machinery used in connection with the modern printing plant." By 2016 the building had been sold multiple times and converted into modern office space.

311 West Forty-Third Street

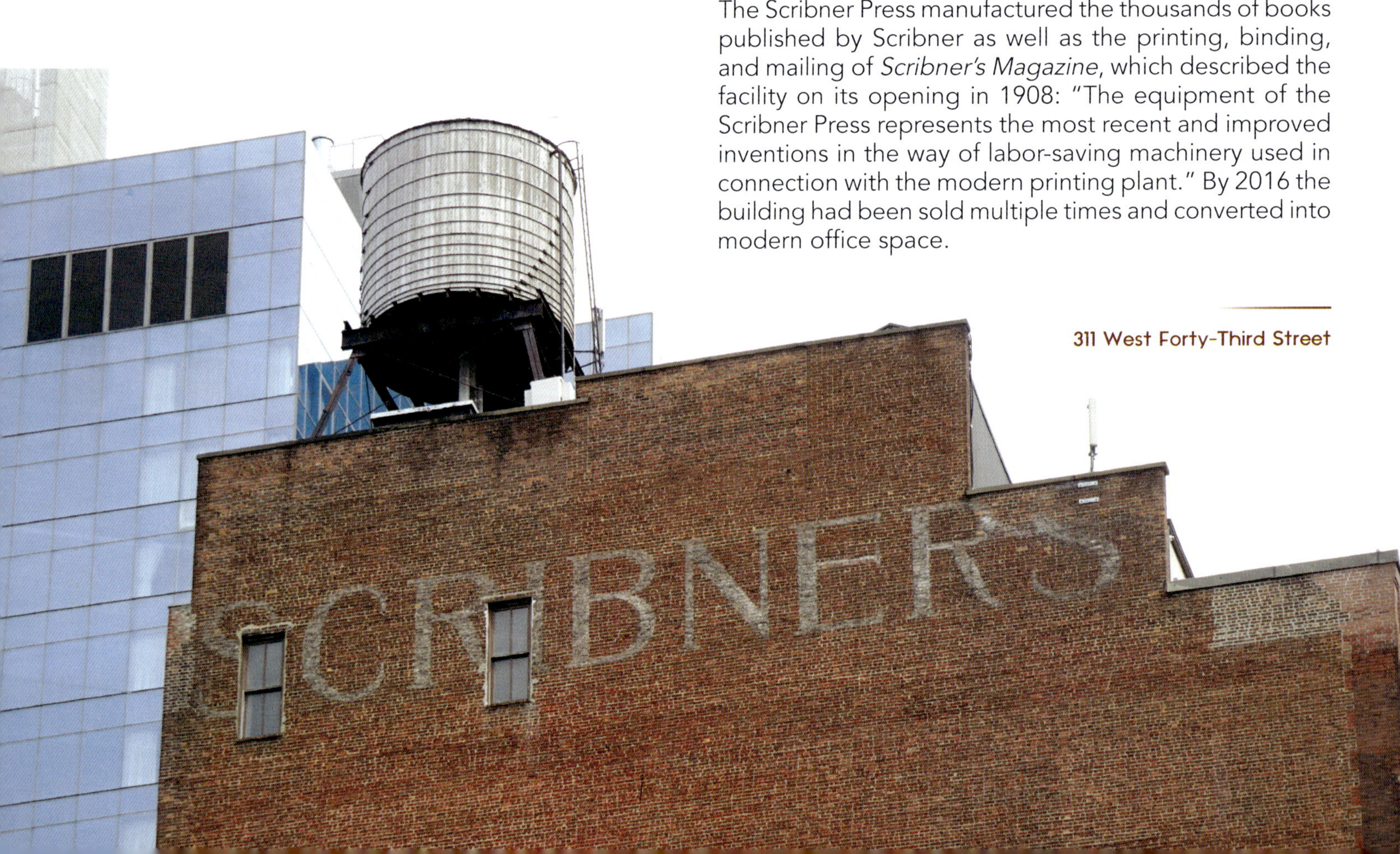

BARTLETT-ORR PRESS

The Printing Crafts Building opened in 1916, the "largest structure in the country devoted to the publishing and printing interests," according to the *New York Times.* Among the original tenants was the Bartlett-Orr Press, the partnership of Edward Everett Bartlett and Louis Herbert Orr that formed in 1906. Bartlett's expertise was illustration and wood engraving; Orr, an expert on newspaper type, was called "a master of typography." Bartlett-Orr Press remained in the building until 1932.

5 Penn Plaza

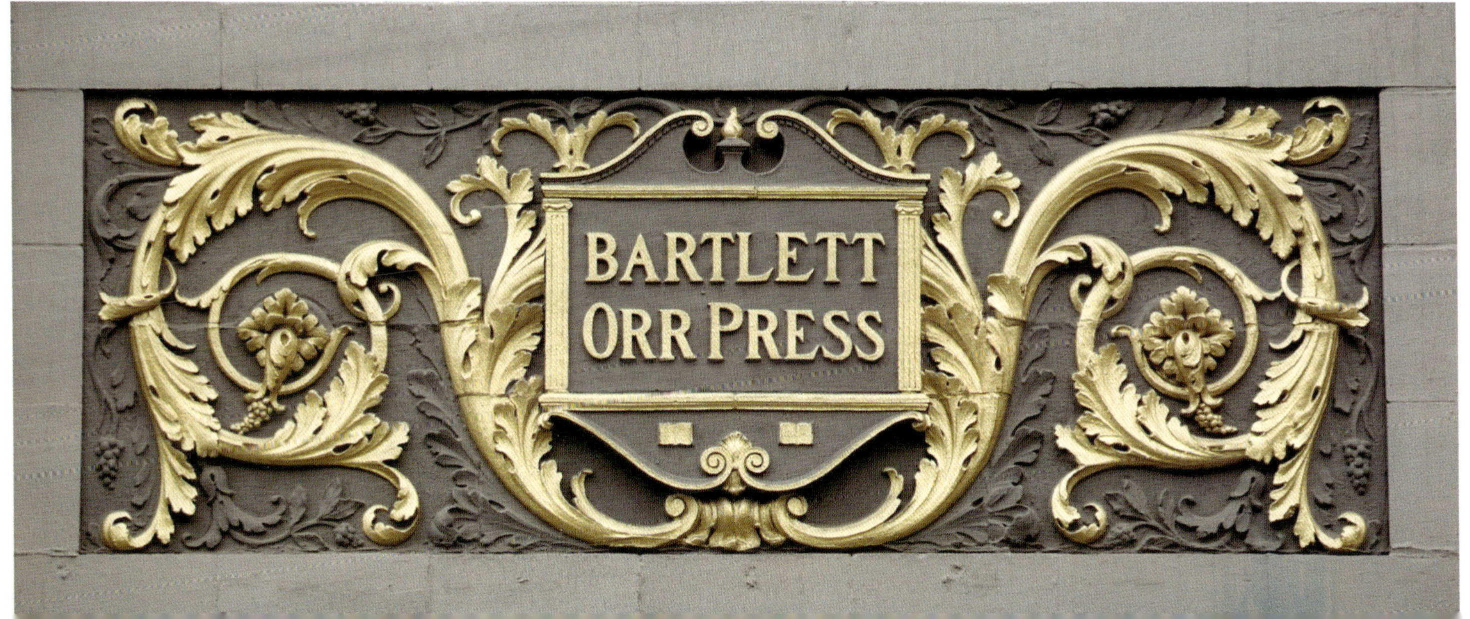

AMERICAN BOOK BINDERY

Louis Satenstein arrived in America from Russia in 1889 and about a decade later founded American Book Bindery. The company merged with the Stratford Press and by 1959 printed 100,000 books a day. Facing financial difficulties in the 1970s, American Book–Stratford Press moved print production to its plant in Saddle Brook, New Jersey. Its massive signage remains both on the Ninth and Tenth Avenue sides of the Chelsea building.

406 West Thirty-First Street

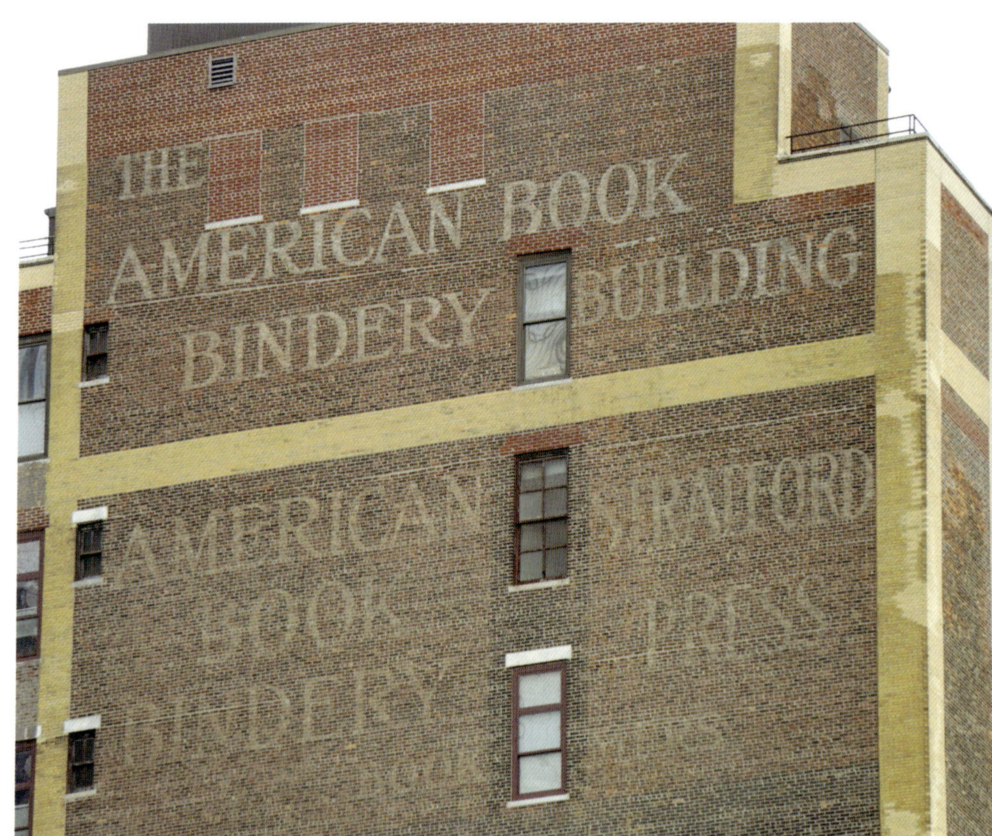

AMERICAN WOOLEN BUILDING

The American Woolen Company, founded in 1899 by William Wood and Charles Fletcher, was a textile business with interests in New England woolen mills. In 1909 the company built the American Woolen Building in Gramercy Park as its headquarters. Five floors of the building on Park Avenue South were used for business offices and sale and sample rooms; freight was delivered on Nineteenth Street.

"A feature of the building which is of special interest is the special freight entrance from Nineteenth Street," noted *Architects' and* Builders' Magazine in 1910. "It is sufficiently large, so that all trucks and delivery wagons may drive right in from the street and unload upon interior platforms." The platforms connected directly to freight elevators. When Textron acquired American Woolen in 1955, the company left the building.

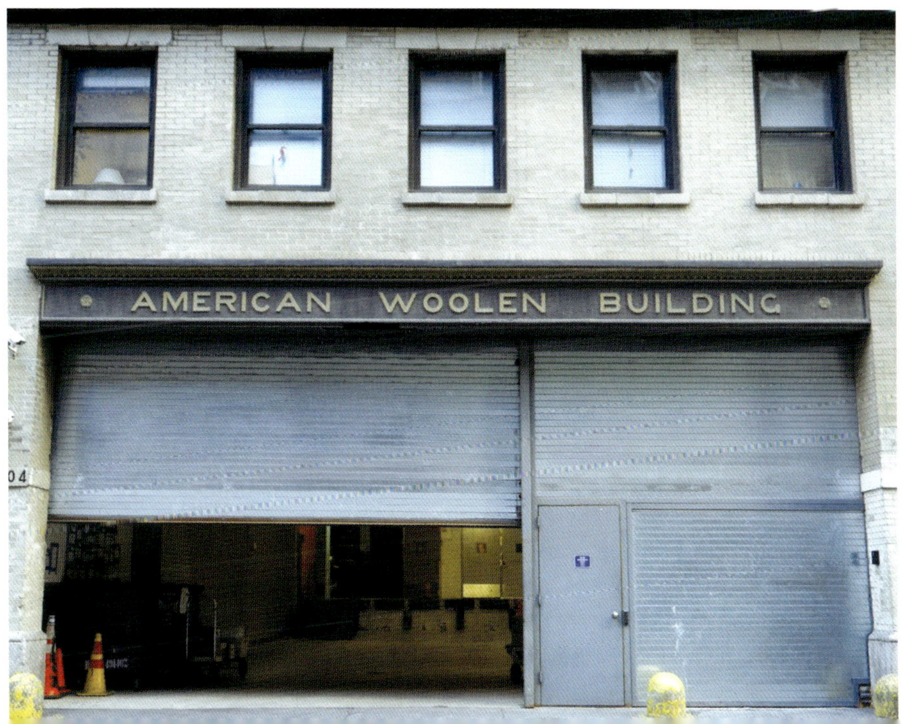

104 East Nineteenth Street

E&J BURKE

Brothers Edward and John Burke founded their Dublin, Ireland, distillery in 1849. By 1913 they established their US headquarters and storage facility in Hell's Kitchen. The Burkes were primarily importers of Guinness Stout in bottles. A stone panel with the company name survives along the roofline, although the business left for , ong Island City, Queens, in 1922. The company closed its doors in 1954.

616–620 West Forty-Sixth Street

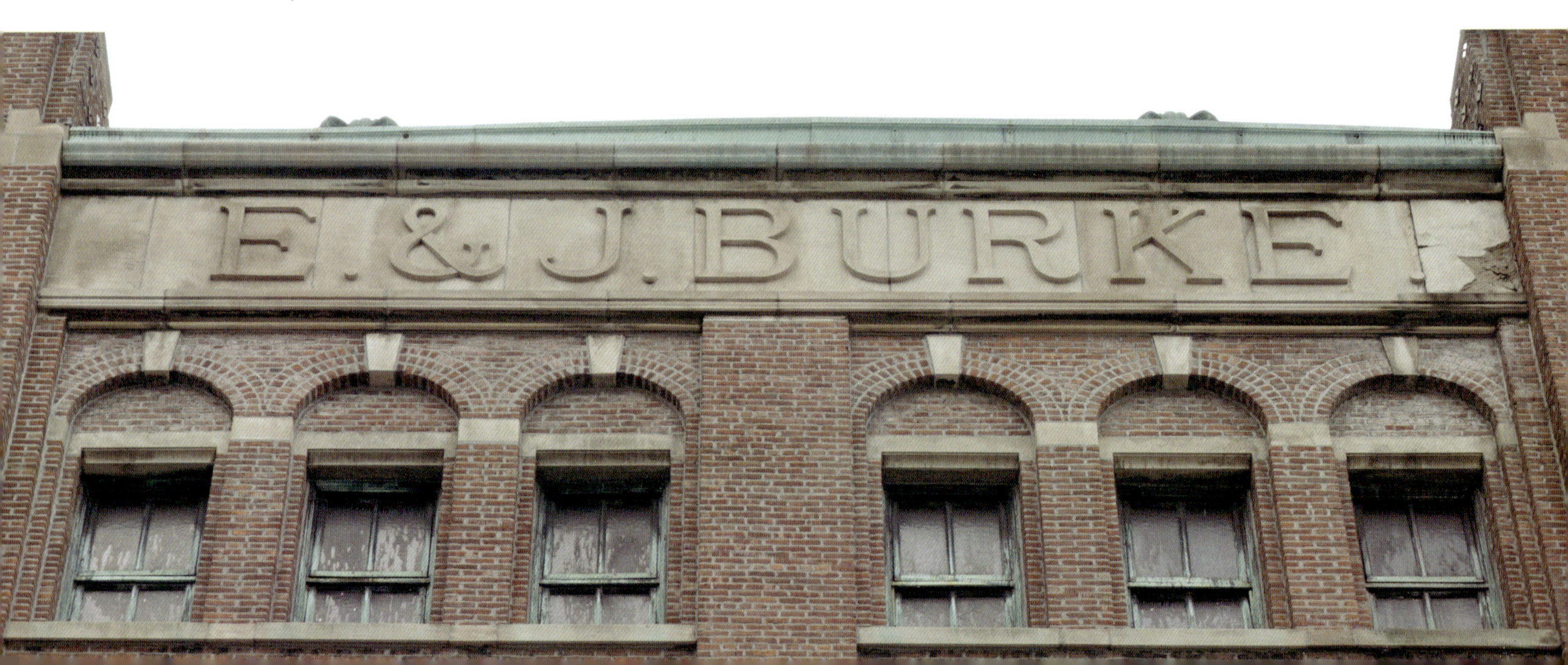

DAIRYLEA

"New Milk Plant to Open: $2,000,000 Dairymen's , eague Unit Is at 12th Ave. and 47th St.," read a 1946 *New York Times* headline. The Dairymen's League was a cooperative of upstate New York dairy farmers founded in 1907. League members, a 1947 *New York Daily News* ad explained, "have a share in an organization which provides each one with a market every day of the year, certainty of payment and facilities for marketing and manufacturing."

The league changed its name to Dairylea in 1969 to reflect its best-known product, Dairylea Milk. In 2014 Dairylea merged with Dairy Farmers of America.

620 Twelfth Avenue

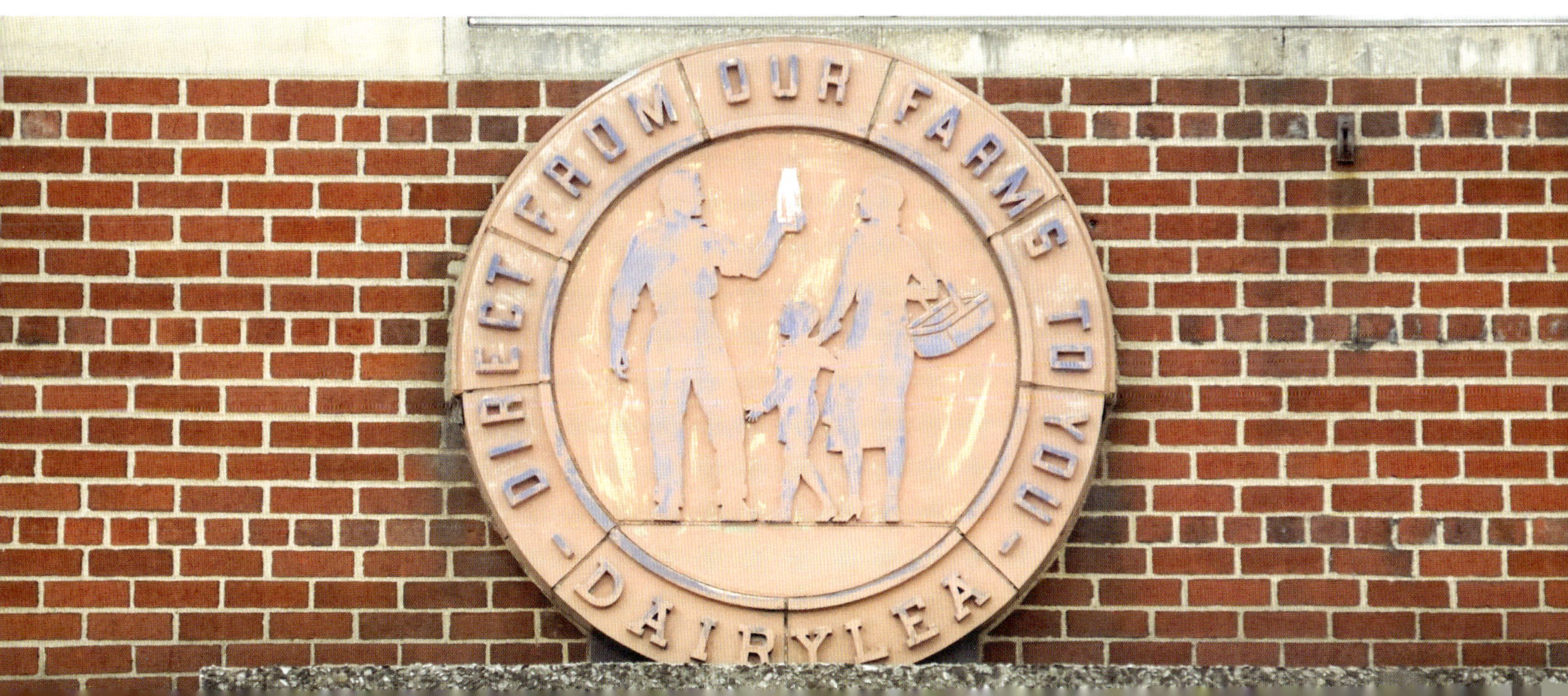

BELL TELEPHONE

Cell phones have made landline calling almost obsolete. Wireless technology has meant that Verizon, one of the companies born of the breakup of the Bell System, no longer needs switching buildings to house equipment required by the outdated technology. Since 2005 Verizon has sold hundreds of millions of dollars in properties to developers, including its central office in Chelsea.

Renamed Walker Tower, the 1929 art deco building has been converted to condominiums. Verizon has kept floors 2 through 7 as offices, which it accesses through this Seventeenth Street entrance that displays the company's former name.

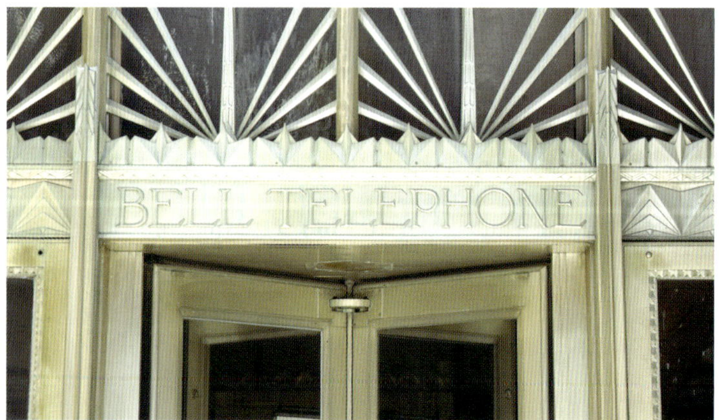

215 West Seventeenth Street

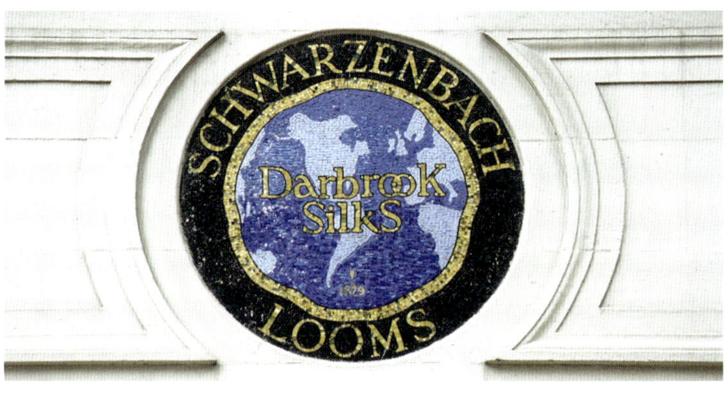

470 Park Avenue South

SCHWARZENBACH LOOMS

"Among the largest manufacturers and producers of broad silk goods in this country are Schwarzenbach, Huber & Co., and with their European mills they are in the front ranks of the largest silk manufacturers in the world," noted the *New York Daily Tribune* in 1903. Schwarzenbach moved here from Broome Street in 1912. Its mosaic sign displays the name of its brand, Darbrook Silks.

Schwarzenbach moved in 1932 but returned in 1946. After World War II, the popularity of synthetic fabrics such as nylon made silk a luxury item. Schwarzenbach remained here until 1974 and, after a move uptown to Sixth Avenue, closed in 1988.

WOOD DOLSON

When Frederick R. Wood and William Hamilton Dolson struck a deal with the Rutgers Presbyterian Church in 1922 to build a real estate office on a small Upper West Side lot next to the church, Broadway's odd angle presented a challenge. "The site selected presented a difficult problem to the architects, in that the facade is designed on a splayed surface, but it has been successfully handled by the architects," reported the *Real Estate Records and Builders Guide* in 1922.

Wood Dolson moved when its lease with the church expired in 1940. Tenants to follow included the Amsterdam Democratic Club and Leslie Records, which produced one of the earliest recordings by Tony Bennett as Joe Bari, his original stage name. Wood Dolson's name remains on the Tennessee marble facade.

2091 Broadway

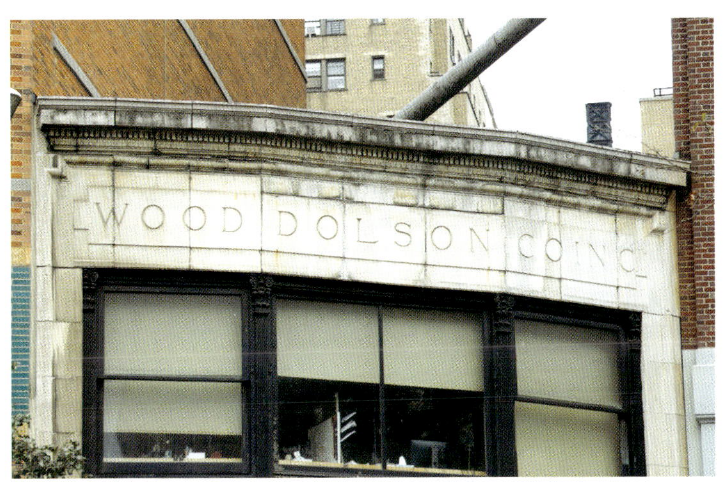

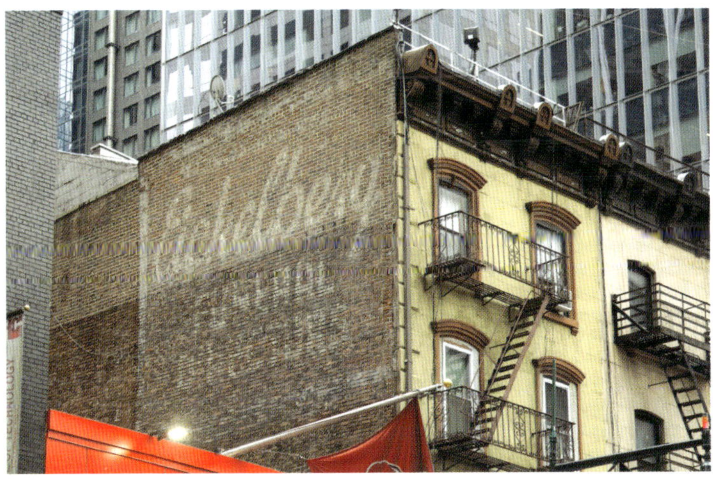

936 Eighth Avenue

EICKELBERG

August Eickelberg was an undertaker in Hell's Kitchen beginning in 1880. After he died in 1923, his sons Elliot and Graham Eickelberg continued the business until 1951.

CHAS. F. NOYES

When he died in 1969, the *New York Times* noted that Charles F. Noyes was "known to many on Wall Street as 'the greatest of real estate brokers,' at one time or another he bought or sold almost every commercial property in Lower Manhattan." Noyes founded his real estate business in 1898 and managed prestigious properties that included the Empire State Building and the Pennsylvania Building, where the sign is still visible.

225 West Thirty-Fourth Street

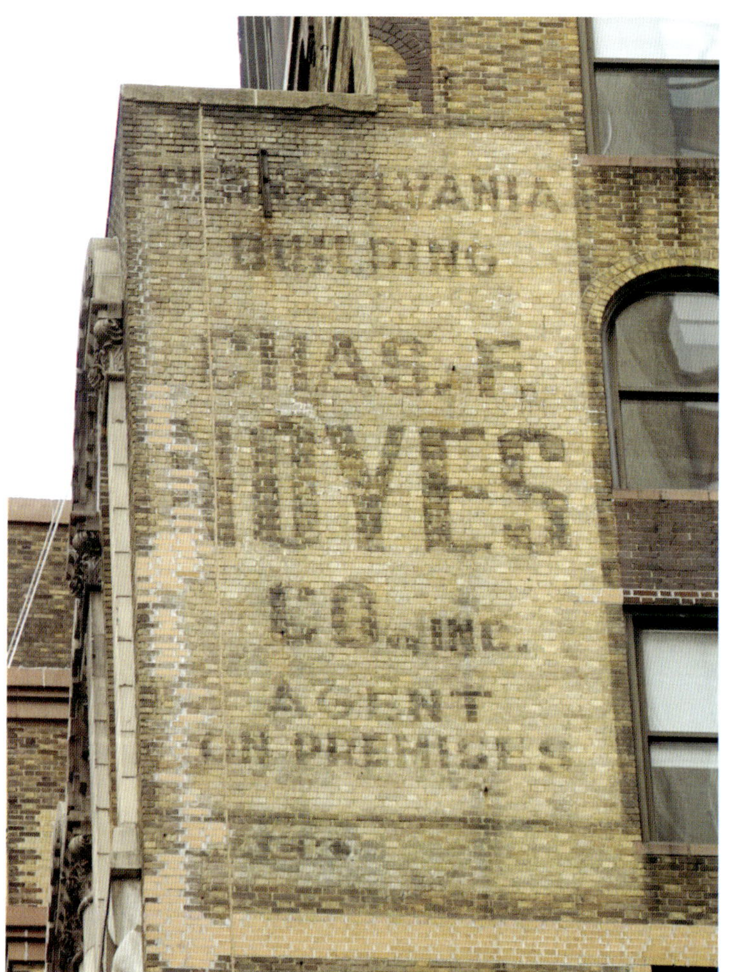

JAMES N. WELLS' SONS

In the early 1800s, Clement Clarke Moore, author of the Christmas poem "A Visit from St. Nicholas," owned a bucolic 100-acre estate named Chelsea. When the city decided to transform the area into a residential neighborhood, Moore collaborated with realtor James N. Wells to develop his estate.

Wells and Moore imposed restrictions on development that forbid stables and manure piles. Their 1835 map, the *New York Times* notes, included a warning that "all kinds of nuisances will be prohibited" (Gray 1996). Their vision can be seen in the Italianate brownstones and broad stoops of Chelsea. Wells maintained his real estate office nearby, where James P. Eadie was a partner. A faded sign remains on a building a few doors down from Wells's house. It reads, "James N. Wells' Sons, James P. Eadie, Real Estate, Sales, Leasing, Management, Insurance, On This Spot Since 1835."

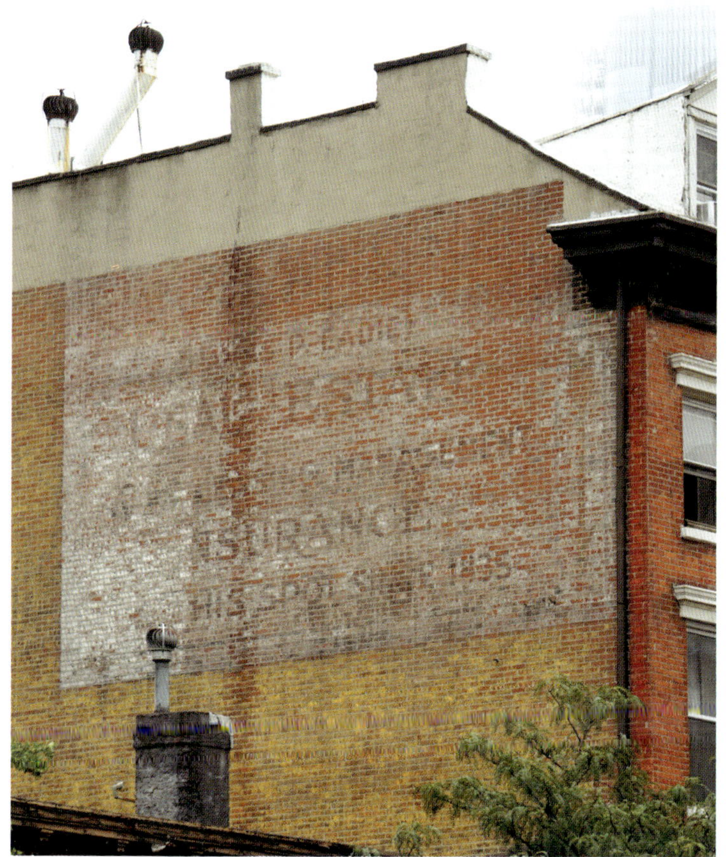

191 Ninth Avenue

TERMINAL WAREHOUSE

Terminal Warehouse was built in 1891 over an entire Chelsea block. Its huge arches on either side were designed to accommodate the freight trains that operated on Eleventh Avenue. Antiques, furniture, stage scenery, works of art, and furs were among the items stored there. Access to the Hudson River made the warehouse an important shipping hub.

269 Eleventh Avenue

As tracks were removed from the streets and freight trains traveled on the elevated High Line, use of the Terminal Warehouse declined. The building housed mini storage units; the Tunnel nightclub operated here from 1986 to 2001. Later restorations added shops, restaurants, and art galleries.

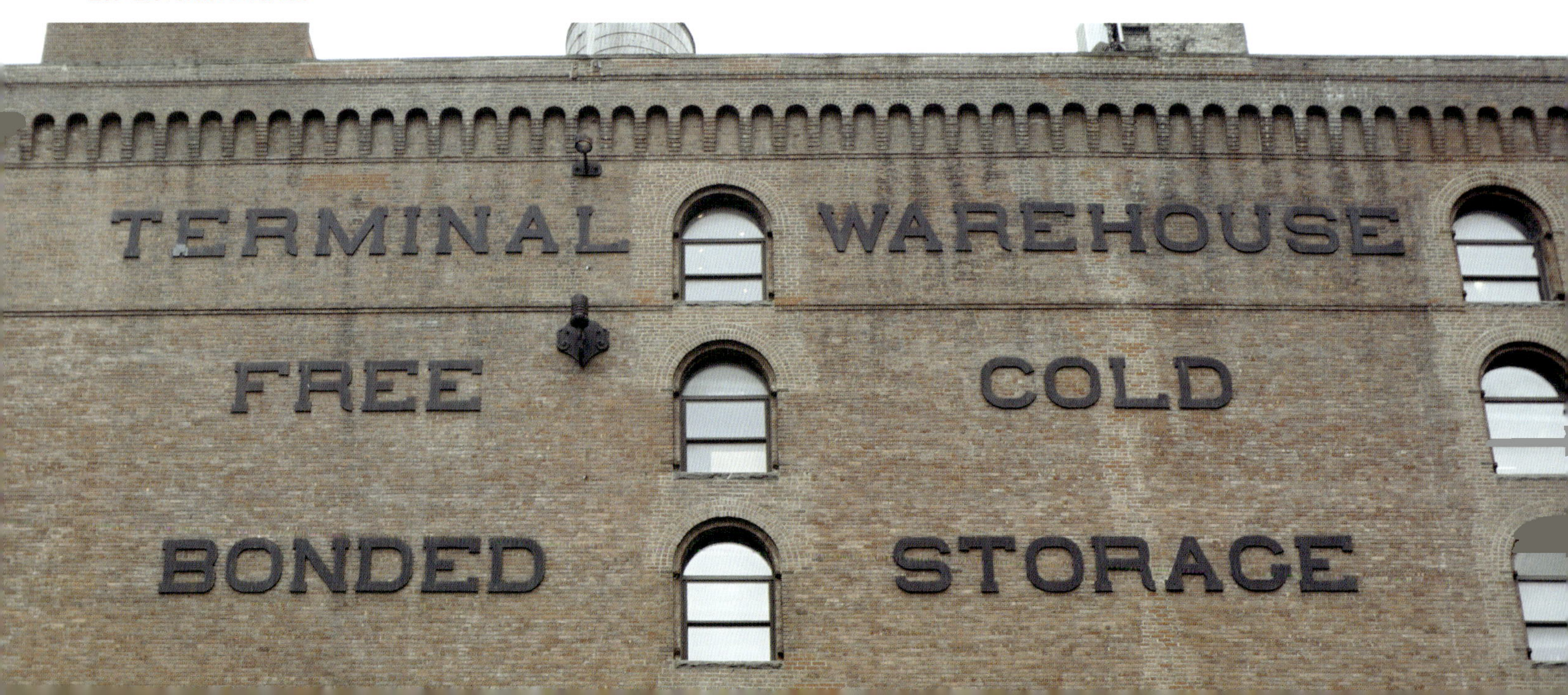

STUDEBAKER

Studebaker manufactured reliable cars with innovative designs from 1904 to 1966. Its storage and distribution building in Manhattanville was built in 1923. The roofline displays two of its terra-cotta "turning wheel" logos. Cars were shipped from here to local dealers, and customers could buy used Studebakers at the site.

"A good car for your vacation can be secured for from $50 to $200," read a 1926 *New York Daily News* ad. "Serviceable, sweet running automobiles—open or closed—are available at wholesale. Studebaker Pledge to the Public on used car sales guarantees you satisfaction."

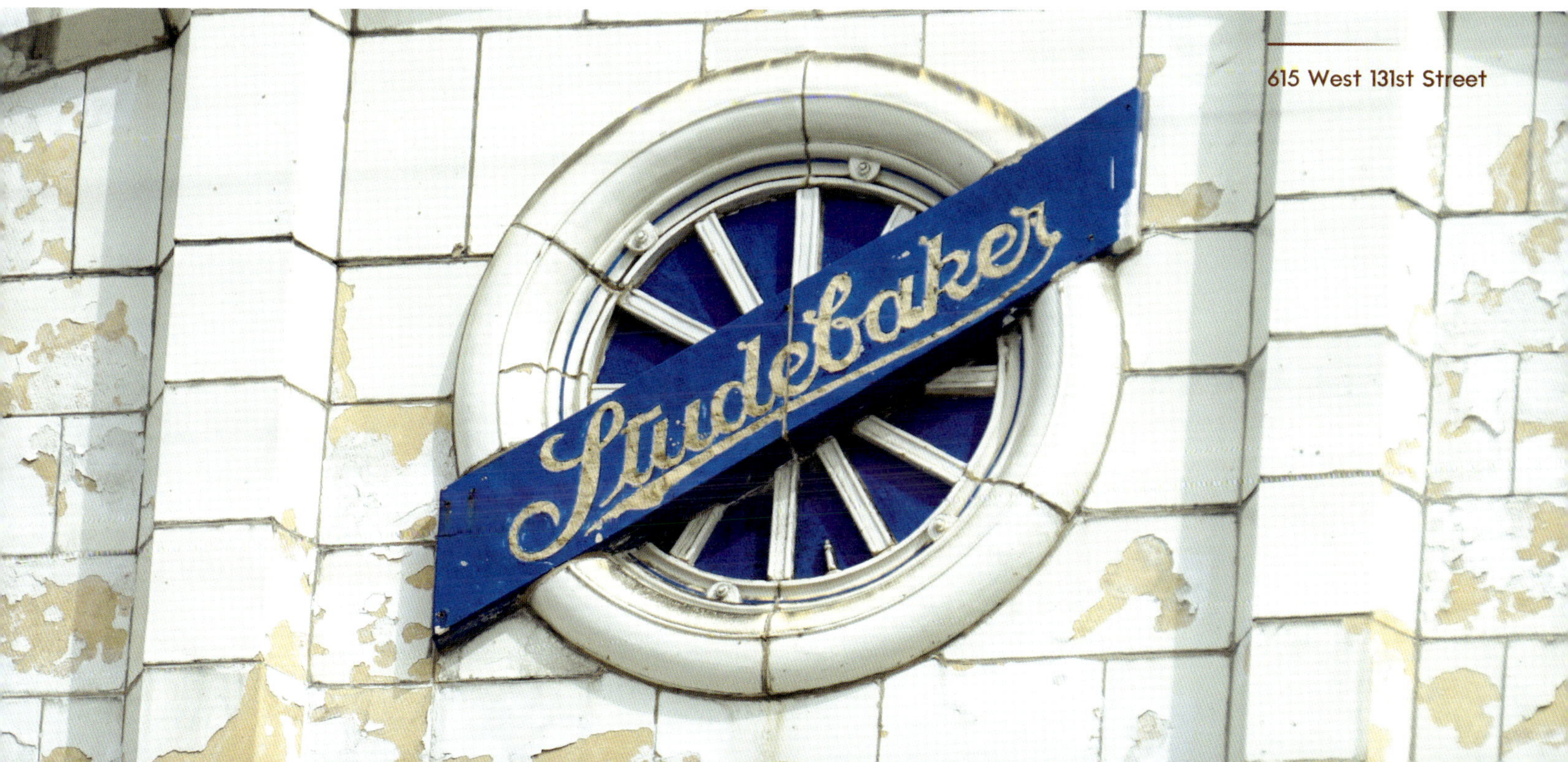

615 West 131st Street

MEETING

HORN & HARDART AUTOMAT

Joseph Horn and Frank Hardart opened their first Automat in Philadelphia in 1902; ten years later, Times Square was the site of New York's first Automat. Automats featured walls of small glass windows displaying prepared food. Customers fed a few nickels into a slot to enjoy favorites such as macaroni and cheese, baked beans, and creamed spinach. "For all the good food, the Automat's real secret weapon was its coffee," noted the *Smithsonian*. "The Automat's smooth aromatic brew flowed regally from ornate brass spigots in the shape of dolphin heads" (Hughes Crowley 2001).

At its peak, Horn & Hardart was the world's largest restaurant chain, serving 800,000 people daily. Changing consumer tastes and the popularity of fast food led to the Automat's demise. The last of the city's Automats closed in 1991.

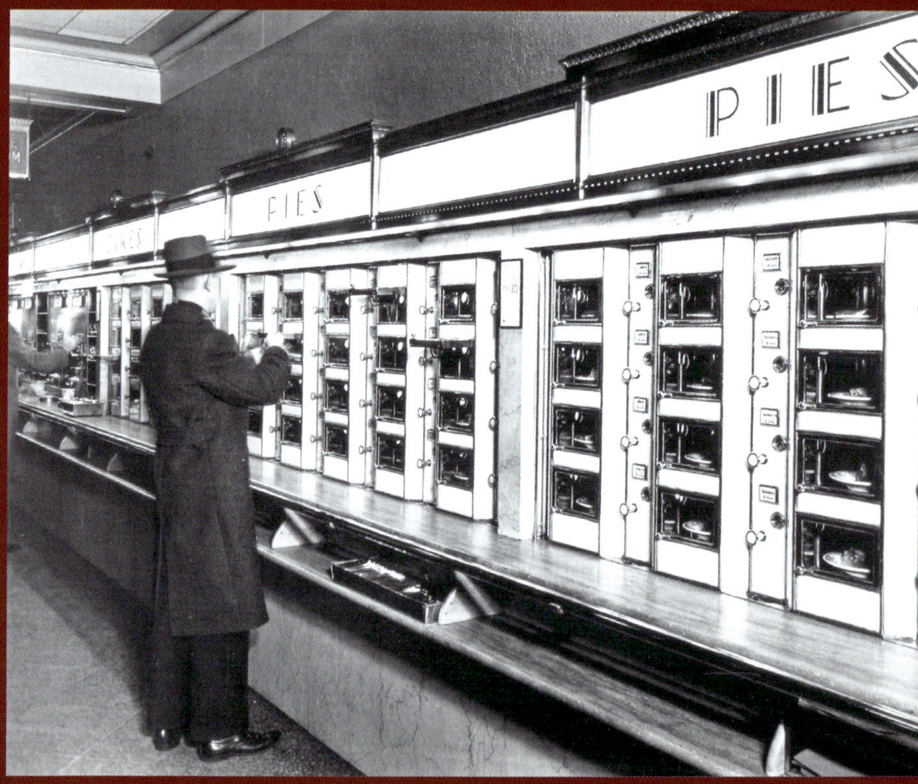

Horn & Hardart Automat, 977 Eighth Avenue, 1936. *Courtesy of the Miriam and Ira D. Wallach Division of Art, Prints and Photographs: Photography Collection, New York Public Library*

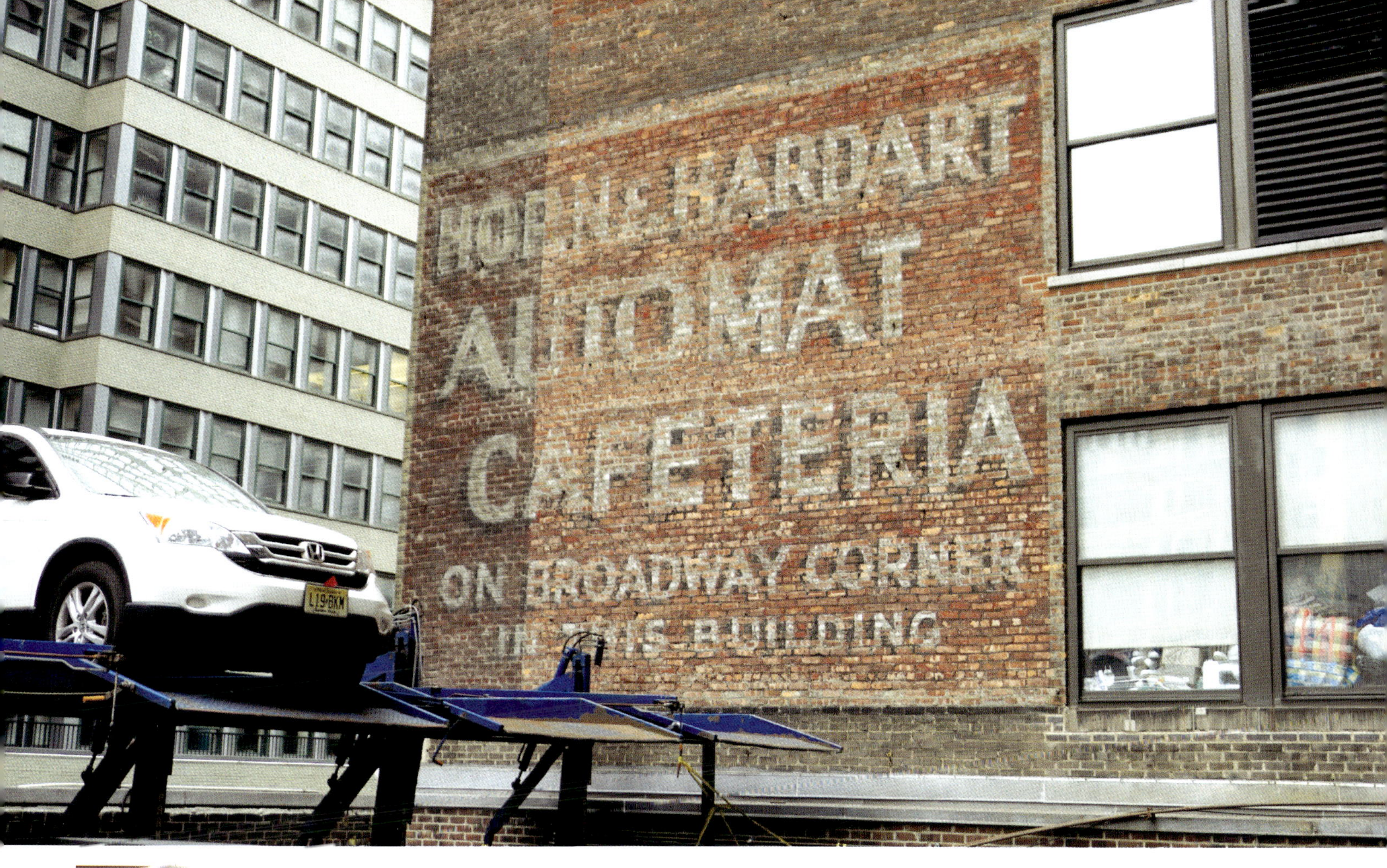

146 West Thirty-Eighth Street

BICKFORD'S

Like the Automat, Bickford's was a New York City institution, serving good food at affordable prices. Samuel Bickford opened his first "lunchroom" in New York in 1922; this Hell's Kitchen location operated from 1929 until the mid-1960s. At its height in 1960, there were forty-eight Bickford's restaurants in New York. The city's last Bickford's closed in 1982.

Bickford's was a favorite haunt of Beat Generation writers of the 1950s. In his poem "Howl," Allen Ginsberg wrote that the best minds of his generation "sank all night in submarine light of Bickford's." When a metal sign was removed from the facade in 2000, the terra-cotta Bickford's logo was revealed over art deco chevrons.

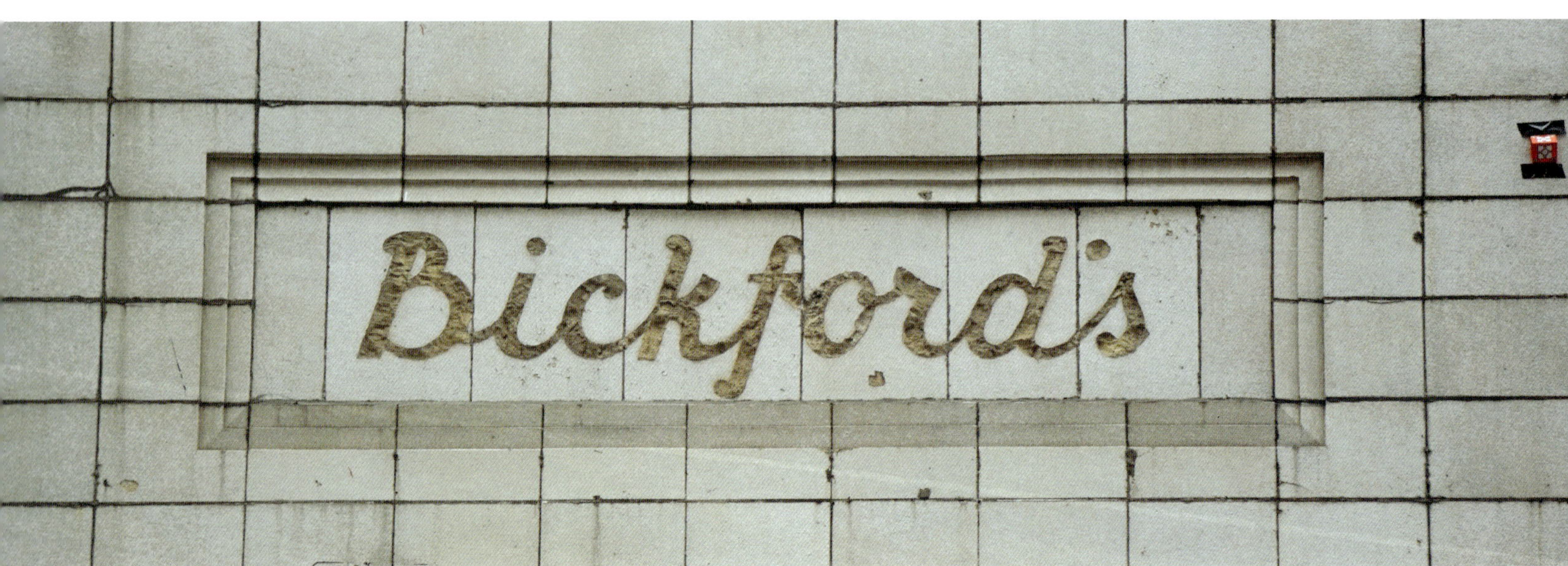

488 Eighth Avenue

COFFEE SHOP

Celebrities, trendsetters, and tourists mourned the closing of the Brazilian restaurant Coffee Shop in 2018. Coffee Shop took its name from its iconic red-lettered neon sign, a holdover from Chase, a working-class luncheonette. Opened in 1990 by a group of former fashion models, Coffee Shop appeared in several episodes of *Sex and the City*. Co-owner Charles Milite told *Forbes* that a rent increase and an impending increase in the minimum wage forced him to close its doors after almost twenty-eight years on Union Square (McGrath 2018).

29 Union Square West

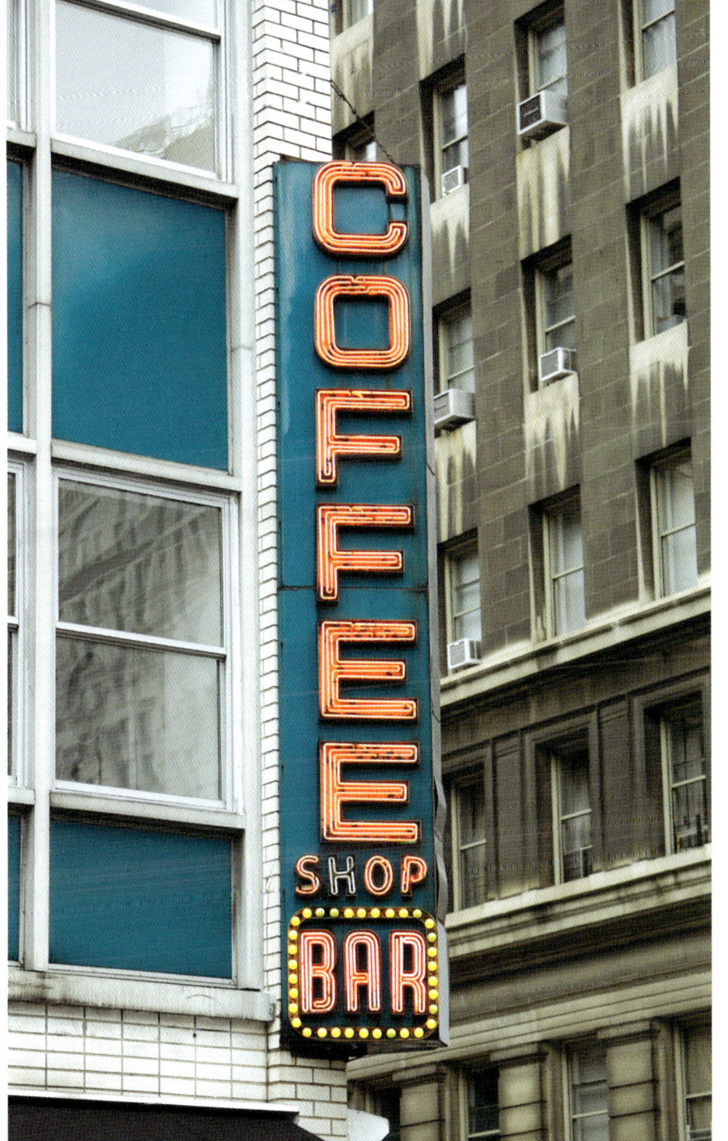

PENNSYLVANIA EXCHANGE BANK

"Bank Gives Away Money," read the eye-catching headline of a 1926 *New York Times* story. To mark the opening of its branch in Chelsea, the Pennsylvania Exchange Bank gave out free dimes to about three hundred schoolchildren. The bank was renamed Gotham Bank of New York in 1959.

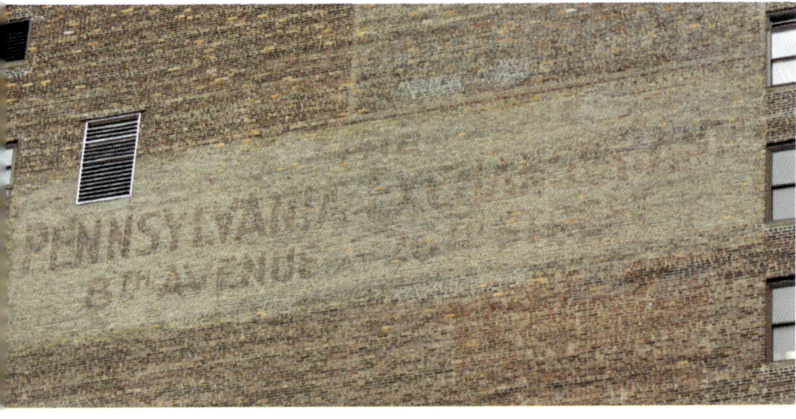

322 Eighth Avenue

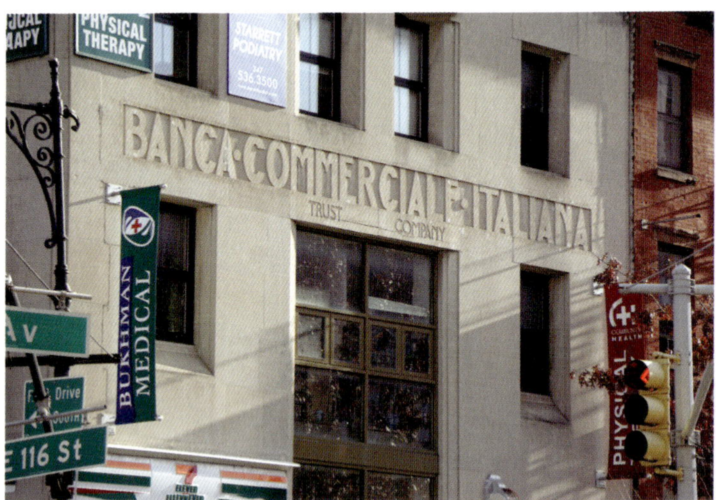

2256 Second Avenue

BANCA COMMERCIALE ITALIANA

Banca Commerciale Italiana (BCI), founded in 1894, enabled immigrants in Italian Harlem to deposit money and send millions of dollars in money orders to Italy. Like other Italian banks during World War II, BCI's assets were seized and the bank was closed. BCI reopened after the war and merged with an international banking group in 1999.

HOTEL HARMONY

"Halfway up the block there was a small fleabag for down-and-outs, the Hotel Harmony," wrote novelist Paul Auster in *The New York Trilogy*. The building opened in 1929 as the headquarters of the Explorers' Club of New York, where it boasted the world's largest collection of books on exploration. The club moved to Central Park West in 1932, and the Hotel Harmony debuted in 1935.

The Hotel Harmony's faded and obscured sign reads, "Hotel Harmony, Where Living Is a Pleasure. Single & Double Rooms, Permanent, Transient." The hotel was open until about 1966. Columbia University purchased the building in the late 1960s and converted it into Harmony Hall, a student dormitory.

544 West 110th Street

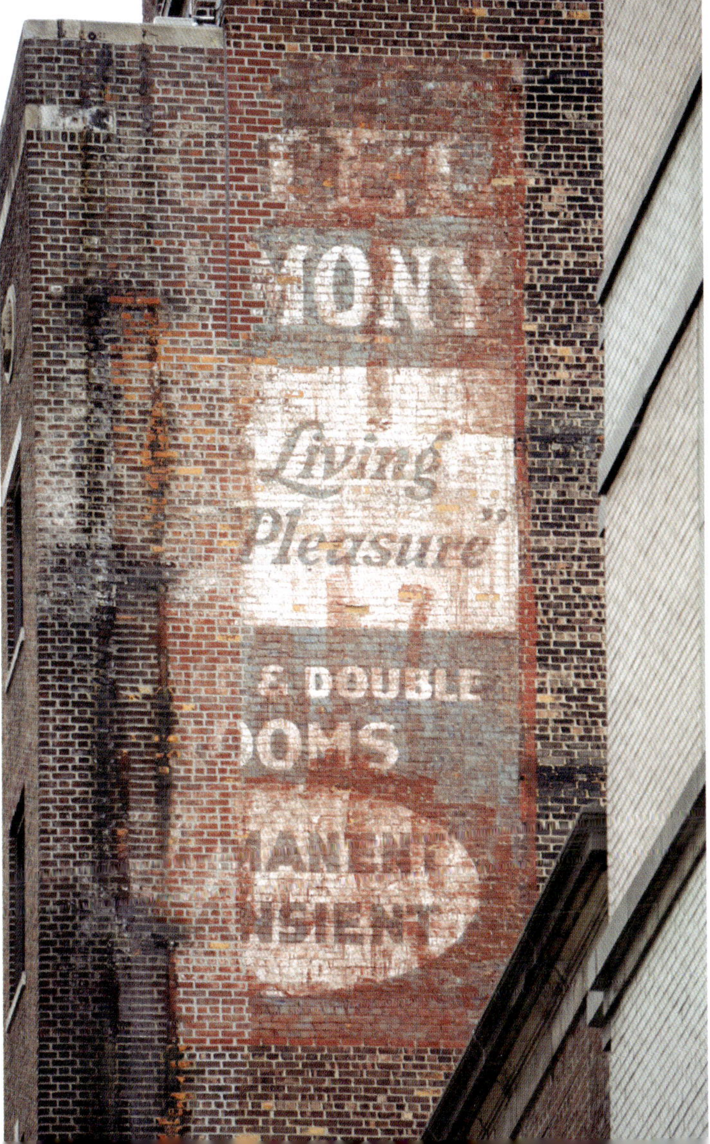

WOODSTOCK HOTEL

Longacre Square, later renamed Times Square, was an emerging theater district in 1903, when Robert Spalding opened the Spalding Hotel. Spalding hoped to satisfy the demand for lodging from singers, actors, and tourists. Spalding died a year later, and the hotel was sold in 1906 to a group of investors that included former governor of Vermont Percival Clement. The lodging was renamed the Hotel Woodstock after a town in the New England state. As the Times Square area became unsavory and crime-ridden in the 1960s, the Woodstock fell into despair and became a welfare hotel. The *New York Times* in 1993 described its ground floor as "dismally gray and decrepit." Project Find, a nonprofit agency, purchased the site in the 1970s and renovated the building. Its Woodstock Senior Center provides housing, food, and counseling for New York's elderly population.

127 West Forty-Third Street

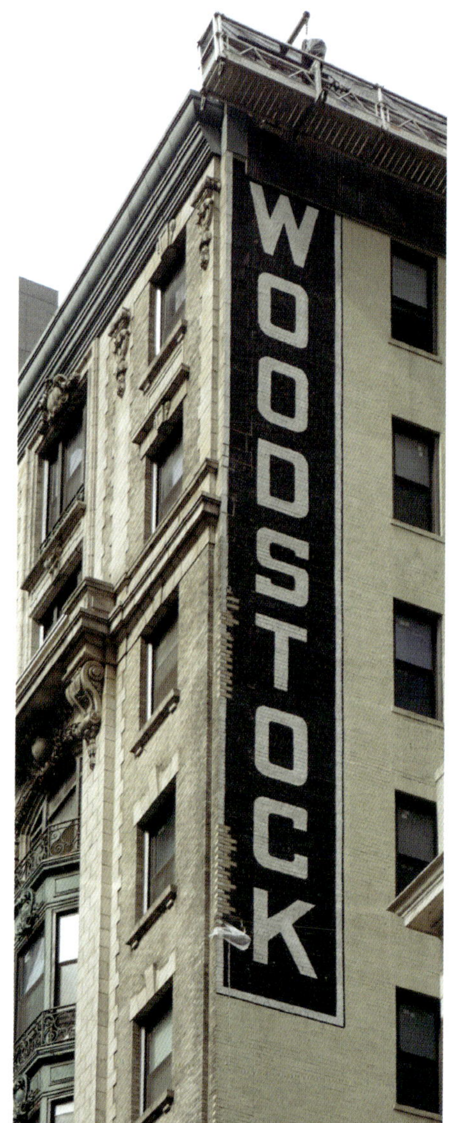

HOTEL 1-2-3

The Gerard Hotel was another elegant apartment hotel in Longacre Square popular among affluent visitors and theater folk staying for long periods. The hotel's reputation suffered by 1914, when the *New York Times* reported that police raided the Gerard, calling it a "disorderly resort." It was renamed the Hotel Langwell by about 1920. As the Hotel 1-2-3, a reference to its address, it was a welfare hotel in the 1970s. After renovations, it became an apartment building.

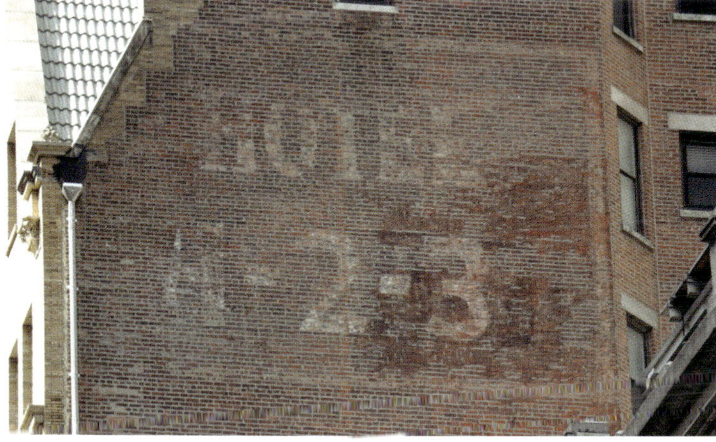

123 West Forty-Fourth Street

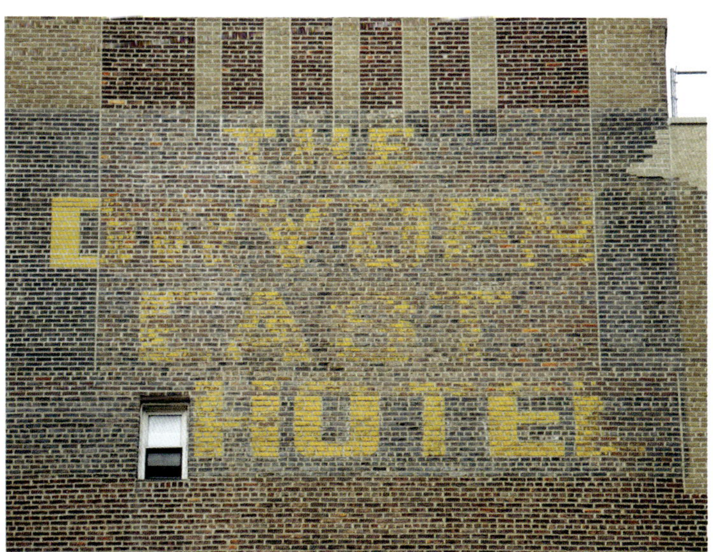

150 East Thirty-Ninth Street

DRYDEN EAST HOTEL

The Hotel Dryden operated in Murray Hill for about thirty years before it was renamed the Dryden East Hotel in the early 1960s. The National Republican Club moved here in 1961; New York's Democratic State Committee followed in 1965. The Dryden East was converted to a luxury apartment building.

MARTINIQUE HOTEL

Named for its owner, William R. H. Martin, the Martinique Hotel was built in 1898 in the Tenderloin. As theaters abandoned the neighborhood for Times Square and stylish stores moved to Fifth Avenue, the Martinique began its decline. By 1973, the city used the Martinique to house homeless families. "Most families spend about a year at the Martinique—with its dimly lit, squalid hallways and a history of problems with asbestos removal—before finding an apartment," reported the *New York Times* (Gray 1987).

The Martinique's era as a welfare hotel ended in 1989, but it remained empty until 1996, when the renovated French Renaissance–style building was reopened as a Holiday Inn. In 2019 it was renamed the Martinique New York on Broadway, Curio Collection by Hilton.

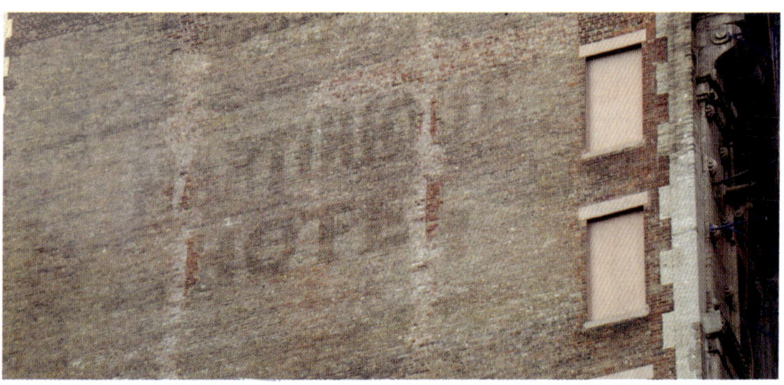

49 West Thirty-Second Street

THE CORNER

In 1881, German immigrants John Koster and Albert Bial opened Koster & Bial's Concert Hall, a vaudeville theater and beer garden on Twenty-Third Street in the Tenderloin. The entrepreneurs opened the Corner one block north in 1887. The Corner served as a saloon and offices for their beer-bottling business. Since the buildings were joined, patrons could enter the theater from the Corner through a passageway.

Frequent police raids and the exodus of theaters from the neighborhood convinced Koster and Bial to close the theater and saloon and move to Herald Square. When that theater closed in 1901, it was demolished and became the site of Macy's department store..

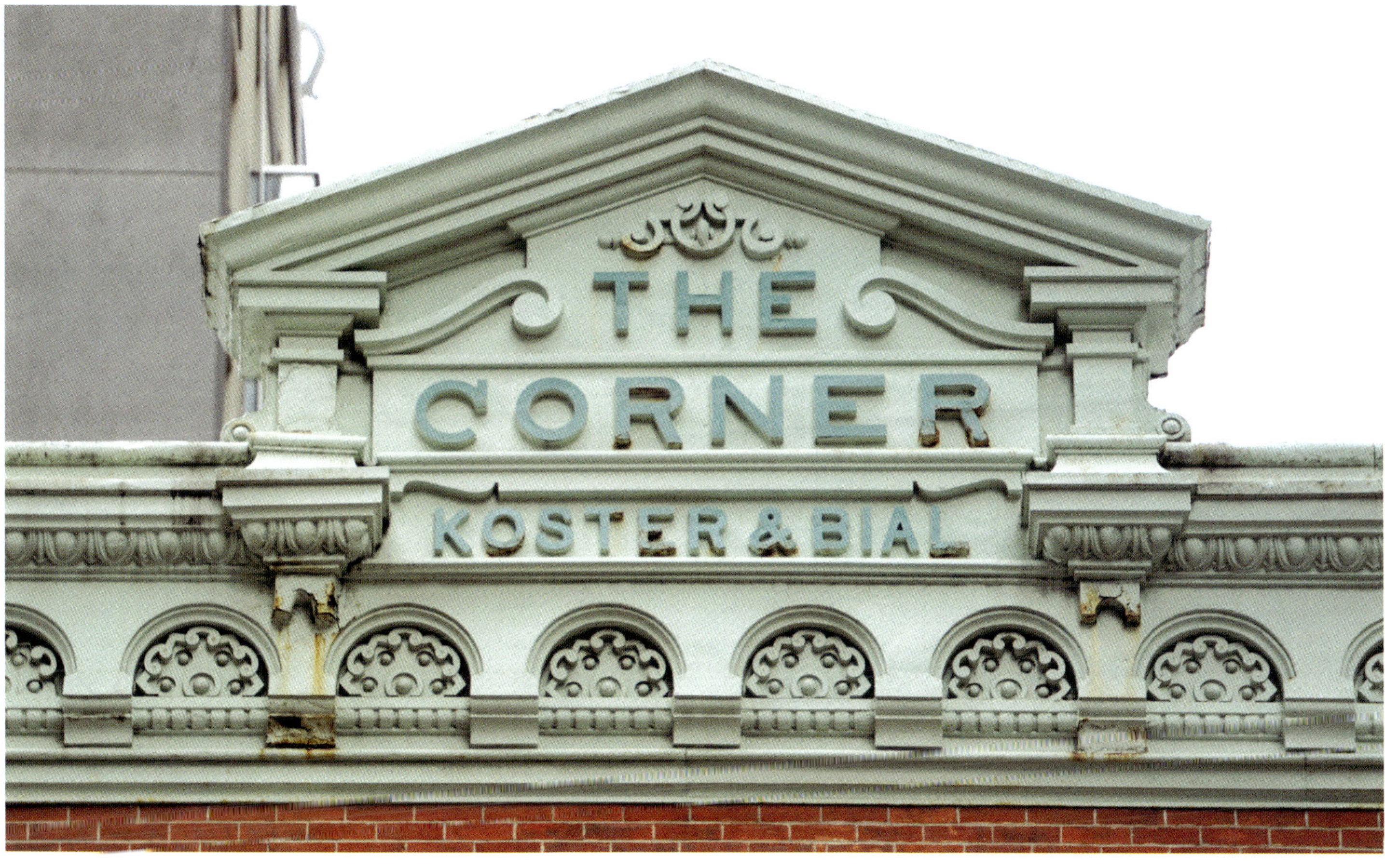

729 Sixth Avenue

HOTEL MCALPIN

When the Hotel McAlpin opened in 1912 it was considered the largest hotel in the world. The *New York Times* noted that at twenty-five stories, "it is so high above the street that the hotel seems isolated from other buildings."

The Alpine Cellar, open from 1970 to 1975, was one of a succession of restaurants in the McAlpin's basement. The hotel was converted to rental apartments in the late 1970s and later to condominiums.

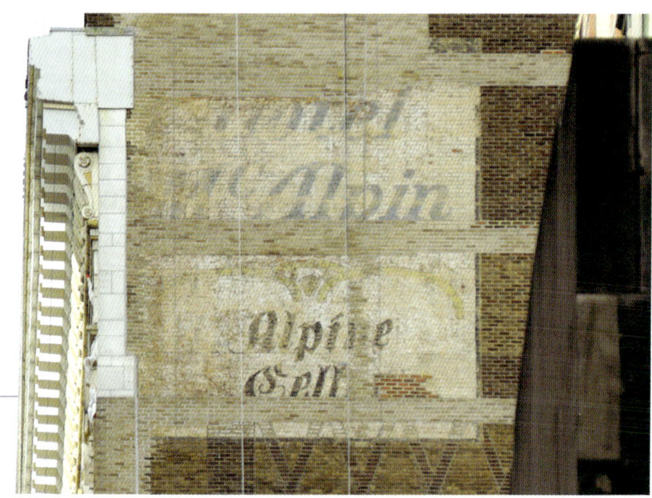

1282–1300 Broadway

ODEON 145TH STREET THEATRE

The Odeon 145th Street Theatre in Central Harlem was built in 1910 and presented vaudeville shows. In the early 1920s Frank Schiffman and Leo Brecher, later owners of the Apollo Theater, converted the theater to a movie house. The Odeon 145th Street Theatre was named to differentiate it from the Odeon Theatre on the Lower East Side.

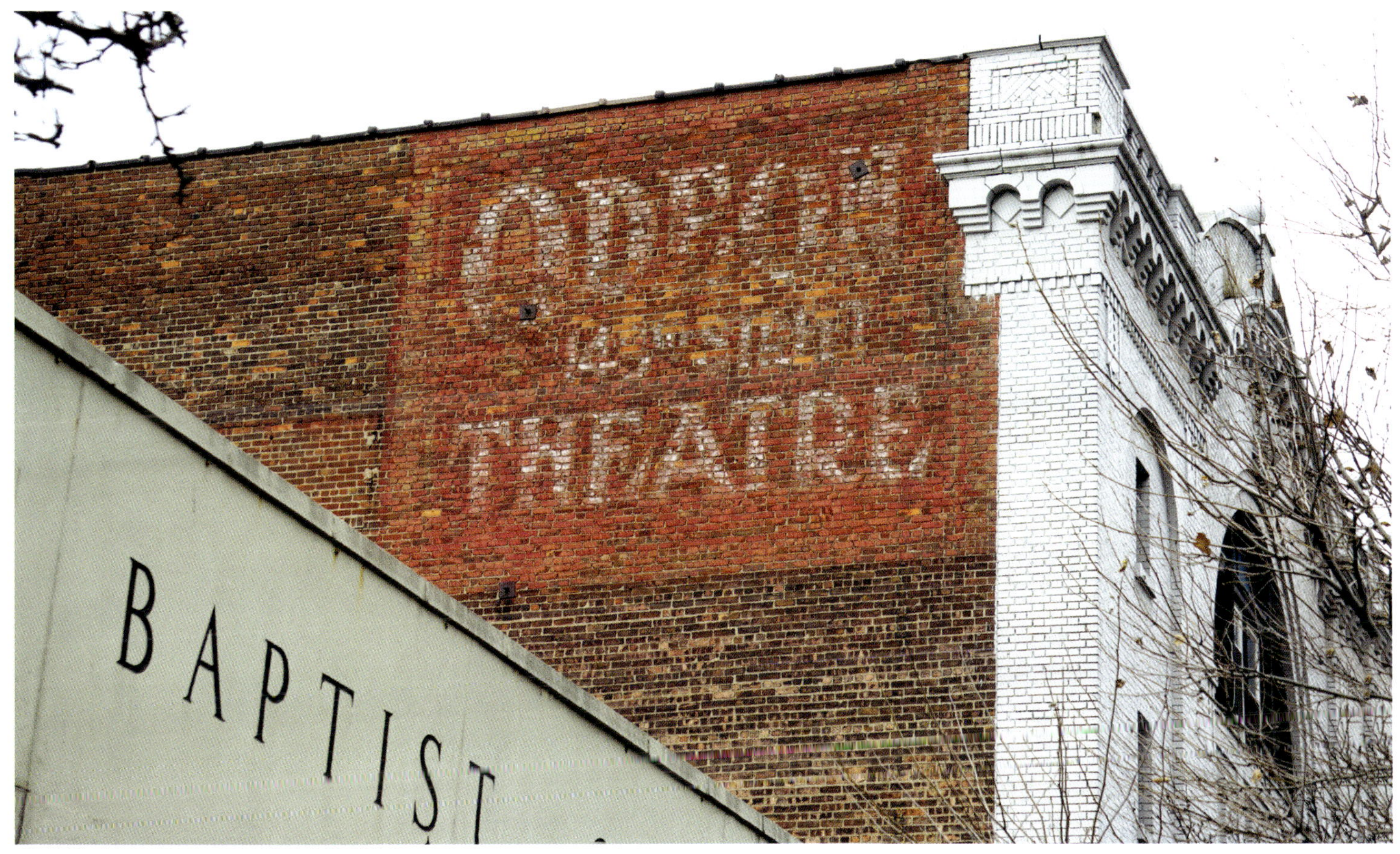

256 West 145th Street

SCHEFFEL HALL

By the 1880s, much of the Lower East Side was known as Kleindeutchland, or Little Germany. Beer halls, restaurants, theaters, and music halls lined the Bowery to serve the 250,000 German-speaking people there. A few blocks north in Gramercy, Carl Goerwitz opened Scheffel Hall. The rathskeller was named for German poet and novelist Joseph Victor von Scheffel.

In 1904, Scheffel Hall merged with Allaire's, a restaurant next door. Both names remain on the facade. The bar was a favorite haunt of writer O. Henry. The 1909 short story "The Halberdier of the Little Rheinschloss" gave Scheffel Hall the name Old Munich and described its "smoky rafters, rows of imported steins, portrait of Goethe, and verses painted on the walls."

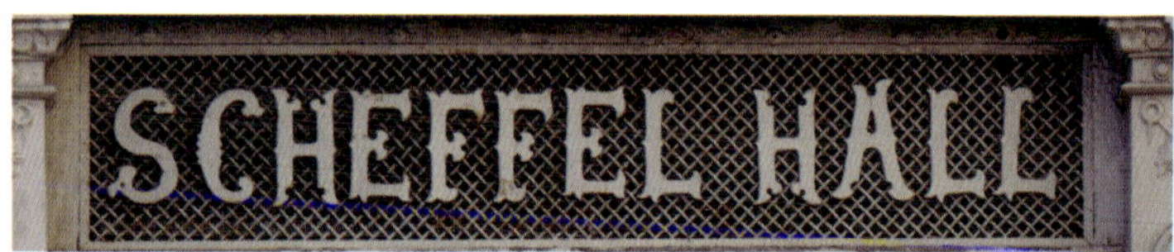

190 Third Avenue

CARRIAGE HOUSE

Thomas Lord was a prominent merchant who built a carriage house in 1870 to house his driver and horses. A third floor was added in 1897, when the Chelsea building may have become a boarding and livery stable. Its ghost sign, among the oldest in the city, probably dates from that time.

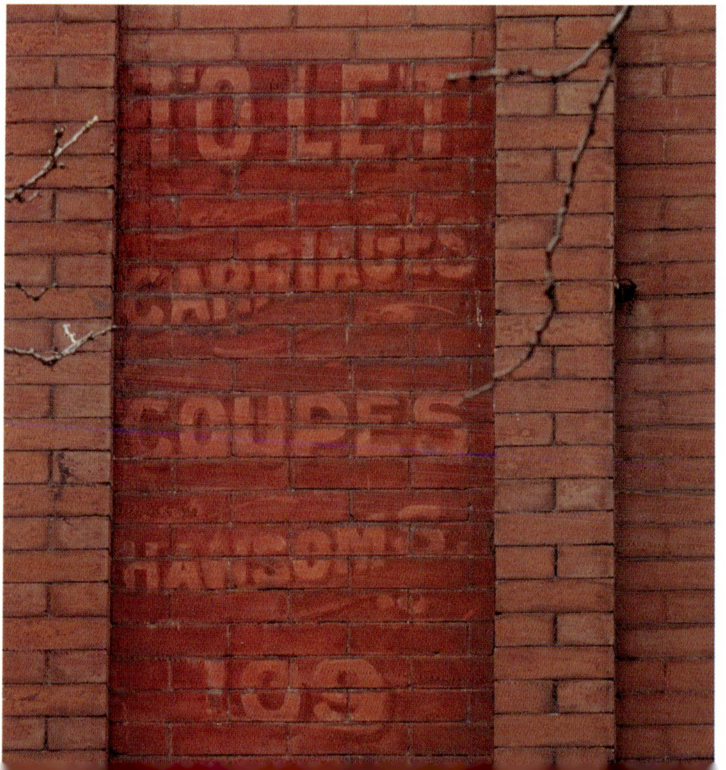

109 West Seventeenth Street

MANUFACTURERS TRUST

Manufacturers Hanover Trust began as Citizens Trust Company of Brooklyn in 1905 and, through acquisitions, became one of New York's largest banks. In 1915 it adopted the name Manufacturers Trust. The steel doors bearing its name were the entrance to its branch in the New Yorker Hotel in Hell's Kitchen.

Manufacturers Trust merged with Central Hanover Bank & Trust in 1961 to become Manufacturers Hanover Trust. Its MHT logo survives above its former branch in Gramercy. Manufacturers Hanover became a division of Chemical Bank in 1992.

481 Eighth Avenue

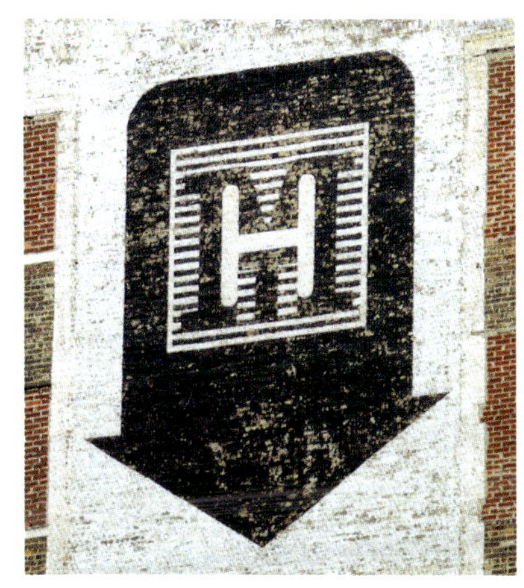

131 East Twenty-Third Street

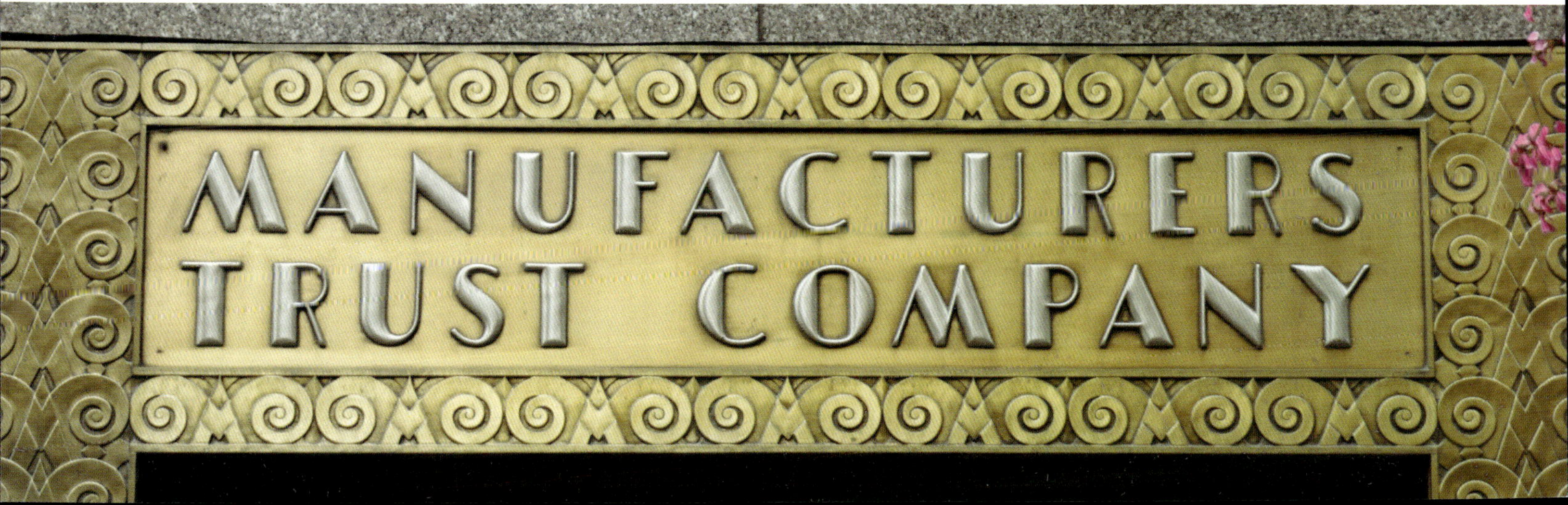

BROADWAY SAVINGS BANK

"There are few happy days where there is worry over money matters," read a 1932 Broadway Savings Bank ad in the *New York Daily News*. "Put your extra dollars where they will be safe and where they will work for you." The bank built what would become its headquarters in Chelsea from 1946 to 1948.

Broadway Savings acquired the Prudential Savings Bank in 1973 and adopted the Prudential name. Other acquisitions followed, and the building has remained a bank.

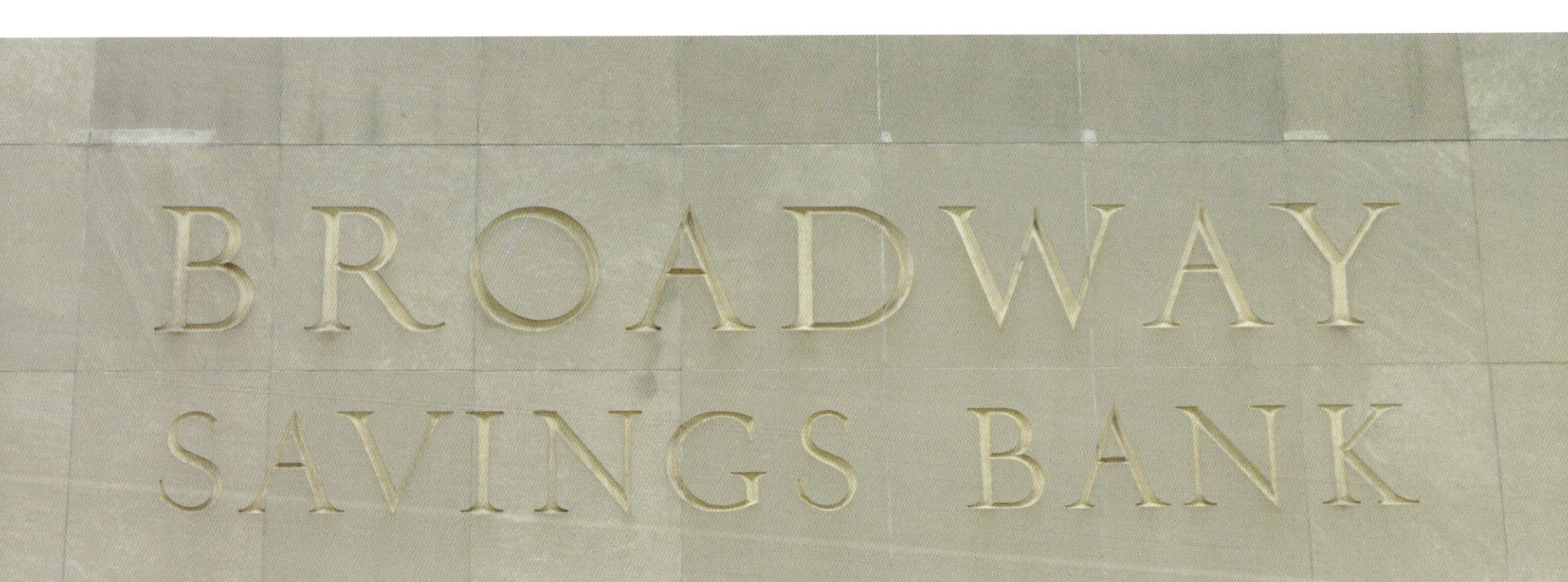

250 West Twenty-Third Street

PRIME BURGER

When Prime Burger closed in 2012, it marked the end of seventy-four years as a moderately priced restaurant across the street from St. Patrick's Cathedral. Hamburger Heaven opened here in 1938; the DiMiceli family took over in 1965 and renamed it Prime Burger. The slogan above the door read, "The Gates of Heaven—Never Closed."

Rita Hayworth, Henry Fonda, Sammy Davis Jr., and Sarah Jessica Parker enjoyed its fare. The James Beard Foundation recognized Prime Burger as an "American Classic" in 2004. A rent increase spelled the end of Prime Burger's run. Its sign was revealed during renovations.

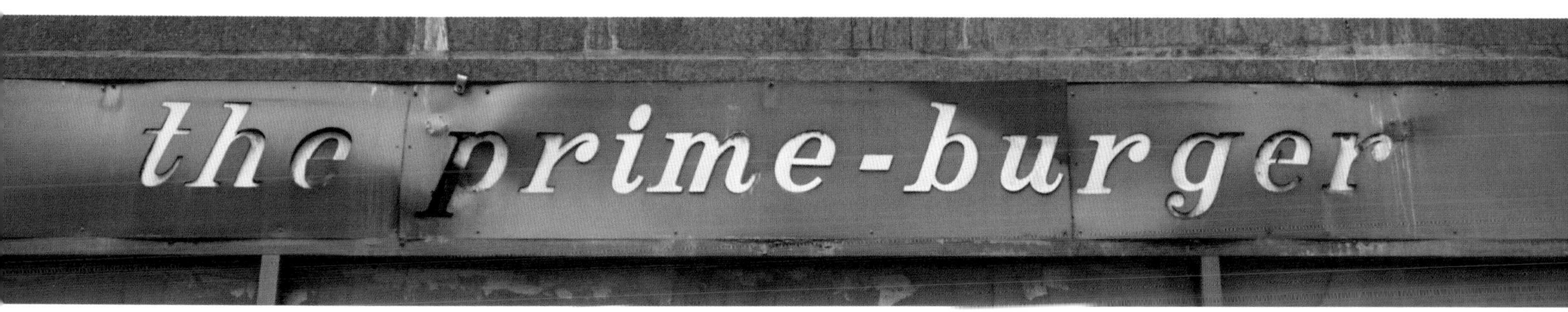

5 East Fifty-First Street

PUZZLING SIGNS

REAL ESTATE ADVERTISEMENT

The removal of an exterior wall in Hell's Kitchen during construction in 2016 revealed this puzzling sign that dates to the early twentieth century. What survives of the sign reads, "From 100 to 230, On Easy Terms, Discount for Gas, Electric Cars Pass Premises to Depot, Commutation Grand Central, 60 Rides for $7.00, Call for Map." The sign advertises real estate, perhaps promoting homes north of Midtown Manhattan.

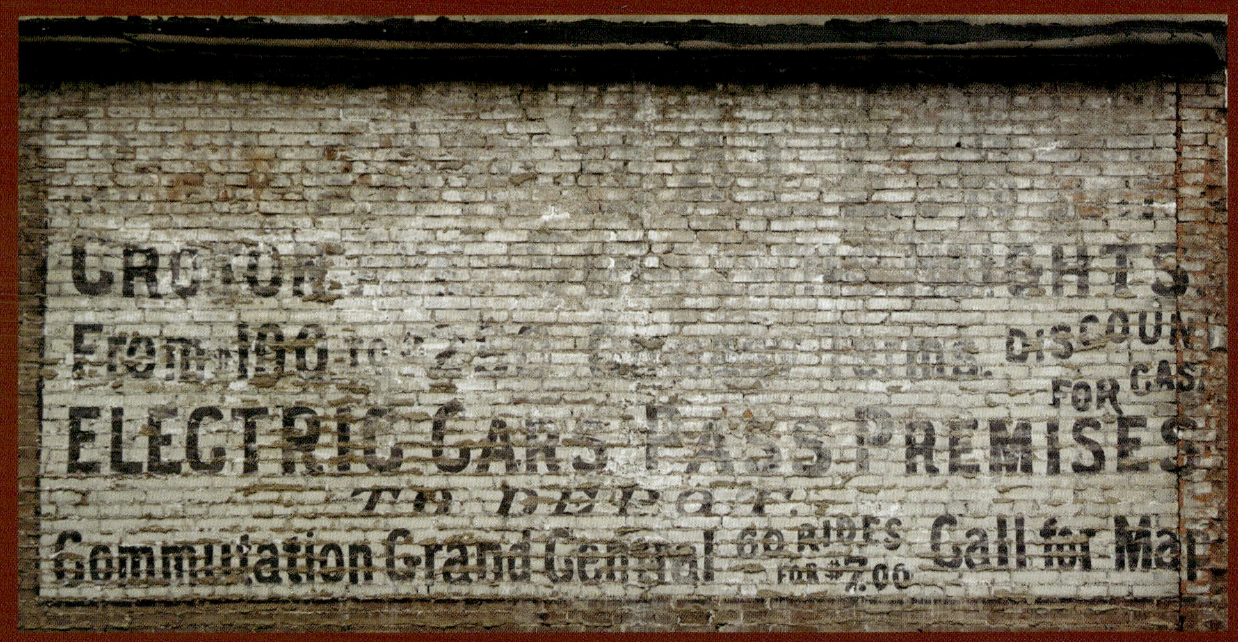

315 West Fifty-Third Street

The reference to a depot offers a clue to its age. When it opened in 1871, the rail terminal on Forty-Second Street was named Grand Central Depot. By 1900, the depot was rebuilt and renamed Grand Central Station. The easy access to electric cars is a reference to the electric streetcars, or trolleys, that ran on tracks along New York's streets beginning in 1909.

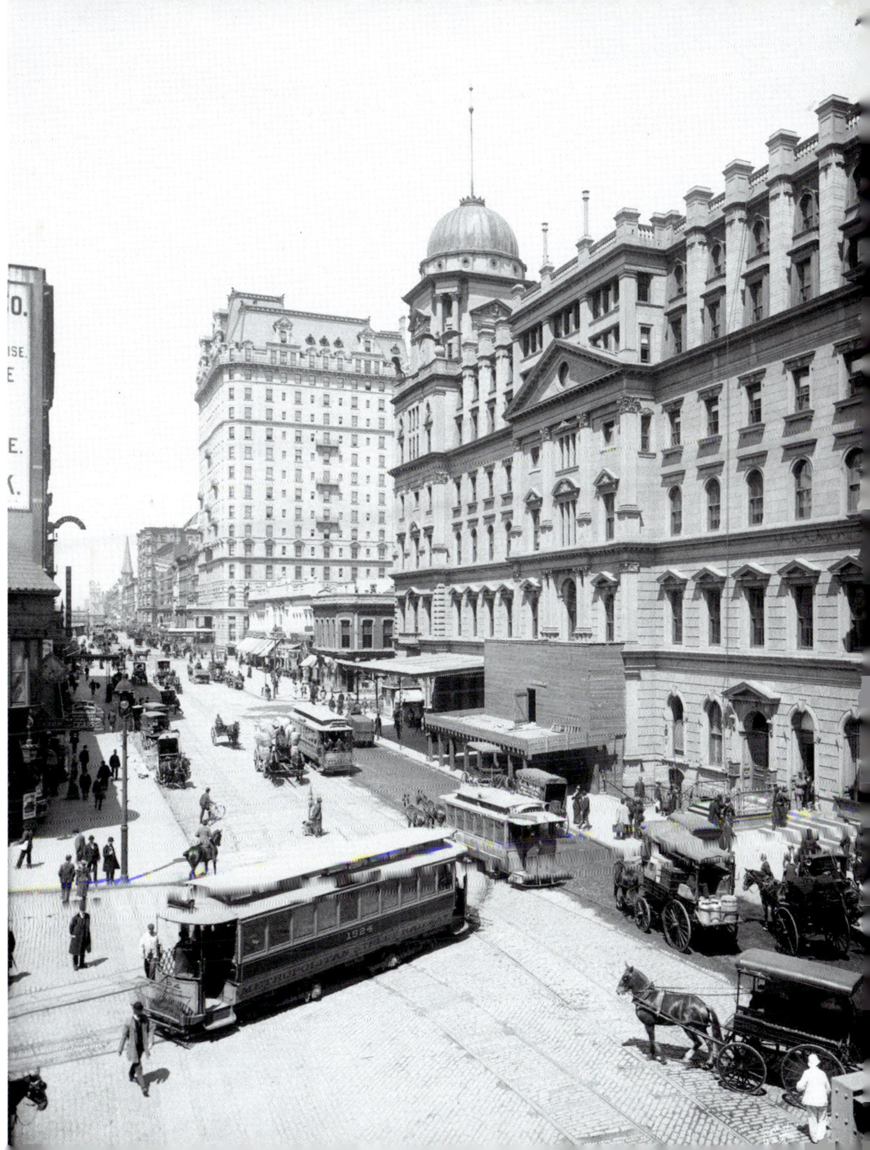

Grand Central Station and Hotel Manhattan, ca. 1900–1906. *Courtesy of the Detroit Publishing Company photograph collection, Library of Congress*

INTERBOROUGH SUBWAY

When New York's subway system was built in the early 1900s, its lines were operated by two private companies, Interborough Rapid Transit (IRT) and Brooklyn-Manhattan Transit (BMT), along with the Independent (IND), run by the city's Board of Transportation. The IRT's Twenty-Eighth Street Station, part of the Lexington Avenue line, has two ornate signs at its entrance.

The city took over control of the bankrupt IRT and BMT lines in 1940. The IRT, BMT, and IND names are no longer used, although their signs remain throughout the system.

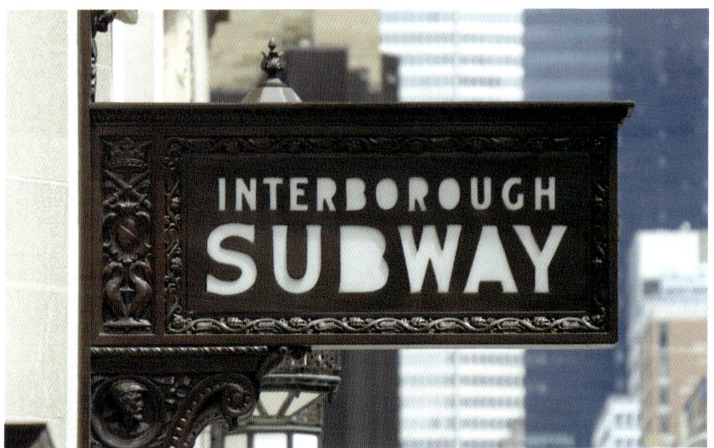

372 Park Avenue South

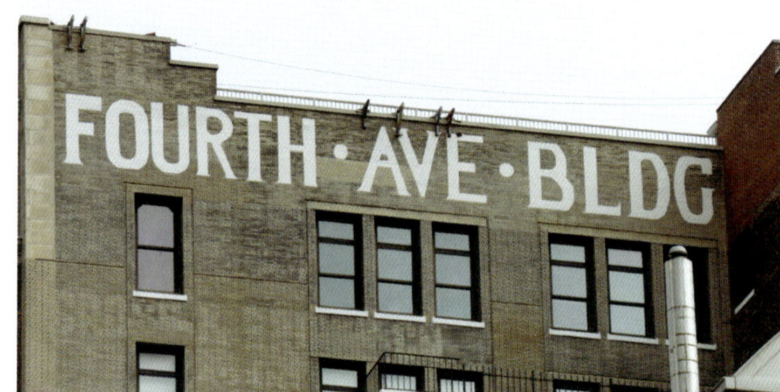

381 Park Avenue South

FOURTH AVENUE BUILDING

Fourth Avenue is a short six-block stretch from Astor Place to Fourteenth Street, but in the 1800s, Fourth Avenue ran as far north as Forty-Second Street. The steam engines of the New York and Harlem Railroad ran along the route until trains were forced to move underground in the late 1800s.

Landscaped gardens replaced the tracks, and the uptown portion of Fourth Avenue above Thirty-Second Street was renamed Park Avenue. In 1959, the stretch between Seventeenth and Thirty-Second Street became Park Avenue South. The Fourth Avenue Building, built in 1909, changed its address to 381 Park Avenue South as a result. The ghost sign along its roofline is regularly repainted.

TUTT'S LIVER PILLS

A confusing sign in East Harlem reads, "Liver." An 1888 story about Dr. W. H. Tutt in *Illustrated New York: The Metropolis of To-Day* explains that "'Tutt's Liver Pills' have been extensively advertised in newspapers and on almost every wooden and stone fence in the country; and they have undoubtedly been used by hundreds of thousands of the population with positive and appreciated benefit." The brand promised to cure "loss of appetite, and all the troubles of the bowels."

The Henry Ford Museum analyzed Tutt's Liver Pills, one of the patent medicines in its collection, and found that the pills contained mercury, which may have toxic effects on the nervous, digestive, and immune systems.

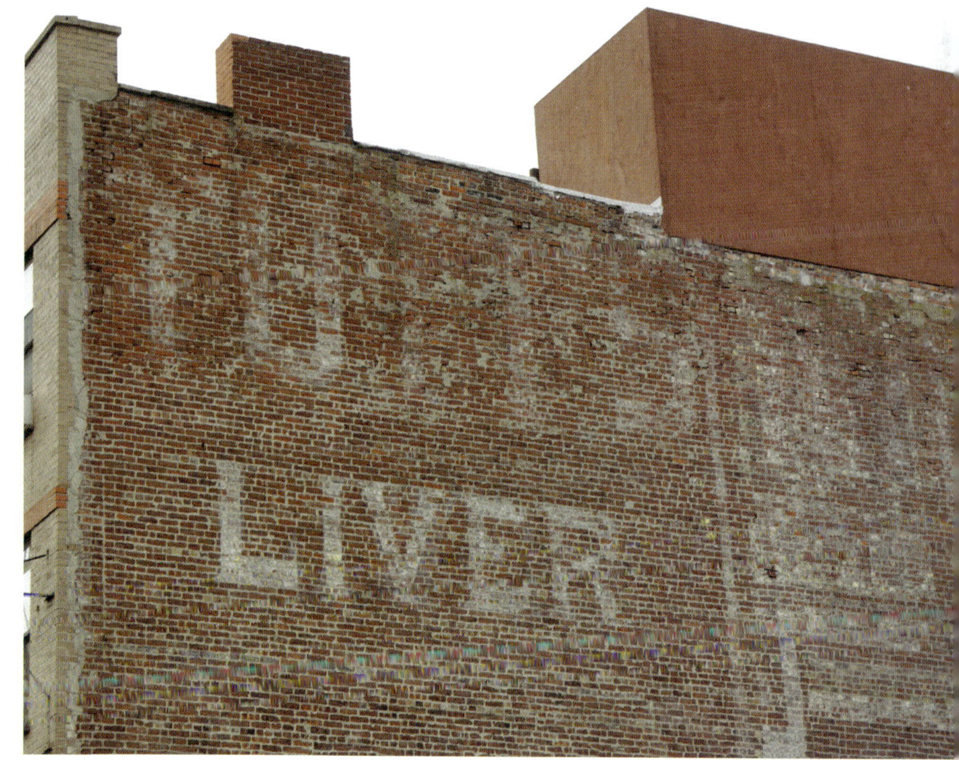

2026 Third Avenue

THE PARK

Diners entered the Park restaurant through an atrium of trees into a dining room filled with tropical plants that created the atmosphere of a rainforest. Outside the trendy Chelsea bistro hung a neon "Park" sign, a reminder of the parking garage that was here before it was converted into a restaurant. The Park closed in 2019 after twenty years of service.

118 Tenth Avenue

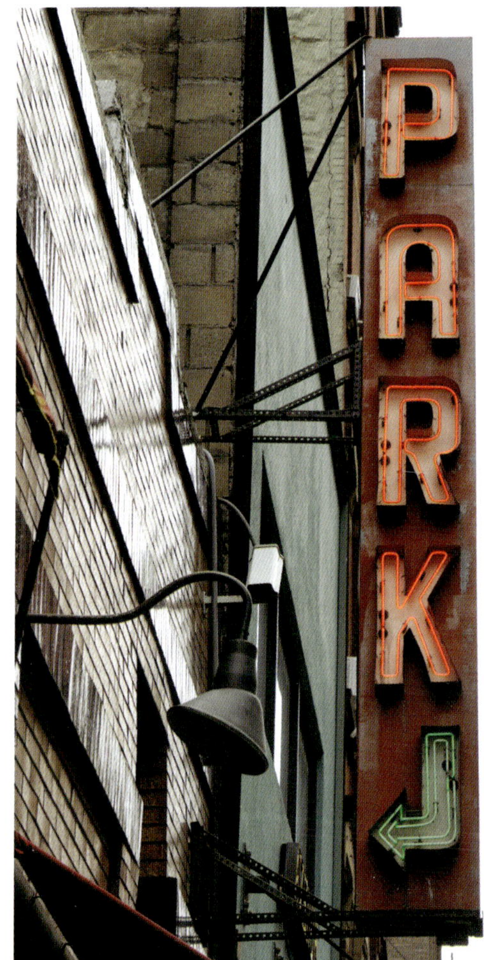

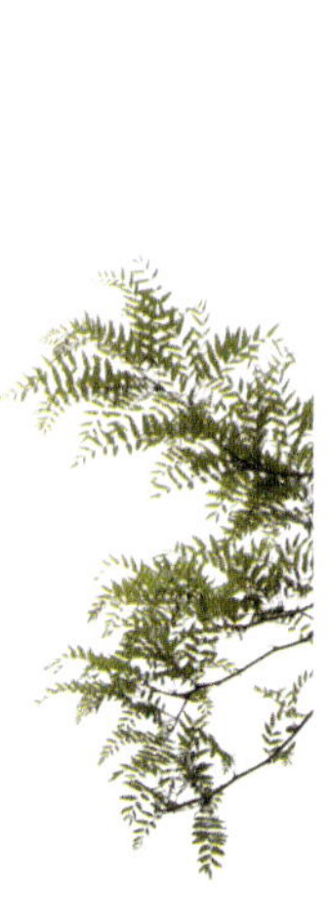

AVENUE A STREET SIGN

New Yorkers know Avenue A as a busy East Village street lined with bars and restaurants. Yet, engraved on the facade of Public School 158, 3 miles uptown on York Avenue, is an Avenue A street sign.

Manhattan's street grid, established in 1811, began with First Avenue on its east side. Avenue A was one of four lettered avenues for smaller sections east of First Avenue; part of its original length ran from Fifty-Third to Ninety-Second Street. In 1928 the uptown section of Avenue A was renamed York Avenue in honor of World War I hero Sgt. Alvin York.

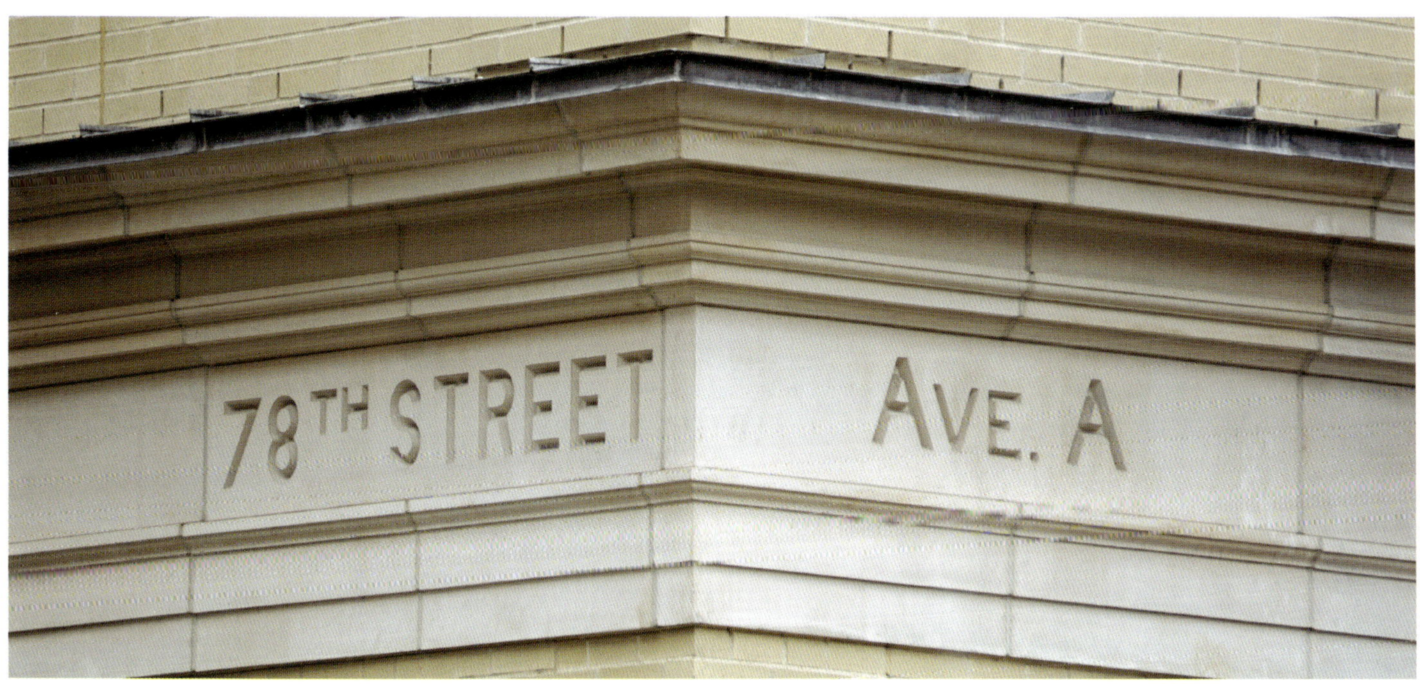

1458 York Avenue

BEEFBURGER FAIR

"Surely everyone has heard of Beefburger Fair," read an article in Baruch College's newspaper *The Ticker*. "Beefburger also boasts a variety of sandwiches, cold platters, and salads that some people enjoy more than their burgers. Portions are generous and satisfying, especially the tuna and chicken salads" (Cuccinello 1979).

Beefburger Fair was a small chain of Manhattan restaurants. The Gramercy coffee shop operated from 1974 to about 1990.

110 East Twenty-Third Street

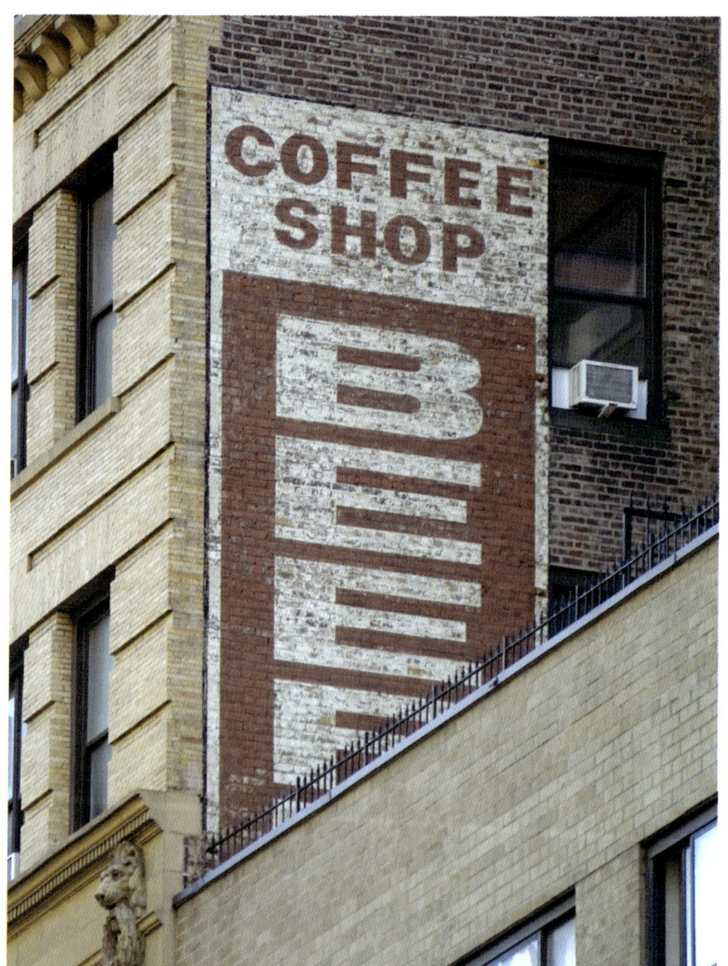

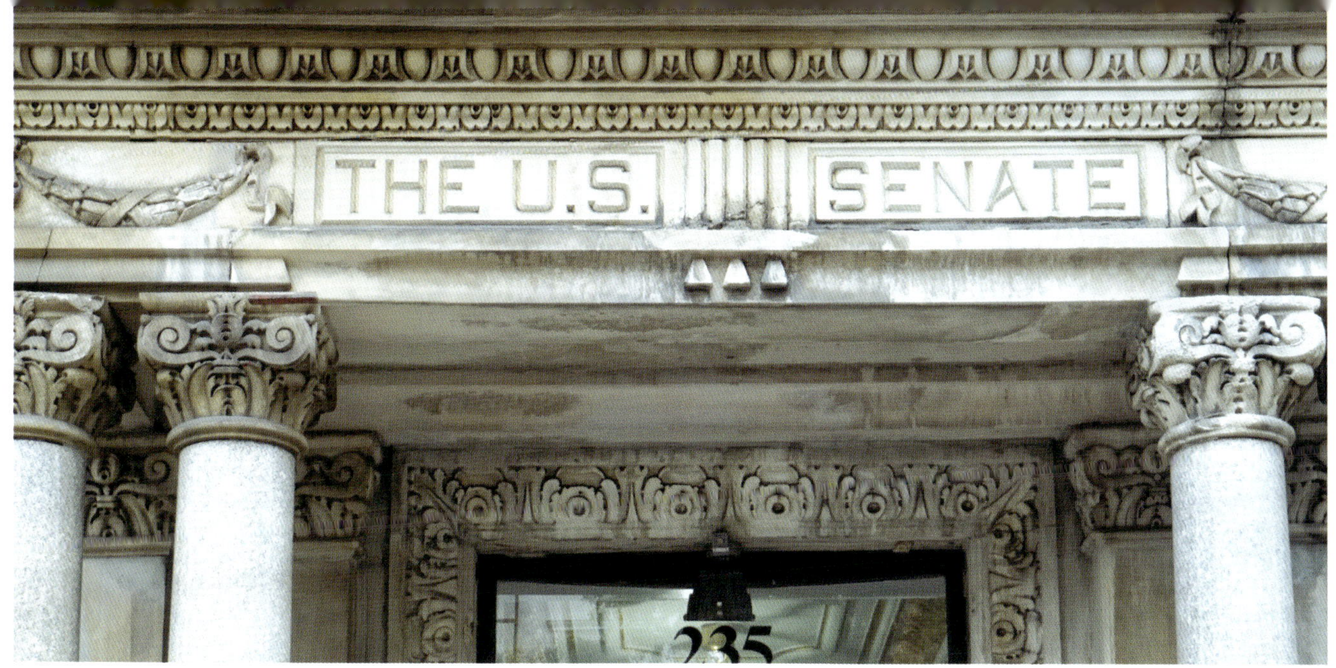

235 Second Avenue

US SENATE

New York City was the nation's first capital after the Constitution was ratified in 1788. George Washington was inaugurated as the nation's first president in 1789 at Federal Hall in Lower Manhattan. An imposing Gramercy ghost sign gives the impression that the United States Senate once convened here.

Sen. William Maxwell Evarts of New York, who served in the upper chamber from 1885 to 1891, died here in 1901. When a new building was erected on the site in 1910, Evarts's career was recognized with the Senate engraving. His name is engraved over the adjacent doorway.

ELSWORTH BUILDING

"Elsw" is a common abbreviation for "elsewhere," but that's not its meaning on this Hell's Kitchen building. It was the Elsworth Building until 2008, when it was cut in half to clear room for construction of the Avalon Clinton apartments.

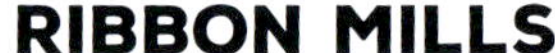

RIBBON MILLS

Ribbon Mills was one of many clothing and fabric companies advertised on the side of the Martin Building in NoMad. The company operated here from 1933 to 1939. Its obscured ghost sign reads, "Ribbon Mills Corp. 'Eventually Your Ribbon House.'"

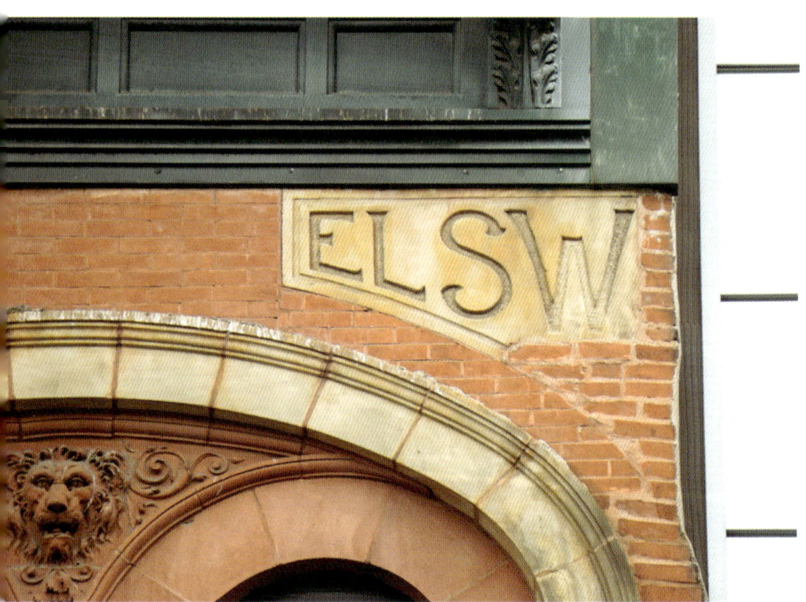

777 Tenth Avenue

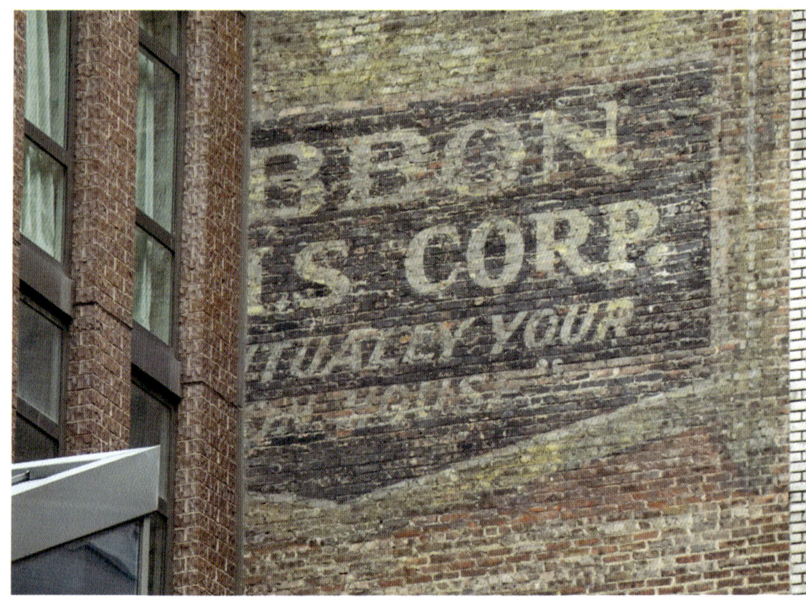

102 Madison Avenue

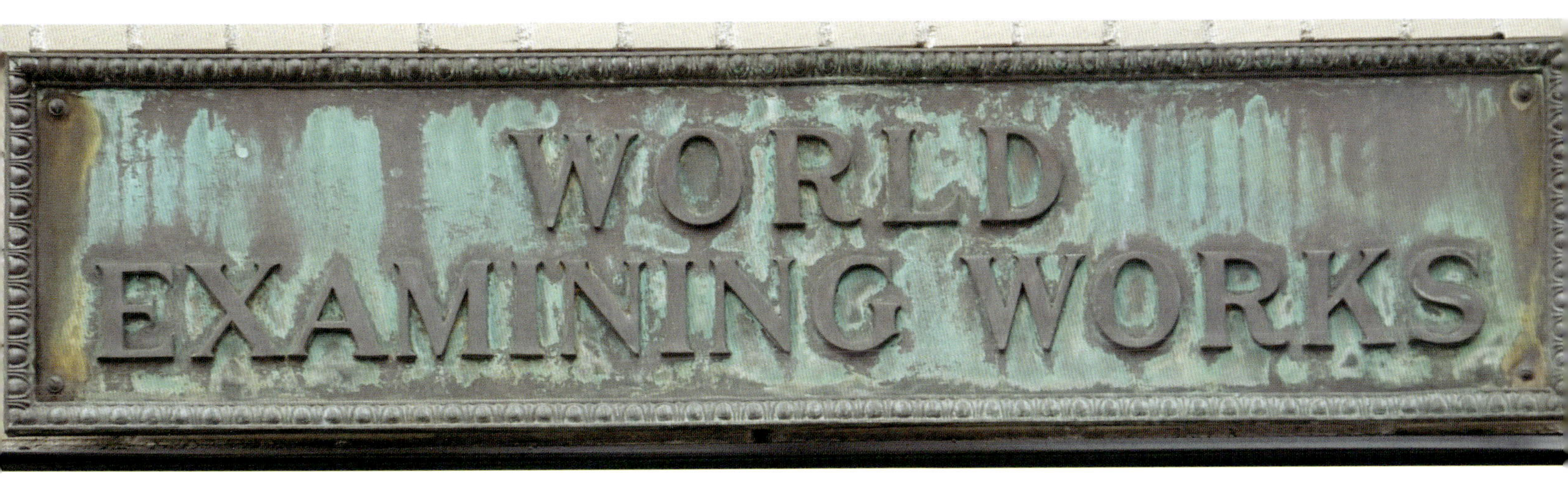

401 West Fourteenth Street

WORLD EXAMINING WORKS

The World Examining Works sign on the Ninth Avenue side of the Western Beef Building offers little clue to the type of business that was once here—unless you are in the textile industry. World Examining Works was a firm that did fabric cleaning, dyeing, and sponging in the Meatpacking District. Sponging is a method of shrinking wool fabrics by applying water, then drying with heat.

GOING . . . GOING . . . ALMOST GONE

Thankfully, the owners of some New York shops and restaurants have resisted change and preserved their iconic, decades-old signs.

OLD TOWN BAR

The Old Town Bar's history dates to 1892, when it was a German American saloon named Burckel Brothers' Cafe. Prohibition saw the bar become Craig's Restaurant, a speakeasy that served food. "You would stow your drinks under the bottom of the booths," owner Gerard Meagher told the *Village Voice* (Kessler 2014). In 1933, the bar was renamed Old Town.

Old Town retains much of its 1890s atmosphere. Its bar, booths, and cabinets are made from the original mahogany, making it a favorite location for television and films. *The David Letterman Show* featured the bar's sign in its opening montage. "We had ten years of visibility each day on the *David Letterman* show," Meagher told *Gothamist*. "That really put us on the map" (Fishbein 2017).

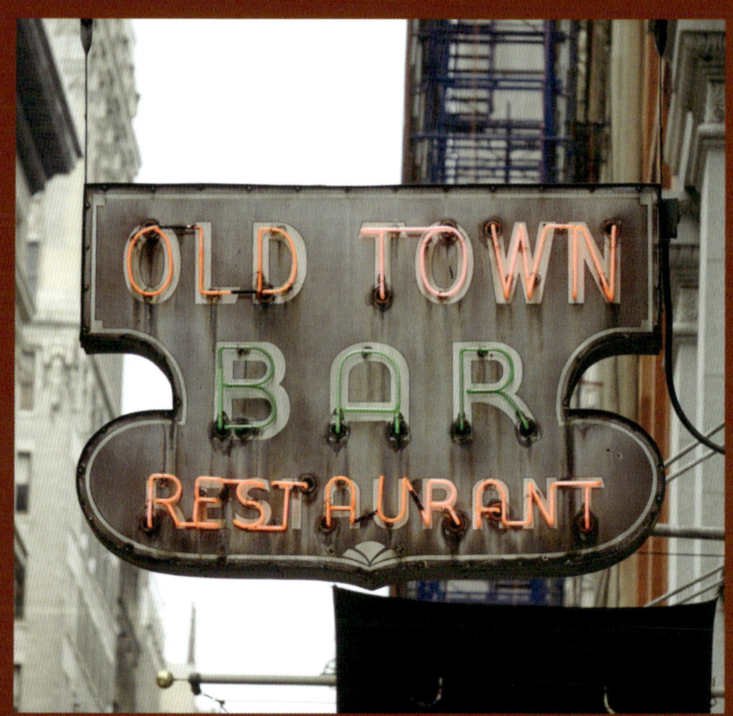

45 East Eighteenth Street

LEXINGTON CANDY SHOP

The Lexington Candy Shop opened in 1925, making it one of the oldest family-owned luncheonettes in New York. Greek immigrant Soterios Philis originally sold chocolate and other sweets made in the basement, but by 1948 the shop became a luncheonette, serving burgers, eggs, milkshakes, and egg creams. The shop's coffee urns, milkshake mixers, and iconic signage date from 1948, when it was last renovated.

"We're a part of the living history of the city," third-generation owner John Philis told *Gothamist*. "There was a time when there were luncheonettes like this on every other block. Everybody grew up with them, they're part of the fabric of the city and they've all disappeared. Now it's up to us to sort of keep up the legacy and history of the business" (Heins 2017).

1226 Lexington Avenue

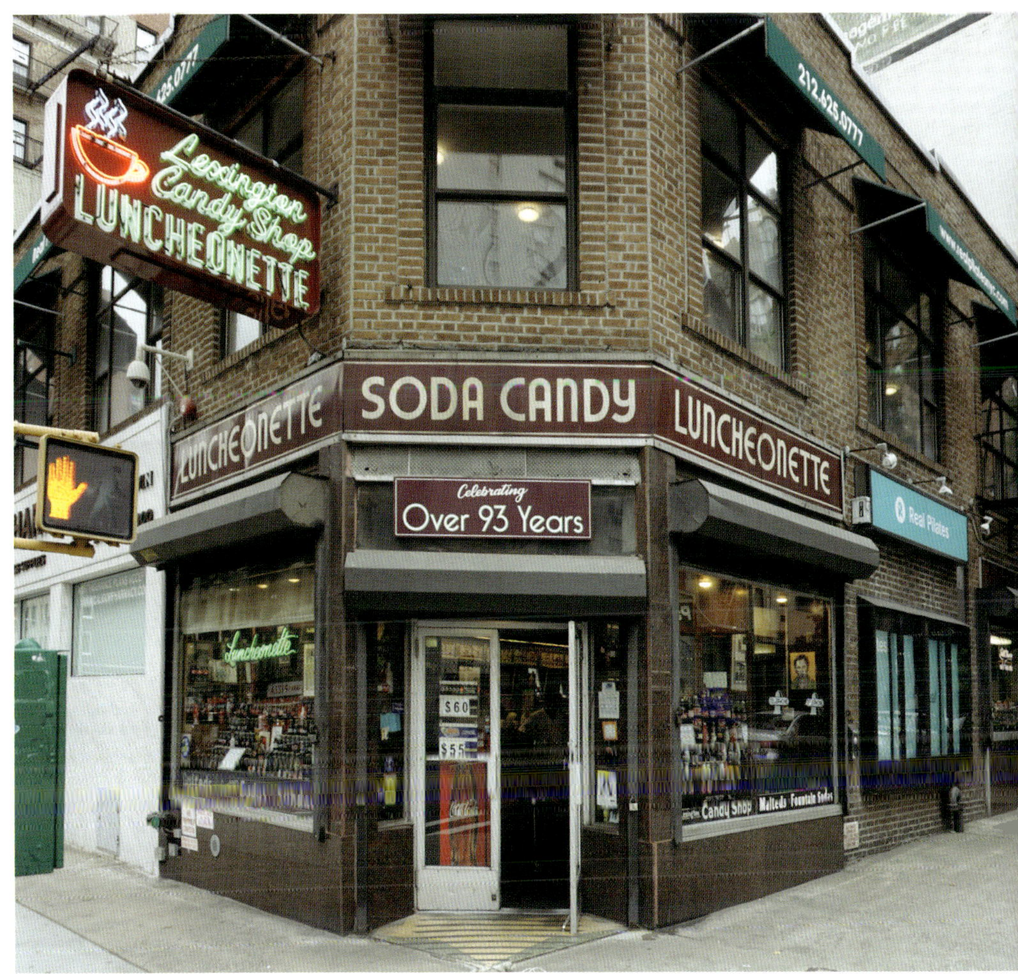

RUDY'S BAR & GRILL

Rudy's calls itself "New York's most famous dive bar, right through the original wood door, carved down the center with the name of the first owners, the Rudy family." The Hell's Kitchen bar, opened in 1883, is named for German immigrants Helen and Ewon Rudy. "Helen Rudy kept two big German Shepherds to mind the door," Rudy's website explains. "If a customer fell asleep, or became unruly, she'd give a signal and the dogs would join the customer at the bar and growl. If that didn't work, the dogs would bark and bare their teeth."

Rudy's remains unpretentious, but its celebrity clientele includes Paul McCartney, Julia Roberts, and Halle Berry. Drew Barrymore was a regular until the owners learned she was not old enough to legally drink.

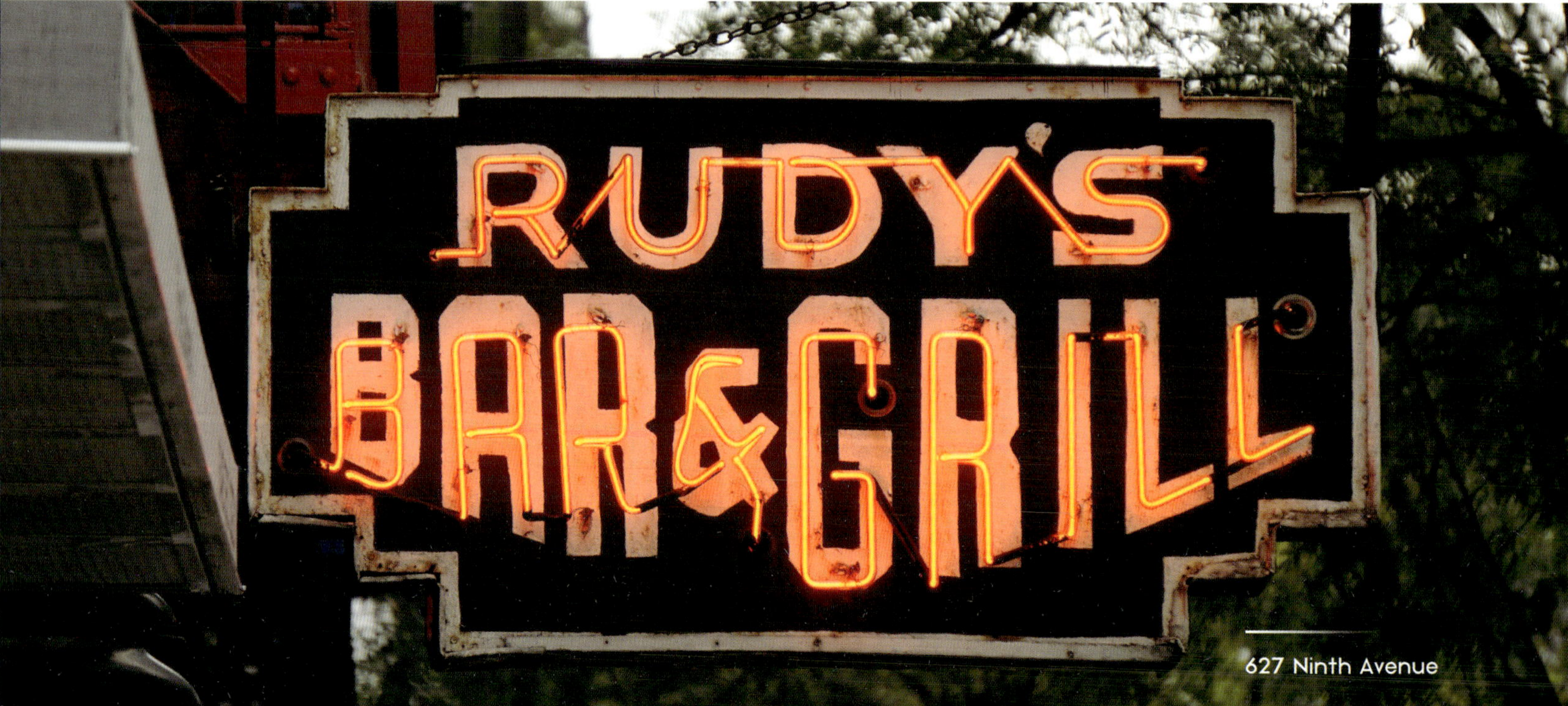

627 Ninth Avenue

BARBETTA

Sebastiano Maioglio opened Barbetta on Thirty-Ninth Street in 1906. One of New York's oldest family-owned Italian restaurants, it serves the cuisine of Italy's Piedmont region and moved to four contiguous brownstones in the Theater District in 1925. The letters of Barbetta's incandescent sign are made of opal glass, a type of lighted sign popular before neon was introduced in 1923.

"Opal glass signs were built from the 1910s through the 1930s," notes *Vintage Signs of America*. "The letters were made of translucent glass and backlit with light bulbs inside the sign. Many people refer to these letters as 'milk glass' since most of them were white. However, other colors were produced as well."

321 West Forty-Sixth Street

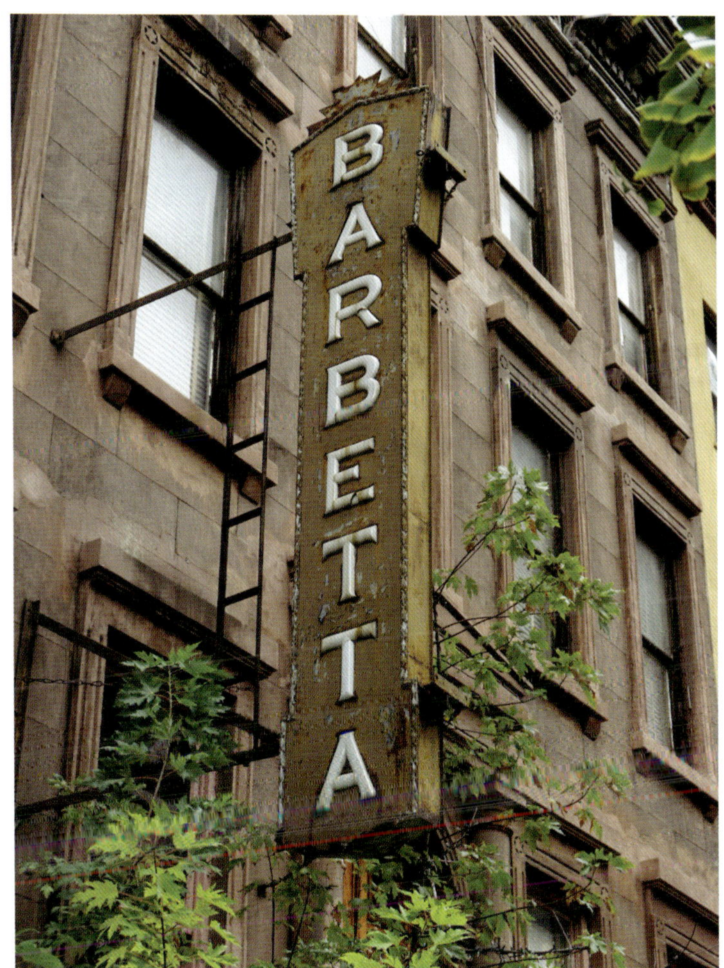

P. J. CLARKE'S

P. J. Clarke's is an Irish pub that opened in 1884. Patrick J. Clarke worked as a bartender for ten years before buying and renaming the bar in 1912. Clarke's is housed in a two-story building surrounded by skyscrapers. The pub's website proclaims the owner's refusal to sell the building "to evil, no-good developers razing the neighborhood's buildings left and right."

Clarke's has hosted celebrities that include Nat King Cole, Jackie Kennedy, Richard Harris, and Elizabeth Taylor. In 1958, Buddy Holly proposed to his fiancée, Maria Elena Santiago, at Clarke's while on their first date.

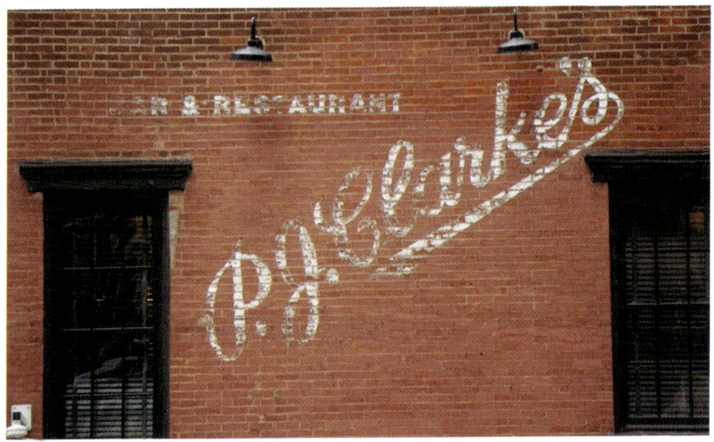

915 Third Avenue

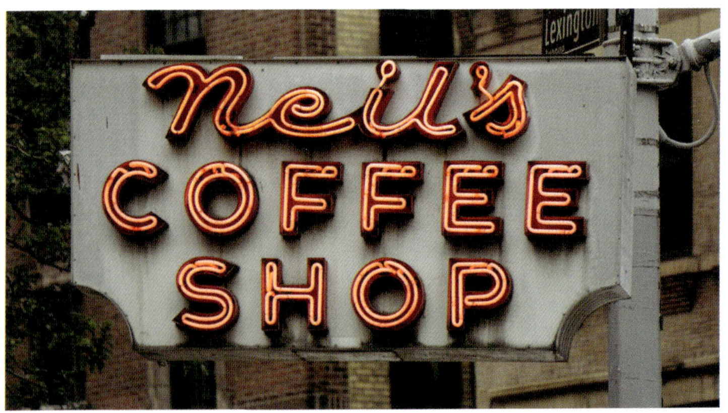

961 Lexington Avenue

NEIL'S COFFEE SHOP

Neil's Coffee Shop opened on the Upper East Side in 1940; its neon sign has hung in front since FDR was president. Greek immigrant Cristo Kaloudis bought the restaurant from the Neil family in 1980. Kaloudis's son Nicholas runs Neil's today.

"My father didn't change the name or the look when he bought it," Kaloudis told *Financial Review*. "Nothing you see here today has been changed from the time he bought the diner apart from the upholstery in the booths, which we change every couple of years. We even use the same old 1951 cash register and the Hamilton milkshake blender is from 1954. They still work fine" (Divola 2020).

TOM'S RESTAURANT

Tom's Restaurant has been a favorite of Columbia University students and faculty since it opened in the 1940s. President Barack Obama dined here when he was a student at Columbia. The neon sign of Tom's Restaurant is familiar to fans of the long-running sitcom *Seinfeld*. When Jerry, George, Elaine, and Kramer gathered at Monk's Café, an exterior shot of Tom's iconic sign was shown, cropped to read "Restaurant." Owner Mike Zoulis told *Traveller* that the restaurant was paid nothing when the *Seinfeld* film crew arrived in 1989. "That doesn't bother me. Think about it. It's all been free publicity. . . . *Seinfeld* made us known to millions. But you can only sit eighty people in here at a time" (Divola 2016).

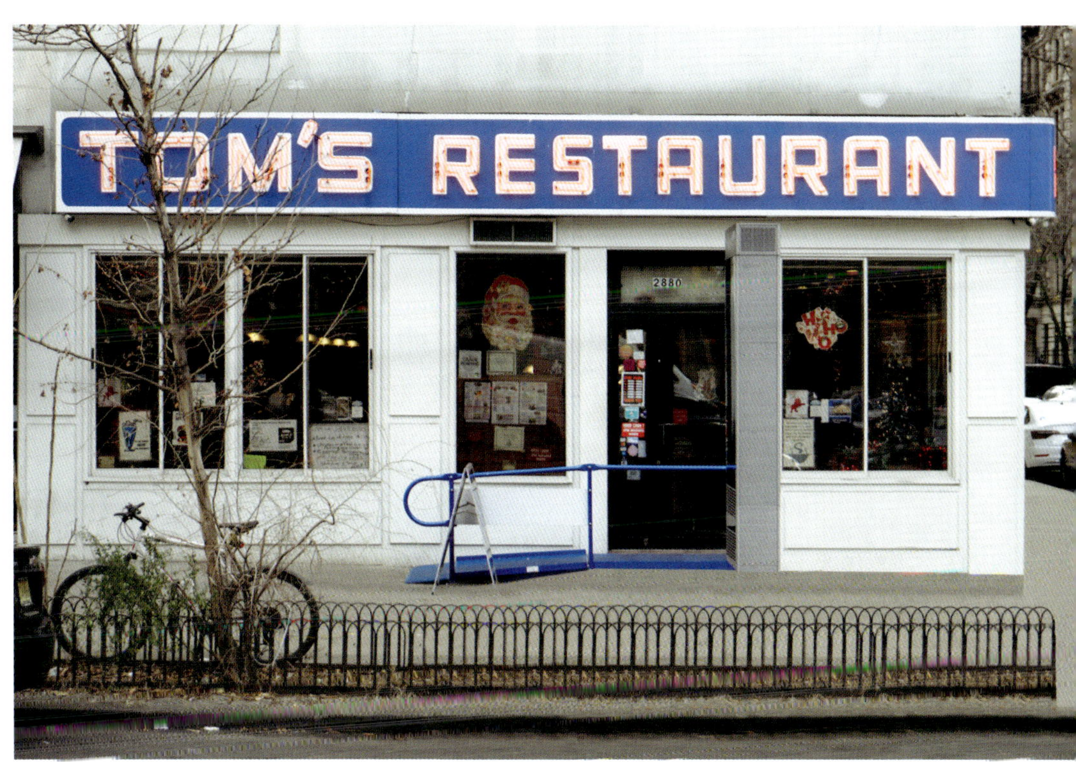

2880 Broadway

SMITH'S BAR

"Smith's Bar and Restaurant has held down the northwest corner of 44th Street and Eighth Avenue for fifty years, its name written in soot-coated neon script outside, in a style of sign once seen above countless New York bars and liquor stores but now largely extinct," noted the *New York Times* in 2005. "A bright green menu panel above the steam tables opposite the bar advertises pigs' knuckles, knockwurst and lamb stew, and the Irish barmen, in ties and white shirts, serve their lunchtime customers—a scattering of men bent over newspapers and racing forms—with curt, dishrag-snapping efficiency" (McAninch 2005).

The Hell's Kitchen bar, which draws many of its customers from Times Square, opened in 1954. Smith's closed in 2014 but reopened under new management a year later, with an updated menu and its classic neon sign restored.

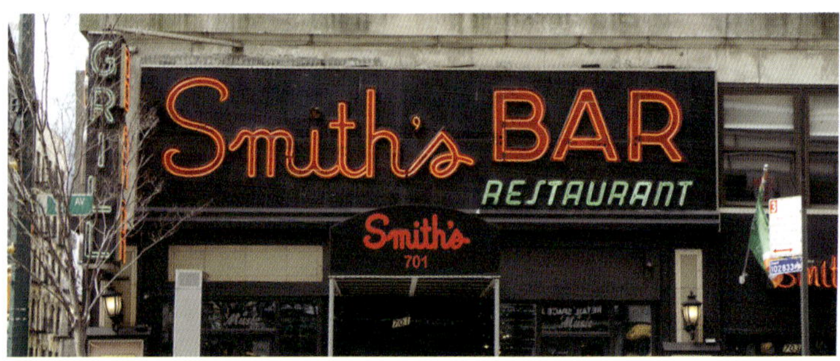

701 Eighth Avenue

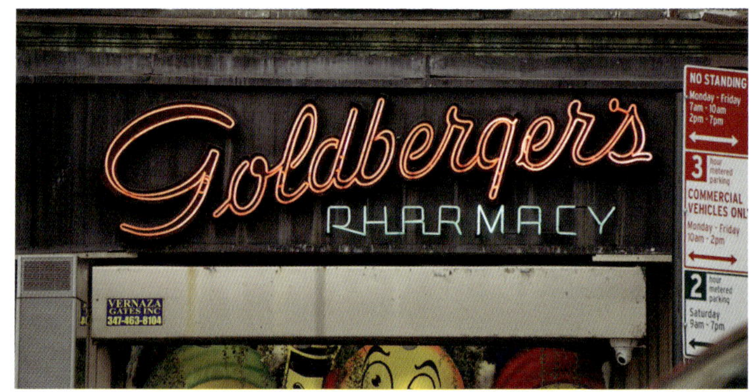

1200 First Avenue

GOLDBERGER'S PHARMACY

Goldberger's Pharmacy was founded by Hungarian immigrant Aaron Goldberger more than a century ago. Its neon signs, thought to be from about 1960, are installed on both sides of its Upper East Side corner. "Its neon fascia sign stands out as something of an antique in the twenty-first century," writes Thomas E. Rinaldi in *New York Neon*, "but it must have struck some as a bold new look for an establishment that had already been in business more than fifty years before the sign appeared."

SUBWAY INN

Subway Inn, named for its proximity to the Lexington Avenue / 59th Street subway station, opened in 1937 on Sixtieth Street and Lexington Avenue, across from Bloomingdale's. The building's owner refused to renew Subway Inn's lease in 2014. A year later, owner Marcelo Salinas reopened the bar two blocks east and brought its iconic neon signs with him, along with the booth where Marilyn Monroe and Joe DiMaggio used to sit in the 1950s. Steve Salinas, Marcelo's son, took over after his father died in 2016. "The heart and soul of the Subway Inn was that it brought everyone together, whether you were a celebrity or just a plain old New Yorker," Salinas told the *Washington Post*. "Nobody felt uncomfortable. No matter where you worked or what your status is in life, we're all the same at the Subway Inn" (Carman et al. 2017).

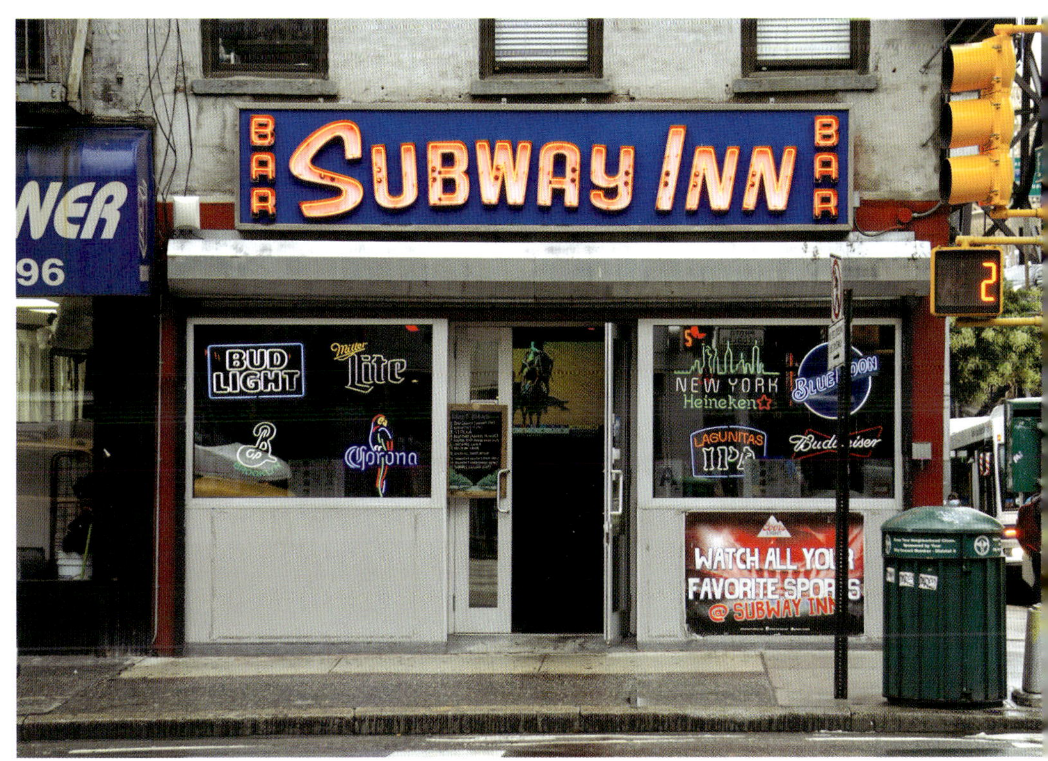

1140 Second Avenue

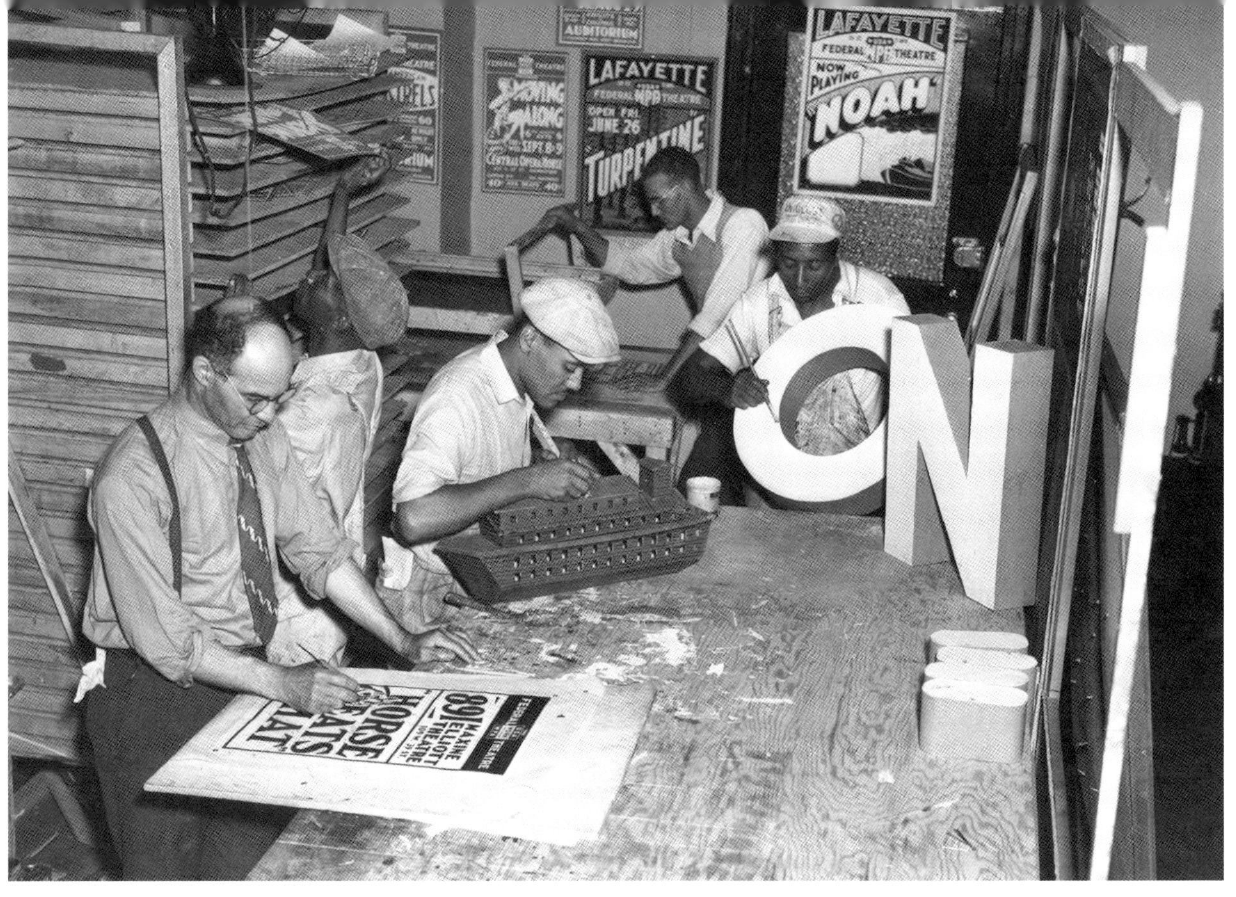

Federal Theatre Project, Negro Theatre, Sign Painting Department, headed by Tipp Beavers. Workshop employees producing posters, display letters, and a cardboard ark for various New York–based Federal Theatre productions, 1936. *Courtesy of Schomburg Center for Research in Black Culture, Photographs and Prints Division, New York Public Library Digital Collections*

BIBLIOGRAPHY

"American Woolen Building." *Architects' and Builders' Magazine*, October 1910. www.books.google.com.

Appleton, Jean. "Needles, Threads and New York History." *New York Times*, August 1, 2012. www.nytimes.com.

"The Architectural Treatment of Side Walls." *Brick and Clay Record*, September 15, 1914. www.books.google.com.

"Arrest Gerard Proprietor." *New York Times*, November 17, 1914. www.nytimes.com.

A. S. Beck advertisement. *New York Daily News*, February 20, 1925. www.newspapers.com.

Associated Press. "US Protests Barclay Ad." *New York Times*, July 8, 1983. www.nytimes.com.

Auster, Paul. *The New York Trilogy*. London: Faber & Faber, 1985.

"Avenue A Now York Avenue from 59th to 93rd Street." *New York Times*, April 11, 1928. www.nytimes.com.

Baker, William Henry. *A Dictionary of Men's Wear*. Cleveland, OH: William Henry Baker, 1908.

"Bank Gives Away Money." *New York Times*, September 21, 1926. www.nytimes.com.

Barbetta. "History of Barbetta." www.barbettarestaurant.com.

Barmash, Isadore. "A Kresge–McCrory Reunion." *New York Times*, April 4, 1987. www.nytimes.com.

Bennett, James. "Recamier Manufacturing Company." *Cosmetics and Skin* (blog). www.cosmeticsandskin.com.

Berger, Joseph. "Painted Signs, Relics of a Bygone New York, Become Even More Rare." *New York Times*, November 5, 2005. www.nytimes.com.

Besonen, Julie. "The Elegant Relic of Restaurant Row." *New York Times*, February 2, 2018. www.nytimes.com.

———. "Gramercy Park: Steeped in History and Grandeur." *New York Times*, June 29, 2016. www.nytimes.com.

Blogg & Littauer advertisement. *New York Times*, July 30, 1922. www.newspapers.com.

Bloomingdale's. "Our History." www.bloomingdales.com.

"Bloomingdale's Inc. History." *Funding Universe* (blog). www.fundinguniverse.com.

Bradley, Austin. "City History: The History of the Upper East Side." *Triplemint* (blog), September 22, 2014. www.triplemint.com.

———. "City History: The History of the Upper West Side." *Triplemint* (blog), September 22, 2014. www.triplemint.com.

Brewer, Daryln. "Repair and Restoration of Lighting." *New York Times*, April 12, 1990. www.nytimes.com.

Broadway Savings Bank advertisement. *New York Daily News*, March 11, 1932. www.newspapers.com.

"The Business of a Great Publishing House." *Scribner's Magazine*, January–June 1908. www.books.google.com.

Byrne, Christopher. "They Came to Play." Toy Industry Association, 2003. www.toyassociation.org.

Cain, Corrine. "Artwork by Robert Bestién." *Savvy Collector* (blog). www.savvycollector.com.

Carman, Tim, Fritz Hahn, and Shelly Tan. "America's Most Authentic Dive Bars." *Washington Post*, April 20, 2017. www.washingtonpost.com.

Centers for Disease Control and Prevention. "Legislation." www.cdc.gov.

Chapman, Pat. "Separates for Night and Day." *New York Daily News*, January 27, 1973. www.newspapers.com.

"Charles F. Noyes, 91, Is Dead." *New York Times*, September 4, 1969. www.nytimes.com.

"Charles F. Noyes, Real Estate Tycoon." *Hackensack* (NJ) *Record*, September 5, 1969. www.newspapers.com.

Clarke, Katherine. "A Developer with Vision: One Landlord Is Naming a Whole Building after Trendy Tenant Warby Parker." *New York Daily News*, November 6, 2014. www.nydailynews.com.

Clines, Francis X. "About New York." *New York Times*, July 14, 1977. www.nytimes.com.

"Colgate Acquires Omega Chemical." *Munster* (IN) *Times*, May 15, 1931. www.newspapers.com.

Crane, Esther. *The Gilded Age in New York, 1870–1910*. New York: Black Dog & Leventhal, 2016.

Cuccinello, Susan. "Did Someone Mention Food?" *Ticker*, October 12, 1979. www.academicworks.cuny.edu.

Cuozzo, Steve. "Life Magazine Building to Be Reborn as Boutique Hotel." *New York Post*, February 20, 2017. www.nypost.com.

Dairymen's League Co-Operative Association advertisement. *New York Daily News*, January 6, 1947. www.newspapers.com.

Dales, Douglas. "National Republican Club Moves to East Side Hotel Tomorrow." *New York Times*, April 2, 1961. www.nytimes.com.

"Discover Flatiron: The Fortune of Fourth Avenue," *Flatiron 23rd Street Partnership* (blog), June 20, 2017. www.flatirondistrict.nyc.

"Discovering the History of Rose Hill." *88 & 90 Lexington Avenue* (blog). www.88and90lex.com.

Divola, Barry. "The Last of the New York Diners." *Financial Review*, February 7, 2020. www.afr.com.

———. "The Real Seinfeld Diner in New York: Inside Tom's Restaurant." *Traveller*, February 28, 2016. www.traveller.com.au.

"Doehler-Jarvis Company Collection, 1940–1972." Ward M. Canaday Center for Special Collections, University of Toledo. www.utoledo.edu.

"Dougherty, John E." *Brooklyn Daily Eagle*, May 25, 1948. www.newspapers.com.

"Dr. W. H. Tutt." *Illustrated New York: The Metropolis of To-Day*, 1888. www.books.google.com.

Dunlap, David W. "At Restored Landmark in Times Square, Mixing 'Brash and Beautiful.'" *New York Times*, January 29, 2014. www.nytimes.com.

———. "G.E. Gives Midtown Tower to Columbia University." *New York Times*, June 3, 1993. www.nytimes.com.

———. "Old York; Look Close, and in This Ever-New Town You Will See Traces of the Past Peeking Through." *New York Times*, December 10, 2000. www.nytimes.com.

———. "Tracking 'Privilege' Signs as They Vanish." *New York Times*, October 16, 2013. www.nytimes.com.

"E. & J. Burke." *Eating in Translation* (blog), February 6, 2017. www.eatingintranslation.com.

Ewing, Michael. "Can You Afford Me Now: Converting an Old Telephone Tower into Ornate Luxury." *The Observer*, March 9, 2012. www.observer.com.

Feldman, Benjamin. "All Cars Transfer There." *New York Wanderer* (blog), October 27, 2006. www.newyorkwanderer.com.

Feldman, Jamie. "Cheesecake, an Immigrant Fable." *Politico* (blog), October 23, 2012. www.politico.com.

Fields, Sidney. "Old Life Goes On." *New York Daily News*, June 26, 1972. www.nydailynews.com.

"A Fiendish Wife Murder." *New York Times*, December 12, 1881. www.nytimes.com.

Fishbein, Rebecca. "Old Town Bar Owner Talks about the Classic Tavern's 125th Anniversary." *Gothamist* (blog), September 19, 2017. www.gothamist.com.

"Flock to Inspect the Biggest Hotel." *New York Times*, December 30, 1912. www.nytimes.com.

Fodor's See It New York City, Fifth Edition. New York: Fodor's Travel Publications, 2012.

"Forty Years of Progress." *Fabrics, Fancy Goods and Notions* 46, no. 6 (June 1912).

"Frank Schiffman, Co-founder of Harlem's Apollo, Dies at 80." *New York Times*, January 17, 1974. www.nytimes.com.

Galbraith, Robert. "How Italy and New York Shaped Banking." *Intesa Sanpaolo* (blog), October 4, 2018. www.world.intesasanpaolo.com.

Gallagher, Jay. "Designer's Best Sellers Are Real 'Bags.'" *Alexandria* (LA) *Daily Town Talk*, April 7, 1972. www.newspapers.com.

Gannon, Devin. "A Mecca of African American History and Culture, Central Harlem Is Designated a Historic District." *6sqft* (blog), May 29, 2018. www.6sqft.com.

"Garment Industry History Initiative." *Gotham Center for New York City History* (blog). www.gothamcenter.org.

Geier, Stephanie. "The Top 10 Secrets of NYC's Herald Square." *Untapped New York* (blog), December 11, 2015. www.untappedcities.com.

"General Electric Building." *Lookze* (blog). www.lookze.com.

"A General Shopping Directory." *New York Tribune*, December 12, 1920. www.newspapers.com.

Ginsberg, Allen. *Howl and Other Poems*. Eastford, CT: Martino Fine Books, 2015.

Goicochea, Julia. "A Brief History of Union Square, New York City." *Culture Trip* (blog), December 21, 2017. www.theculturetrip.com.

Gray, Christopher. "The Home of the Man Who Planned Chelsea." *New York Times*, October 20, 1996. www.nytimes.com.

———. "Streetscapes: The Herald Square Hotel; Old Life Building Getting a New Look." *New York Times*, November 5, 1995. www.nytimes.com.

———. "Streetscapes: The Hotel Martinique; Grimy Grande Dame Housing the Homeless Off Herald Square." *New York Times*, September 27, 1987. www.nytimes.com.

———. "Streetscapes: Irving Place; A 19th-Century Street Honoring Washington Irving." *New York Times*, May 18, 2003. www.nytimes.com.

———. "Streetscapes: The McAlpin Marine Grill; The Fate of a Polychrome Grotto Hangs in Balance." *New York Times*, July 23, 1989. www.nytimes.com.

———. "Streetscapes: Readers' Questions; The Old U.S. Army Building on Whitehall Street." *New York Times*, March 5, 1995. www.nytimes.com.

"Greater New-York's Representative Business Firms." *New-York Tribune*, January 30, 1897. www.newspapers.com.

Griffon advertisement. *New York Daily News*, February 2, 1947. www.newspapers.com.

Grutchfield, Walter. "Berley & Co." *Walter Grutchfield* (blog). www.waltergrutchfield.net.

———. "Illfelder Importing Co." *Walter Grutchfield* (blog). www.waltergrutchfield.net.

———. "Martin Building." *Walter Grutchfield* (blog). www.waltergrutchfield.net.

———. "Metropolitan Wines / Longo Bros." *Walter Grutchfield* (blog). www.waltergrutchfield.net.

———. "Miss Weber Millinery." *Walter Grutchfield* (blog). www.waltergrutchfield.net.

———. "Schwarzenbach Buildings." *Walter Grutchfield* (blog). www.waltergrutchfield.net.

———. "Weber & Heilbroner." *Walter Grutchfield* (blog). www.waltergrutchfield.net.

"Guinness in America." *Guinness in America* (blog). www.sites.google.com.

Hamlin, Suzanne. "Who Is Baby Watson?" *New York Daily News*, March 12, 1980. www.newspapers.com.

"Harlem." *Encyclopedia Brittanica*, July 20, 1998. www.brittanica.com.

"Harlem History." *Harlem World* (blog). www.harlemworldmagazine.com.

"Harlem Renaissance." *History* (blog). www.history.com.

Heins, Scott. "Inside the UES's Legendary Lexington Candy Shop Lunch Counter." *Gothamist* (blog), October 23, 2017. www.gothamist.com.

"Hell's Kitchen, Manhattan (History)." *Urban Areas* (blog). www.urbanareas.net.

The Henry Ford. "Dr. Tutt's Liver Pills, circa 1907." www.thehenryford.org.

Henry, O. *The Halberdier of the Little Rheinschloss.* New York: Charles Rivers, 2012.

Herman, Gabe. "Historic Terminal Warehouse in Chelsea Is Set to Undergo Major Renovations to Make It a Business Hub." *amNY*, September 20, 2019. www.amny.com.

High Line. "History." www.thehighline.org.

"History." *Carnegie Hill Neighbors* (blog). www.carnegiehillneighbors.org.

"History." *Meatpacking* (blog). www.meatpacking-district.com.

"History of Harlem." *Harlem Heritage Tours* (blog). www.harlemheritage.com.

"The History of Koreatown." *Macaulay Eportfolio* (blog). www.eportfolios.macaulay.cuny.edu.

"The History of Murray Hill." *Murray Hill Neighborhood Association* (blog). www.murrayhillnyc.org.

Horn & Hardart. "History." www.hornandhardartcoffee.com.

Horsley, Carter B. "The Upper East Side Book." *City Review* (blog). www.thecityreview.com.

Hughes, C. J. "Dial C for Condos." *New York Times*, March 8, 2012. www.nytimes.com.

———. "East Harlem: Bodegas, Botanicas and New Buildings." *New York Times*, October 5, 2016. www.nytimes.com.

Hughes Crowley, Carolyn. "Meet Me at the Automat." *Smithsonian*, August 2001. www.smithsonianmag.com.

Jacobson, Aileen. "Carnegie Hill: A Quiet Enclave Bordering the Park." *New York Times*, November 9, 2016. www.nytimes.com.

———. "NoMad: A Rapidly Evolving Neighborhood with a Storied Past." *New York Times*, January 9, 2019. www.nytimes.com.

Jessie Smith Noyes Foundation. "Legacy." www.noyes.org.

Jump, Frank. *Fading Ads of New York City*. Charleston, SC: History Press, 2011.

Kessler, Kevin. "Drink in New York City History at Old Town Bar." *Village Voice*, September 11, 2014. www.villagevoice.com.

Kimmelman, Michael. "When Manhattan Was Mannahatta: A Stroll through the Centuries." *New York Times*, May 13, 2020. www.nytimes.com.

Koshetz, Herbert. "Amerotron Opens Wool Experiment." *New York Times*, February 27, 1956. www.nytimes.com.

Kress Foundation. "The Kress Legacy." www.kressfoundation.org.

"Ladies' Mile Marks 25 Years as Historic District," *Flatiron 23rd Street Partnership* (blog), April 30, 2014. www.flatirondistrict.nyc.

La Farge, Annik. "High Line Architecture: The Spears Building." *Livin' the High Line* (blog), July 23, 2014. www.livinthehighline.com.

Lasky, Julie. "Kips Bay: An Anonymous Neighborhood with Fringe Benefits." *New York Times*, October 11, 2017. www.nytimes.com.

"Last Minute News from the Style Fronts Proves to Be Practical." *Honolulu* (HI) *Star-Bulletin*, September 27, 1947. www.newspapers.com.

"The Latest from Paris." *Silent Hollywood* (blog). www.silenthollywood.com.

Lerner Shops advertisement. *New York Evening World*, March 9, 1922. www.newspapers.com.

Life Hotel. "Our History." www.luxehotels.com.

Lively, Amy. "The History of the Martinique Hotel near Times Square." *USA Today*, March 24, 2019. www.usatoday.com.

"Koster and Bial's Music Hall." *Nomad Alliance* (blog), September 25, 2015. www.experiencenomad.com.

"Macy's." Encyclopedia.com. www.encyclopedia.com.

"Macy's Department Store." *A View on Cities* (blog). www.aviewoncities.com.

Marketing Team. "History of the Flatiron District." *Triplemint* (blog), March 3, 2017. www.triplemint.com.

Marton, Janos. "Today in NYC History: In 1904, Longacre Square Renamed 'Times Square.'" *Untapped New York* (blog), April 8, 2015. www.untappedcities.com.

Marzlock, Ron. "A. S. Beck Was a Real 'Shoe-In.'" *Queens* (NY) *Chronicle*, March 12, 2015. www.qchron.com.

Mastropolo, Frank. *Ghost Signs: Clues to Downtown New York's Past*. Atglen, PA: Schiffer, 2019.

"Max Blauner, 79, of Suzy Perette." *New York Times*, June 8, 1962. www.nytimes.com.

Maxwell, Connie. "Landmark Scribner Bookstore Closes." United Press International, January 22, 1989. www.upi.com.

McC., A. "Expert Says Dress Ages Gracefully If It Has the Right Accessories." *New York Times*, June 28, 1956. www.nytimes.com.

McAninch, David. "Here Is New York, Right Where We Left It." *New York Times*, February 27, 2005. www.nytimes.com.

McCrory's advertisement. *New York Evening World*, November 5, 1912. www.newspapers.com.

McGrath, Maggie. "Remembering the Coffee Shop: A New York Institution Is Closing after 28 Years." *Forbes*, October 12, 2018. www.forbes.com.

Miller, Tom. "The 1922 Wood, Dolson Co. Building." *Daytonian in Manhattan* (blog), August 14, 2018. www.daytonianinmanhattan.blogspot.com.

———. "The 1929 I. Miller & Sons Building." *Daytonian in Manhattan* (blog), January 31, 2014. www.daytonianinmanhattan.blogspot.com.

———. "Bazar Francais." *Daytonian in Manhattan* (blog), November 1, 2011. www.daytonianinmanhattan.blogspot.com.

———. "Gimbels Department Store." *Daytonian in Manhattan* (blog), December 20, 2014. www.daytonianinmanhattan.blogspot.com.

———. "The Goliath 1891 Terminal Warehouse Buildings." *Daytonian in Manhattan* (blog), September 28, 2012. www.daytonianinmanhattan.blogspot.com.

———. "The Price Building." *Daytonian in Manhattan* (blog), June 27, 2018. www.daytonianinmanhattan.blogspot.com.

———. "Scheffel Hall." *Daytonian in Manhattan* (blog), June 16, 2010. www.daytonianinmanhattan.blogspot.com.

Mitgang, Herbert. "Scribner Book Store, 75, Will Close Next Month." *New York Times*, December 7, 1988. www.nytimes.com.

"MM Morris Moskowitz." *Bag Lady U.* (blog). www.bagladyemporium.com.

"Museum Mile, New York City." *NY.com* (blog). www.ny.com.

"The Neighborhood." *34th Street Partnership* (blog). www.34thstreet.org.

"New Building for Wood, Dolson Co." *Real Estate Record and Builders Guide*, December 9, 1922. www.rerecord.library.columbia.edu.

"New Milk Plant to Open." *New York Times*, November 24, 1946. www.nytimes.com.

"New Sixth Avenue Firm." *New York Times*, July 24, 1910. www.nytimes.com.

New York City Department of Parks & Recreation. "Herald Square." www.nycgovparks.org.

———. "Union Square Park." www.nycgovparks.org.

New York City Landmarks Preservation Commission. "Explore the Central Harlem–West 130th–132nd Streets Historic District." www.nyc.gov.

———. "The Gerard, Later Hotel Langwell, Later Hotel 1-2-3." www.nyc.gov.

———. "Richard Webber Harlem Packing House." www.nyc.gov.

Nonko, Emily. "How the Manhattan Neighborhood of Turtle Bay Got Its Name." *6sqft* (blog), January 26, 2018. www.6sqft.com.

Olejniczak, Julian M. *To Be a Soldier: A Selective American Military History*. Bloomington, IN: Xlibris, 2015.

"The Omega Chemical Company, New York, Omega Oil." *Bay Bottles* (blog), February 10, 2017. www.baybottles.com.

Omega Oil advertisement. *New York Daily News*, October 31, 1934. www.newspapers.com.

"Our Lecture Notes: A Physical History of the Garment District." *NBC New York* (blog), March 17, 2011. www.nbcnewyork.com.

"The Park." *Open Table* (blog). www.opentable.com.

Paumgarten, Nick. "The Mannahatta Project." *New Yorker*, September 24, 2007. www.newyorker.com.

P. J. Clarke's. "Our Roots." www.pjclarkes.com.

Popik, Barry. "Millinery District." *Barry Popik* (blog), November 20, 2006. www.barrypopik.com.

"Postings: Woodstock Renovation; Brightening the Scene Just off Times Square." *New York Times*, August 22, 1993. www.nytimes.com.

Price, Lauren. "From Swamps to Swank: A Brief History of Gramercy Park Hotel and the Garden's Highly Coveted Keys." *6sqft* (blog), August 19, 2014. www.6sqft.com.

Price, Nancy J. "A Manhattan Mini-Mystery." *Click Americana* (blog), January 2, 2014. www.clickamericana.com.

"Printing Crafts Building." *New York Times*, May 14, 1916. www.nytimes.com.

Project FIND. "Woodstock Hotel." www.projectfind.org.

Randall, David K. "Only the Store Is Gone." *New York Times*, February 19, 2006. www.nytimes.com.

"Real Estate Notes." *Real Estate Records and Builders Guide*, February 11, 1922. www.rerecord.library.columbia.edu.

Redman, Laura Dannen. "NYC's Life Magazine Building Is Reborn as a Boutique Hotel." *Conde Nast Traveler*, April 20, 2017. www.cntraveler.com.

"Renovations Underway at Dryden East Hotel." *New York Times*, June 30, 1964. www.nytimes.com.

Richard Webber Harlem Packing House advertisement. *Hackensack* (NJ) *Record*, June 24, 1910. www.newspapers.com.

Rinaldi, Thomas E. *New York Neon*. New York: W. W. Norton, 2013.

Rudy's. "History." www.rudysbarnyc.com.

Schneider, Daniel B. "F.Y.I." *New York Times*, March 19, 2000. www.nytimes.com.

Schulz, Dana. "East Harlem: From Manhattan's First Little Italy to El Barrio to a Neighborhood on the Cusp of Gentrification." *6sqft* (blog), April 9, 2015. www.6sqft.com.

"Schwarzenbach, Huber & Co." *New York Daily Tribune*, March 29, 1903. www.newspapers.com.

"Scribner Press." *Scribner's Magazine*, January–June 1918. www.books.google.com.

"Scribners in New Home." *New York Times*, May 18, 1913. www.nytimes.com.

Sealy. "A Look Back at Sealy through the Years." www.sealy.com.

Seltzer, Debra Jane. *Vintage Signs of America*. Gloucestershire, UK: Amberley, 2017.

Small, Matthew. "Harlem's Hidden History: The Real Little Italy Was Uptown." *Medium* (blog), July 17, 2016.

Songalia, Ryan. "Controversy over Anti-Mormon Rhetoric Nixes Street Co-naming." *Town & Village* (blog), October 14, 2019. www.town-village.com.

Spencer, Luke J. "Israel Miller's 'Show Folks Shoe Shop' Building." *Atlas Obscura* (blog). www.atlasobscura.com.

"Sponging." *Fabric Dictionary* (blog). www.fabricdictionary.com.

"State Democrats Move." *New York Times*, November 5, 1965. www.nytimes.com.

Steinmann, Sonia. "A Sense of Place: Preserving Morningside Heights." *Columbia Spectator*, October 11, 2017. www.columbiaspectator.com.

Stokes, Colin. "Subway Inn." *New Yorker*, March 25, 2016. www.newyorker.com.

Strausbaugh, John. "Turf of Gangs and Gangsters." *New York Times*, August 17, 2007. www.nytimes.com.

Studebaker advertisement. *New York Daily News*, September 27, 1926. www.newspapers.com.

"The Studebaker Building." *Columbia University Computing History* (blog), April 21, 2017. www.columbia.edu.

"Subway FAQ: A Brief History of the Subway." *NYC Subway* (blog). www.nycsubway.org.

Sullen, Henry L. "A Master of Typography Passes into History." *Inland Printer*, April–September 1916. www.books.google.com.

Tarver, Denton. "From Farmland to High Rises." *The Cooperator New York* (blog), June 2006. www.cooperator.com.

Tebbel, John William. *A History of Book Publishing in the United States*. 4 vols. New York: R. R. Bowker, 1972–1981.

"Ten Things You Didn't Know about the NYC Garment District." *The Knickerbocker* (blog). www.theknickerbocker.com.

"Theater District." *New York Preservation Archive Project* (blog). www.nypap.org.

Thilman, James. "After 74 Years, Prime Burger Will Flip Its Last Burger on Saturday." *Gothamist* (blog), May 22, 2012. www.gothamist.com.

"A Times Square Hotel Now Home for the Elderly." *New York Times*, March 13, 1978. www.nytimes.com.

"To Keep the Hands Clean." *American Inventor*, September 15, 1903. www.books.google.com.

Trapnell, Kelli. "History of NYC Streets: Strivers' Row." *Untapped Cities* (blog), December 20, 2012. www.untappedcities.com.

"Turtle Bay History." *Turtle Bay Association* (blog). www.turtlebay-nyc.org.

29th Street Neighborhood Association. www.29streetassociation.org.

Upadhyaya, Kayla Kumari. "Union Square's Iconic Diner Coffee Shop Will Close in October." *Eater New York* (blog), July 12, 2018. www.ny.eater.com.

Van Gelder, Lawrence. "Shop Talk." *New York Times*, January 3, 1976. www.nytimes.com.

Wallenfeldt, Jeff. "Times Square." *Encyclopedia Brittanica*, July 20, 1998. www.brittanica.com.

Walsh, Kevin. "Bloomingdale's." *Forgotten New York* (blog), May 10, 1998. www.forgotten-ny.com.

———. "Chelsea-Clinton." *Forgotten New York* (blog), April 12, 2011. www.forgotten-ny.com.

———. "Fourth Avenue Building." *Forgotten New York* (blog), January 21, 2014. www.forgotten-ny.com.

Waxman, Sarah. "The History of New York City's Upper West Side." *NY.com* (blog). www.ny.com.
Weaver, Shaye. "As Lord & Taylor's Flagship Closes, We Look Back at Department Stores of the Past." *amNY*, March 18, 2018. www.amny.com.
"Weekend History: The Story behind an Upper West Side Ice Cream Sign; 3 Million Gallons!" *West Side Rag* (blog), August 22, 2015.
"Welcome to West Harlem." *Macaulay Eportfolio* (blog), February 2011. www.eportfolios.macaulay.cuny.edu.
Williams, Keith. "How the Upper East Side Grew out of Three Historic Enclaves." *Curbed New York* (blog), February 20, 2014. www.ny.curbed.com.
Wilson, Reid. "14-Story Scribner Printing Plant Building at 311 West 43rd Street Getting Office Renovation, Hell's Kitchen." *New York Yimby* (blog), May 17, 2016. www.newyorkyimby.com.
Young, Jan B. *Tales of Studebaker: The Early Years*. Raleigh, NC: Lulu, 2011.
Zaczkiewicz, Arthur. "Herald Square Draws More Than Two Million Visitors Annually." *WWD*, March 15, 2018. www.wwd.com.

INDEX